SARDEGNA

Puglia Calabria

Basilicata CAMPANIA

ABRUZZi e MOLiSE

LAZIO Marche

Umbria TOSCANA

Emilia-Romagna

Liguria Veneto

Friuli-Venezia Giulia

Trentino-Alto Adige

LOMBARDIA

Piemonte e Valle d'Aosta

ALHAMBRA
EDITIONS

Antonio Carluccio's

ITALIA

photography by Alastair Hendy

Publishing director **Jane O'Shea**
Creative consultant **Priscilla Carluccio**
Project editor **Janet Illsley**
Photographer **Alastair Hendy**
Editor **Susan Fleming**
Production **Rebecca Short**

notes

All spoon measures are level unless otherwise stated:
1 tsp = 5 ml spoon;
1 tbsp = 15 ml spoon.

Always use fresh herbs unless dried herbs are specifed in a particular recipe.

For seasoning, use sea salt and freshly ground black pepper unless otherwise suggested.

Free-range eggs are recommended. Egg sizes are stated where critical; otherwise use large eggs.

Firstly I would like to dedicate this book to Milton Patrick, my 10-year-old step grandson, in recognition of his fascinating, young, creative mind.

Secondly I dedicate it, with a huge thank you, to Pellegrino Artusi, an Italian gastronome of the last century who united the cooking of the Italian regions.

This edition first published in 2005 by
Alhambra Editions
Alhambra House
27-31 Charing Cross Road
London WC2H 0LS

Cataloguing in Publication Data: a catalogue record for this book is available from the British Library.

ISBN 1 84400 247 0
Printed in Italy

CONTENTS

TRENTINO-ALTO ADIGE
FRIULI-VENEZIA GIULIA
VALLE DiAOSTA
LOMBARDIA
VENETO
PIEMONTE
EMILIA-ROMAGNA
LIGURIA
TOSCANA
MARCHE
UMBRIA
ABRUZZI
MOLISE
LAZIO
PUGLIA
CAMPANIA
BASILICATA
CALABRIA
SARDEGNA
SICILIA
A l p i
A p p e n n i n e s
Adige
Po
Arno
Tiber
Lago Maggiore
Lago di Como
Lago d'Iseo
Lago di Garda
Lago Trasimeno
Lago di Bolsena
Lago di Bracciano
Trento
Udine
Trieste
Verona
Venezia
Milano
Torino
Parma
Bologna
Genova
La Spezia
Rimini
Pesaro
Ancona
Firenze
Pisa
Livorno
Siena
Perugia
Norcia
Pescara
L'Aquila
Roma
Napoli
Salerno
Bari
Taranto
Sassari
Cagliari
Palermo
Catania
Reggio di Calabria
Golfo di Venezia
Golfo di Genova
Golfo di Taranto
ADRIATIC SEA
TYRRHENIAN SEA
MEDITERRANEAN SEA

Introduction

I have always been fascinated by the regionality of Italy's cooking. This probably has something to do with my roots, which lie in various distant parts of the country. My father was a stationmaster and each of his six children was born in a different station according to his posting at the time! As a consequence, I have developed a keen interest and appreciation of the culture and cooking of the whole of Italy.

Italian food is distinctly regional, partly because the country was only united politically in 1861 – less than 150 years ago. Before then it was comprised of disparate (often warring) regions, states and cities, all of which differed marginally, sometimes radically, from their neighbours, in customs, politics, mentality – and in styles of food and cooking. But it is the geography that played, and still plays, the most determining role in defining culinary styles. Italy has no less than 1500 miles of coastline and seafood is obviously more important to those regions that abut the Adriatic and Mediterranean than to those which are landlocked. Italy is almost entirely composed of mountains – the Apennine range which forms the country's backbone, stretching from Piedmont in the north right down to Calabria in the south. In the mountains basic ingredients are quite unlike those of the coastal plains, and the basic style of cookery differs enormously as a result. The sheer length of the country, from the Alpine north right down to the 'toe' of the Italian 'boot', dictates that styles differ radically – that of the north being more Germanic, cold-weather cooking characterised by the use of butter; that of the sun-baked south, more Mediterranean, often veering towards its sunny neighbours in Greece and North Africa where olive oil is the main ingredient used for cooking.

Indeed Italy, like many other countries, has absorbed influences from other civilisations and cuisines, and this too has contributed to that unique regionality. The French house of Savoy, for instance, possessed the land from Nice to Genoa as well as the regions of Piedmont, Sardinia, Sicily and Campania at one point in the early 19th century, and the pesto of Genoa is inextricably linked with the Provençal pistou. Which came first, the Italian or French, is a constant source of argument, but I know it was the Italian! The use of capers, pine nuts, dried fruit and couscous in the cooking of the south, particularly Sicily, is a custom acquired from Arab cuisines, the Saracens (North African Berbers and Spanish Muslims) having invaded and ruled from the 9th century.

As if politics, geography and outside influences were not enough, the regionality of Italy's cooking is further reinforced by the very nature of the Italians themselves, by something called *'campanilismo'*. This is an echo of the times when neighbours would pull together to defend the church and its bell from invaders, and the concepts of loyalty and adherence to locality, church and people, has extended to other areas – including food. Most Italians are obsessed by food anyway (I have to admit to being no different), and much of our conversation involves talk of meals, of ingredients and of specific recipes – with much raising of voices and hand waving when we disagree. For not just individual regions, but towns and villages, individual families and even individuals within families, will adhere to their idea of the right way to prepare a certain dish. In spite of this devotion and passionate interest in food, a certain inter-regional fusion has taken place, as products from the south and north are imaginatively cooked together to produce still wonderful Italian food. I firmly believe, however, that the culinary patrimony of the twenty regions is too powerful – and too historically ingrained in their peoples – to be ousted.

Piemonte e Valle d'Aosta

Situated in the very far, landlocked north of Italy, these two regions share many geographical, historical and culinary characteristics. They are mountainous, with the Alps forming a formidable border with France and Switzerland, and the cooking is substantial – rich in carbohydrates with a good variety of sustaining dishes to help survive the cold winters. It was here that I grew up, and so I have a particular affection for the area.

I have come to appreciate how privileged I was to live here during my early formative years. When I was seven months old, my father decided that the future for our large family would be more secure in the industrial north rather than in the sunny south, so we moved to Castelnuovo Belbo in Monferrato, with its acres of vineyards, vegetable and fruit fields, and its famous hills. Later we settled in Borgofranco d'Ivrea on the border between Piemonte and Valle d'Aosta, and it was here that I stayed until I flew the nest. Those happy years helped shape the Antonio of today.

The hills and mountains around Borgofranco were my childhood playground and I used to spend hours exploring with my friends. Usually we would take with us a *merenda* (snack), perhaps a *cacciatorino* (small salami) with some bread, cheese, fruit, and chocolate if we were lucky. Occasionally we would find a café or *trattoria* in a village and have a plate of hot polenta and mushrooms, or some soup, or simply *pane, burro e acciughe* (bread, butter and anchovies). On the way there and back we would collect foods from the wild – still a great passion of mine. We picked chestnuts or mushrooms, or wild herbs from the fields, proudly bringing our spoils back home. My mother was a genius at transforming these simple ingredients into tasty and nourishing meals for her brood, so my food tastes were formulated in this area as well.

Piedmont and the Aosta Valley have many other happy memories for me. As a child, I was fascinated by the fortified buildings. Every town has its *castello, fortezza* or *palazzo*, which was once the centre of local commerce and also a defence against invasion. Built by dukes or local rulers on top of hills, many are still intact and now used for theatrical performances and festivities. They are almost all visible from the road in the Aosta Valley – once, of course, the route through to France, and to romance!

CULINARY TRADITIONS & SPECIALITIES

In a sense, the way of life with which I was so familiar is still preserved in Piedmont and the Aosta Valley. It is the countryside and its produce that characterise the area – the grape vines for the many wonderful wines, the rich mountain pastures where cows produce excellent milk for the region's fine cheeses (see page 15), and the vast damp and fertile Po Valley, stretching from the Alps through Lombardy and Veneto to the Adriatic, where rice and maize (for polenta) are grown. Piedmont is made up of a multitude of little artisans producing exceptionally good things, from cheese to meat, to vegetables, fruits and wines. Each town and village still has its weekly or monthly market, where specialities of the area and the season are on sale. Many of the vendors are small producers, offering foods from their own gardens – perhaps a basket of eggs or courgettes, or bunches of parsley and basil. To me these people represent the soul of good living.

Some years ago, with a view to maintaining the traditional way of life, a dedicated Piedmontese by the name of Carlo Petrini invented 'slow food' as an antidote to 'fast food' and all that it represents. 'Slow food' aims to preserve classic ways of agriculture in order to protect the environment, and to make sure that local and artisan products remain viable in today's competitive, commercial world. The movement holds exhibitions and constant tasting sessions, and every second October in Turin, manufacturers and suppliers from the entire Piedmont region, and elsewhere, give seminars, tastings and exhibitions at the *Salone del Gusto* (Hall of Taste), which attracts visitors from all over the world.

Insalata di Carne Cruda Raw beef salad

In all good *trattorie* and restaurants of the Monferrato, near Turin, you will find this dish among many other antipasti. It's usually prepared a day or a few hours ahead, using the famous *sanato*, the meat of a mature veal calf, which has a lovely pink colour, an excellent flavour, and is extremely tender. The Piedmontese are very fond of this raw meat dish, which is not unlike steak tartare, although it has a more subtle flavour. It is normally eaten with *grissini*, the breadsticks of Turin, and is sometimes served topped with a few slices of truffle.

SERVES 4

400 g raw beef or veal rump or fillet
juice of 1 lemon
1 garlic clove, crushed
3 tbsp olive oil
salt and pepper
2–3 tsp very finely chopped flat-leaf parsley
few slices of truffle (optional)

Chop the meat finely, preferably '*a punta di coltello*' (with the tip of a very sharp knife), to maintain a little texture.

Put the meat in a bowl and add the lemon juice, garlic, olive oil and seasoning to taste. Stir well, cover and refrigerate overnight. The lemon juice will colour the beef grey, but it's the flavour that the Italians are after.

Mix in the chopped parsley just before serving. Arrange on plates and top with a few slices of freshly shaved truffle for a truly noble dish. Serve with toasted bread or *grissini*.

Il Gran Bollito Misto Mixed boiled meats

This is a great winter celebration dish for a large gathering. It is found in other regions, but this version is very typical of Piedmont. *Gran bollito* combines at least five different types of meats, and has several little accompanying sauces: *salsa verde* (see below), *salsa rossa* (tomato and onion), *salsa bianca* (onion-based), and *mostarda di Cremona* (fruits candied slowly in a heavy sugar syrup flavoured with essence of mustard), illustrated on page 90.

SERVES 10–12

600 g pork skin without fat
cayenne pepper
freshly grated nutmeg
finely chopped flat-leaf parsley
finely chopped rosemary
salt and pepper
2 uncooked (or pre-cooked) *cotechino* sausages, 300 g each
4 celery stalks, cut into chunks
2 large onions, 1 spiked with 4 or 5 cloves
few black peppercorns
4 bay leaves
1.5 kg beef brisket
1 salted veal tongue, about 600–800 g
1 kg veal brisket
1 boiling chicken, about 1.5–2 kg

Lay the pork skin flat on a surface and sprinkle with cayenne, nutmeg, parsley, rosemary and salt and pepper. Roll up and tie with string. Put into a saucepan with the uncooked *cotechino* sausages and cover with cold water. Bring to the boil, then lower the heat and simmer for about 3 hours. (If using pre-cooked *cotechino*, add them to the pork pan 30 minutes before the end of the cooking time.)

Meanwhile, put 3 celery stalks, the clove-spiked onion, peppercorns and bay leaves in a large pot of lightly salted water and bring to the boil. Add the beef and cook gently for 30 minutes.

Add the tongue and veal brisket to the beef and simmer for 2 hours, skimming regularly to remove any scum from the surface. Top up with boiling water as necessary to ensure the meat is always covered. (If you don't have a large enough pot for all the meat, divide the vegetables and meat between two pans.)

Cook the chicken separately in water to cover, with the remaining celery and onion, for 1–1½ hours, depending on age.

When all the meats are cooked and tender, remove them from the liquor. Peel and trim the tongue. Slice the meats and arrange them on a large serving plate. Serve hot, accompanied by *salsa verde*, a little of the beef or chicken stock, and some *mostarda di Cremona*.

Salsa Verde Green sauce

There are several versions of this Piedmontese sauce, which is derived from *bagnet verd*. It accompanies many different dishes, including *batsoa* and *bollito misto*. Chopped chilli is sometimes added.

SERVES 4–6

1 soft white bread roll
a little white wine vinegar
8 salted anchovy fillets, rinsed and drained
25 g salted capers, rinsed and drained
1 garlic clove, peeled
1 large bunch of flat-leaf parsley
extra virgin olive oil to emulsify

Break up the bread roll and soak in wine vinegar to cover for a few minutes, then squeeze out all excess liquid and whiz in a blender or food processor to make crumbs.

Very finely chop the anchovies, capers, garlic and parsley, using a knife (not the food processor) and mix with the breadcrumbs. Stir in enough olive oil to emulsify and make a very dense sauce. Serve with bread or *grissini* as an antipasto, or as an accompaniment to meat dishes.

Both Piedmont and the Aosta Valley are influenced by their French neighbours. In Aosta, both French and Italian are spoken – as well as a diabolical patois, which only the locals can understand! Piedmont was once part of the French kingdom of Savoy with Turin, the present-day capital of Piedmont, Savoy's capital. Culinary influences are evident too. More cream and butter, for instance, are used in Piedmont than anywhere else in Italy, and some of the creamy pastries and desserts served in cafés in the old part of the Turin originated with the cooks at the court of Savoy.

The antipasti of Piedmont is an echo of French influence as well. Often served as *assaggi* (or tastings), it may feature thin slices of salami (the region is famous for its goose and young donkey versions), or ham, or *violini* (salted and cured venison), or *mucetta* (cured chamois) in Aosta. These would be served with a pickle of some sort, perhaps mushrooms or artichokes, to stimulate the taste-buds. Antipasti vegetables include *cipolle ripiene* (stuffed onions), and in season a rare and special salad of *ovoli* (Caesar mushrooms) and porcini or the famous white truffle.

Being landlocked, the Piedmontese do not have many fish dishes, but they have a passion for anchovies. Indeed, in a valley in the province of Cuneo, the locals have made a business out of salting the imported fish (from Liguria). These anchovies and local vegetables come together in one of Piedmont's most renowned dishes, *bagna cauda* (literally 'hot bath', see page 17). This is served with plenty of bread – often grissini, a Turin speciality – and plenty of wine! An important element of *bagna cauda* is garlic, and the regional motto of Piedmont is *L'aj a l'e spesiari d'paesan* (Garlic is the peasant's pharmacist), which perhaps goes a little way towards explaining why garlic features so much in local and traditional specialities!

Piedmont is also home to a wonderful range of desserts, including the well-known zabaglione, stuffed peaches and pears, peaches and pears cooked in Barolo wine, a compote of local chestnuts, and *marrons glacés* (candied chestnuts), which are made around Turin. This city is now famous throughout Italy for its chocolate, brought together magnificently with the local hazelnuts in *giandujotti* – a Turinese speciality.

The cheeses of Piedmont and the Aosta Valley are renowned. As soon as the last snow has melted, herds of cows, sheep and goats are taken up into the alpine valleys, where they crop the lush, herb-rich pastures. Their fragrant milk is used to make a variety of cheeses (see right). These are typically served to round off a meal, although some are also served as an antipasto.

Many Piedmontese towns and villages have a yearly *sagra* or festival, at Easter perhaps, or to celebrate the local seasonal produce. I remember particularly the *fagiolata di carnevale* in Biella and Ivrea, with its famous bean and pork soup – cooked in huge containers and available to all. In spring, asparagus is lauded in Cabiano; in summer peaches and sweet peppers are celebrated in Canale and Carmagnola respectively. In Alba, there is a huge festival in October dedicated to the famous white truffle, and weekly truffle markets through until December. In Nomagloi, there is a chestnut festival on the first Sunday in November. And last but not least in Montalto in November, there is a *sagra* of the famous local cabbage.

Cheeses of Piedmont & the Aosta Valley

Bra A semi-hard cheese, made from semi-skimmed cow's milk, from the town of Cuneo in Piedmont. There is a fresh cheese and an aged one, good for grating.

Bris Also known as brôs, brüs and brussu, this is made with a variety of cheeses, which are cut up into small pieces and fermented with grappa. Used for spreading on bread or polenta.

Caprini Goat's cheeses are found in both regions. There is a log cheese in Aosta, one called sora from Cuneo in Piedmont, the *caprino piemontese* and a fresh *caprino di remella*.

Castelmagno A blue cheese made around Cuneo in Piedmont from cow's and ewe's milk. Semi-hard, it is eaten as a table cheese.

Fontina An unpasteurised cow's milk cheese, which is semi-hard, with a high fat content. It is produced only in the Aosta Valley, near the French border, during the summer. Fontina comes in large wheels, up to 18 kg in weight. It is good eaten with fruit, and melts well (notably in *fonduta*). Fontal is the industrial copy.

Murazzano A soft fresh full-fat ewe's milk cheese made around Cuneo in Piedmont. Good as a table cheese, or it can be used in sauces.

Pagliarina A soft, full-fat cheese produced near Turin, from cow's milk. It is named after the little straw mat or *paglia* on which it is briefly matured. A wonderful table cheese.

Ricotta Most regions in Italy produce ricotta because it is a by-product of the cheese-making process; it uses the whey left after the curds have been removed. Fresh and mild, ricotta has a low fat content and can be made from any milk. The *ricotta piemontese* is reputed to be one of the best.

Robiola A soft, fresh and rindless cheese from Cocconato, which is most usually made with cow's milk, but some versions use ewe's or goats' (or a mixture). It is also eaten after maturing, when it becomes drier and harder.

Toma A hard table cheese made from cow's milk in both regions (and also in Liguria). The fresh version is known as tometta. Tomino is another fresh toma, which is often flavoured and immersed in oil; the most highly prized is flavoured with truffle.

Bagna Cauda Hot garlic and anchovy dip

The Piedmontese love garlic and anchovy, and this is a wonderful combination of both, to be served in a fondue dish in the middle of the table, or in little individual pots each with a candle underneath. My recipe is milder than usual – the garlic isn't too pungent – so that everyone can enjoy it.

The vegetables for dipping should be very fresh and tender. Choose from celery, Jerusalem artichokes, small globe artichokes, cardoons, yellow and red peppers, cucumber, fennel, radicchio and asparagus. Trim and cut into small pieces.

SERVES 6 OR MORE

16 garlic cloves, peeled
milk, to cover
300 g anchovy fillets (preferably salted and rinsed), or 30 anchovy fillets in oil, drained
300 g butter (Alpine is best), cut into pieces
200 ml extra virgin olive oil
100 ml double cream
selection of raw vegetables (see above)
a little beaten egg (optional)

Put the garlic cloves into a small pan, cover with milk and cook extremely slowly over a very low heat until the garlic is soft. Remove from the heat and crush the garlic into the milk until the mixture becomes creamy. Add the anchovies and let them dissolve, stirring over a very low heat. When everything is amalgamated, add the butter and olive oil and stir gently to combine. Finally add the cream.

Pour the *bagna cauda* into little fondue dishes, or into one single one, and keep warm over a lighted candle. Now, one by one, dip the tips of the vegetable pieces into it, and eat with bread. Repeat this until you have finished everything or you are satisfied! At the end, you can stir a spoonful of beaten egg into the last of the sauce and let it coagulate. This will be the last wonderful morsel.

Tajarin all'Albese Pasta Alba style

This recipe is very common in Piedmont. Homemade pasta is rolled into thin sheets, then cut with a knife into small ribbons, characterised by their irregularity. If you like, you can buy ready-made egg *tagliolini*, either fresh or dried, instead. The sauce is made of chicken livers and white truffle is often added, not surprisingly as Alba is the centre for white truffles.

SERVES 4–6

600 g egg tagliatelle (page 251)
salt and pepper
50 g Parmesan, freshly grated
slices of white truffle (optional)

Sauce
80 g butter (preferably Alpine)
50 ml olive oil
1 onion, finely chopped
400 g chicken livers, trimmed and finely chopped
2 ripe tomatoes, skinned, deseeded and diced
80 ml dry white wine

To make the sauce, melt the butter with the olive oil in a sauté pan, then add the onion and fry until it starts to turn golden. Add the chicken livers and fry for 8 minutes. Mix in the tomatoes and wine and bring to the boil. Simmer for a few minutes to reduce to a good sauce consistency and season with salt and pepper to taste.

Meanwhile, cook the pasta in plenty of boiling salted water until *al dente*, then drain and mix with the sauce and grated Parmesan. Serve at once, topped with freshly sliced white truffle if you are feeling extravagant.

Agnolotti in Tovagliolo Ravioli without sauce

I encountered this curious but way of eating ravioli – or *agnolotti* as the Piedmontese call them – during one of my visits to Cocconato in the province of Asti. Here the good things in life are available locally thanks to enthusiastic artisans. The *agnulot* made by *Fabrizio* at the Trattoria del Ponte are served in an immaculate white napkin – the filling is so tasty that they don't need a sauce. Originally made from leftover roast meats, the filling is now made from small cuts of tender pork, rabbit and veal – oven-roasted and then minced. Delicious!

SERVES 4

1 recipe egg pasta dough (page 251)
2 litres vegetable stock (page 251)
few drops of oil
Filling
2 tbsp olive oil
100 g diced veal
100 g diced pork
100 g diced rabbit
80 g finely diced mixed celery, carrot and onion
30 g spinach or Swiss chard
2 tbsp fresh ricotta
1 egg
20 g Parmesan, freshly grated
freshly grated nutmeg
salt and pepper

To make the filling, heat the olive oil in a large pan, add the diced meats and vegetables and fry, stirring, until the meats are evenly browned. Lower the heat and continue to cook, stirring occasionally until the meat is almost cooked, about 45 minutes.

Meanwhile, cook the spinach or chard in a little water until tender, then drain and squeeze out the excess liquid. Mince or finely chop and add to the meat. Continue to stir over the heat until the mixture is quite dry. Leave to cool, then mince, using a mincer or food processor. Add the ricotta, egg, Parmesan and nutmeg. Mix well and season with salt and pepper to taste.

Roll out the pasta into two long thin sheets, about 1.5 mm thick. Using a serrated pasta wheel, cut into 5 cm wide strips. Place small balls of filling (the size of a hazelnut) at 2 cm intervals along the centre of each strip. Brush the edges with a little water, then bring the long edges over the filling and press them together to seal. With the join uppermost, pinch into little pockets between the filling and cut with a serrated wheel to make *agnolotti*.

Bring the stock to the boil in a large pan. Plunge the *agnolotti* into the hot stock, along with a few drops of oil to avoid sticking. Cook for 6–7 minutes, until little more than *al dente*, then drain. Serve immediately, without sauce.

Note You can make the *agnolotti* in advance. Freeze them (to prevent the filling seeping out) and cook from frozen, allowing 10–12 minutes.

Crema alla Panna Pannacotta from the Aosta Valley

This is the original *pannacotta*. According to the Aostani, the recipe originated in Savoy, and it is probably a derivative of the French *crème caramel*, except that there are no eggs in *pannacotta*, only a little gelatine to hold it altogether.

SERVES 8

750 ml single cream
200 ml full-fat milk
250 g caster sugar
seeds from 1 vanilla pod
few drops of vanilla extract
2 tbsp peach liqueur or dark rum
3 gelatine leaves

Put everything except the gelatine in a pan and very slowly bring to the boil.

Soften the gelatine leaves in a little warm water. Lift out, squeeze out excess water and add to the hot cream mixture just before it comes to the boil. Stir with a wooden spoon until the gelatine has dissolved, then pour into 8 ramekins or dariole moulds.

Allow to cool, then refrigerate until set. To unmould, dip the base of each mould into warm water for a few seconds, then turn out onto small serving plates.

You might like to serve the *pannacotta* with crystallised fruit or a little fruit sauce; it is also good with some caramel poured on top.

Zabaione Zabaglione

This classic Piedmontese recipe is said to be named after the patron saint of *pâtissiers*, San Giovanni di Baglion. It's a terrific dessert and very simple to make. This version is one of the oldest, dating back to a chef of King Carlo Emanuele I of Italy.

SERVES 6–8

180 g caster sugar
12 egg yolks
100 ml aged Madeira or Marsala, or Moscato Passito di Pantelleria
pinch of ground cinnamon

Beat the sugar and eggs together (preferably in a round-bottomed copper bowl), using a balloon whisk, to a whitish foam. Add the fortified wine and cinnamon and mix well.

Stand the bowl over a pan of gently simmering water on a low heat and continue to beat and stir until you have a thick, almost firm, foam. Pour into glasses.

Serve at once, while still warm, accompanied by delicate dessert biscuits, or allow to cool and then chill before eating.

REGIONAL PRODUCTS

Cheeses, wines, beef cattle, pork products, vegetables, fruit and nuts, rice, mushrooms and truffles are the primary regional products.

CHEESES Piedmont and the Aosta Valley produce some of the finest cheeses in Italy (see page 15), notably fontina, toma and ricotta, which is especially highly prized.

WINES Many of the most prestigious wines of Italy come from Piedmont. The principal vineyards are in the south, around Alba. Here the Nebbiolo grape reigns supreme, and is made into the famed DOCG reds, Barolo and Barbaresco; the DOC wine, Carema, said to be favoured by Napoleon; Gattinara and a Nebbiolo. Barbera grapes are planted too, and Barbera wine is the ideal accompaniment to *bagna cauda*. These strong and flavoursome reds complement the hearty meat and game dishes of the region perfectly. I find they compare favourably with the reds of Bordeaux.

White wines take second place. A fashionable wine is Gavi, made in the south-west near the border with Liguria. The dry white Arneis is popular too, as is the dry and fragrant Erbaluce, and these wines are ideal with antipasti, fish and light meats. But perhaps the most famous whites are those made from the Moscato grape. The Moscato d'Asti is a fine white; the Naturale version is a great dessert wine; and the sparkling one, Asti Spumante, needs no introduction. These wines are perfect with cakes and puddings – or simply for celebrations. Piedmont is also the birthplace of the most famous of vermouth wines, which the Martini family started to produce in 1863.

Other typical regional dishes

Agnolotti con ripieno di riso Ravioli filled with meat and/or greens and rice

Batsoa Pig's trotters boiled, boned, cut into strips and deep-fried, served with green sauce

Bônet Egg custard enriched with crushed amaretti, cocoa and rum

Brasato al Barolo Beef casseroled in Barolo

Caffè valdostana Coffee with lemon peel, sugar and grappa, served from a communal bowl

Caponet Baked stuffed Savoy cabbage leaves

Carbonade Salted beef, stewed with onions and wine, typical of Brusson

Composta di marroni Compote of chestnuts

Costoletta alla valdostana Veal chop fried, then baked with a topping of sliced fontina

Finanziera di pollo *Ragù* of chicken offal

Fonduta valdostana con tartufi Fondue made with the local fontina cheese, served with truffle

Fritto misto alla piemontese Deep-fried pieces of meat, offal and vegetables

Gnocchi alla bava Potato gnocchi with cheeses

Lardo di Arnaz Cured and dried pork fat, eaten like prosciutto

Lepre in salmi Jugged hare

Lingua in salsa verde Tongue with green sauce

Monte Bianco Chestnut purée enriched with cocoa, vanilla and rum, topped with whipped cream

Paniscia di novara Bean and pork soup

Perette al vino Small pears cooked in Barolo

Polenta concia Polenta with fontina and butter

Rane in padella Fried frogs

Risotto alla piemontese Risotto with truffles

Timballo di pere martine Pear pie

Tofeja Bean and pork rind soup

Trota al vino Trout fried, then braised in wine

Vitello tonnato Veal in tuna sauce

Zuppa alla valpelleuneentze Cabbage, fontina and bread soup

BEEF Piedmontese cattle produce milk for many great cheeses and their excellent meat is used in rich stews and roasts. The Fassone del Piemonte is regarded as the best breed. Every region of Italy has a *brasato* or beef stew, but the Piedmontese keep the piece of meat whole and braise it in the local Barolo (*brasato al Barolo*). For *carne all'albese*, fine raw slices of beef or veal (sometimes *sanato*, milk-fed veal) are dressed as a salad and served in season, often with slices of raw cep or slivers of white truffle. Beef also features in the famous meat dish of the north, *bollito misto* (boiled meats). A Piedmontese version can have up to seven different types of meat in it: among them beef primarily, but also veal, chicken, tongue, a calf's head, pork belly and a *cotechino* sausage (the latter cooked separately). The best *bollito* – the *gran bui* – is accompanied by at least four tangy sauces. In the Aosta Valley, *carbonade* is the classic beef dish (the French influence evident again) and is typically served with polenta.

OTHER MEAT PRODUCTS Most of these are specialities of the Aosta Valley. *Lardo di Arnaz* DOP is thick lard, which is salted, covered with rosemary and air-dried for several months. It is thinly sliced and served raw as an antipasto, or cut thickly and melted on toasted bread in the oven. *Sugna* or pork fat is rendered and used for cooking, and also for preserving. *Boudin noir*, or *sanguinaccio*, is a fresh black pudding made with pig's blood. *Jambon de bosses* DOP is a raw cured ham, similar to Parma ham. *Mucetta* is the dried meat of the chamois, served cut into very thin slices. *Sautissa* is a pork sausage, sold by the metre, which is either grilled or used in *ragùs* with polenta.

LOMBARDIA

Stretching from the Alps in the north to the River Po on its southern border, Lombardy is one of the most industrial regions of Italy and the most highly populated especially around Milan, yet it is also an extraordinarily beautiful region. The famous great lakes are all here, and the region has a rich and varied agriculture, and a wonderful cuisine, which varies from city to city, and village to village.

The original Lombards (also called *Langobards* or *Longobards*) were a Germanic people who invaded northern Italy in the mid 6th century and established a kingdom in the Po Valley. The present-day Lombards are a sophisticated lot, as interested in making a killing (a financial one) as their ancestors. Interestingly, the English phrase 'Lombard Street', referring to the British banking and financial world, originated from the Lombardian money changers who once worked in that particular street in the City of London. Milan, Lombardy's primary city, is certainly thriving today, with a population in excess of nine million. It is Italy's industrial and financial centre, and one of the main fashion centres in the world.

Move away from the cities and you appreciate the natural beauty of this region, especially the well-known lakes Como, Maggiore, Garda and Iseo. Glaciation from the Alps has also left a multitude of lush green valleys and hills, plus the huge and immensely fertile river plain that forms much of the region, that of the River Po. The marshes and fields of this plain were drained and properly irrigated as early as the 10th century. This was carried out firstly by the Church (the region is rich in medieval monasteries and churches), and later by some of the wealthy and noble families who assumed control of the area, among them the Gonzagas, Sforzas and Viscontis. Leonardo da Vinci, although Tuscan by birth, became an advisor to Duke Ludovico Sforza in the late 15th century, and is said to have lent his expertise to the task of drainage.

Not surprisingly, the Lombardian agricultural industry became one of the most successful in Italy. It led to something of a dual society, and indeed cuisine, with a rich diet and dishes for those who could afford it, and a peasant subsistence for those who could not.

CULINARY TRADITIONS & SPECIALITIES

Historical and geographical influences have shaped the Lombardian cuisine of today. In 1535, Phillip, son of the Spanish king, Charles V, became Duke of Milan and the Spaniards went on to rule Lombardy for nearly 200 years. They introduced saffron and rice-growing, hence the famous saffron risotto of Milan. After the War of Spanish Succession, it was the Austrians who took over in northern Italy and Lombardy, and this accounts for the Germanic flavours – the stewed meat and cabbage dishes, the *costoletta alla milanese* (similar to *Wienerschnitzel*) and the cake-breads for which the region is well known. A French influence, filtering through from the House of Savoy in neighbouring Piedmont, is evident in the use of dairy foods such as butter and cream.

Over time, agriculture and eating styles have changed, partly because Lombardy has become more cosmopolitan. During the last 50 years or so, immigrants from the south of Italy have settled in the region, bringing with them their customs and culinary preferences. A proportion of the produce in Milan's markets is brought in from Puglia, so southern ingredients are sold alongside local products, and the Milanese cuisine is more varied – Mediterranean even – than historically it might be. Milan, like any big city, has absorbed influences from all over, and there are too many fast-food establishments for my liking, but you can still eat well here, if you choose carefully. However, traditional Lombardian food is easier to find away in the provinces.

Agriculturally, Lombardy is grain country, with vast acreages given over to rice, wheat and buckwheat, a local variant. The main areas of grain production are in Lomellina (between Milan and Pavia) and the fertile triangle along the north of the Po, between Pavia, Mantua and Cremona. *Grano saraceno* (buckwheat) is produced in the Valtellina Valley, not far from Milan. This is used, along with '00' flour, to make a noodle-type pasta called *pizzoccheri*, probably the only buckwheat pasta used in Italy. Traditionally served with cabbage, potatoes and cheese (that Austrian influence again), it is a rich main-course dish, popular with vegetarians. Meat-eaters like it with sausage. Buckwheat is also used with maize in the local coarse polenta, which was the main food in the peasant diet for centuries. In Brescia and Bergamo, this polenta is often served with grilled and skewered small wild birds. It is known as *polenta taragna*, after the long stick, a *tarello*, which is used to stir it. *Sciatt*, or *frittelle valtellinesi di grano saraceno*, are fritters made with buckwheat.

The local rice is used in a variety of dishes, notably risotto, which is flavoured with all manner of ingredients, including oxtail, marrow, pumpkin (also used in pasta), sausage, quail, lake fish, and the frogs that abound in the rice paddies of the Po Valley. The Spanish influence reveals itself again in the addition of butter towards the end of cooking, a stage known as *mantecare*, after the Spanish for butter, *mantequilla*. Rice is also used in the local peasant *minestre* (rich soups), but the most famous of all – minestrone – uses pasta.

Luccio in Salsa Pike with sauce

This rather curious way of preparing freshwater fish to be eaten cold originates from Mantua. Lakes Maggiore, Como and Garda, and many lesser known lakes and rivers in Lombardy provide plenty of freshwater fish to choose from. I have also tried this recipe with carp and tench, and although these fish both have a muddier taste, they still tasted delicious. You must cook and prepare the dish a day in advance.

SERVES 4–6

1 pike, about 1 kg, gutted, cleaned and scaled
1 carrot, finely chopped
1 celery stalk, finely chopped
1 onion, finely chopped
1 garlic clove, finely chopped
2–3 bay leaves
50 ml white wine vinegar
salt and pepper

Sauce

8 tbsp olive oil
1 small onion, finely chopped
4–5 salted anchovy fillets, rinsed and drained
2–3 tbsp finely chopped flat-leaf parsley
1 garlic clove, finely chopped
2 tbsp capers in vinegar
1 small pickled sweet chilli, cut into little cubes
40 g lard or pancetta fat, finely sliced
50 ml dry white wine

Rinse the fish inside and out. Put the carrot, celery, onion, garlic, bay leaves, wine vinegar and 1.5 litres water in a large shallow pan. Bring to the boil, add salt and pepper, then add the fish. Bring to a low simmer and poach for 30 minutes (or a little longer if the fish is larger). Leave to cool in the liquid.

Meanwhile, for the sauce, heat the olive oil in a pan and fry the onion until softened. Add all the other ingredients and simmer gently for 10 minutes, stirring occasionally.

When the fish is completely cold, lift it out of the liquid on to a board and carefully bone it – use tweezers to remove any small bones. Skin the fish fillets and arrange on a plate. Pour the sauce over the fish, allow to cool, then refrigerate.

Serve the next day, with a green salad and/or a potato salad and some beetroot if you like.

Being landlocked, it is freshwater fish that are most popular in Lombardy, notably eels from the region's rivers, and pike, trout and *alborella* from Lakes Como and Maggiore. A local fish speciality called *misseltit* is made by hanging *alborella* and another local fish, *agoni*, to dry in the sun, then grilling the fish to serve.

Beef and pigs are raised in the fertile Po Valley, and Lombardy is famous for its preserved meats and salami (see page 32). The fresh meats are used in a number of famous local dishes, including *bollito misto*, *ossobuco* and *cassoeula* or *cazzoeula* (a pork and cabbage stew, which takes its name from the Spanish pot, *cazuela*). Cow's and sheep's milk are used in the region's famous cheeses (see page 35).

A large proportion of Italy's fruit comes from Lombardy, including cherries, pears, figs and apricots. A particular speciality of the area is *mostarda di Cremona* – fruits candied slowly in a heavy sugar syrup flavoured with essence of mustard (illustrated on page 90). This is eaten with *bollito misto*, the hearty dish claimed by both Piedmont and Lombardy. Fresh fruits are also dried and used in other Lombardian specialities, including the renowned Milanese Christmas speciality, *panettone*, and the *pane con l'uva*, a fruit loaf usually made by the Milanese at Easter. Almonds form the basis of the famous amaretti biscuits, which have been made in Saronno for more than a hundred years. The Italian almond liqueur, amaretto di Saronno, also originated here.

There are numerous festivals or *sagre* in Lombardy, mostly in honour of the grape. From the beginning of September through to the middle of October you will come across celebrations all over the region, encompassing folklore and local gastronomic specialities. In September, visit the festivities at Grumello in Bergamo; Broni, Canneto Pavese and Cicognola in Pavia; and during the last week, in Gussago in Brescia. In October the Festa dell'Uva is celebrated in Capriano del Colle in Brescia, and Graffignana in Lodi.

Cazzoeula alla Milanese Pork stew

You won't find *cazzoeula* (or casserole) in a posh Milanese restaurant, but rather in a good family-run *trattoria* or – better still – a Lombardian home. On a winter's evening, when it's already dark and foggy in Milan (it usually is), this is the ideal comforting dish to lift your spirits after a hard day's work. There are many local versions of this dish, but I have chosen the one from Milan.

SERVES 4–6

2 pig's trotters, cut into pieces and pre-cooked
800 g meaty spare ribs
4 tbsp olive oil
1 large onion, sliced
400 g carrots, peeled and cut into chunks
400 g celeriac, peeled and cubed
200 g pork skin without fat, cut into squares
salt and pepper
200 g small pure pork sausages
1.5 kg Savoy cabbage, cored and divided into leaves
3 tbsp tomato purée
a few celery leaves

Put the pig's trotters and spare ribs in a pan with water to cover, bring to the boil and boil for 20 minutes to render some of the fat. Drain and put into a large casserole. Add the olive oil, onion, carrots and celeriac.

Season the pork skin squares with pepper, roll up and tie with string. Add the pork skin rolls to the casserole with the sausages. Cover with water, season with salt and pepper and cook gently for 2 hours. Meanwhile, blanch the cabbage leaves in boiling salted water for a few minutes and drain.

Skim off the fat from the surface of the stew. Dilute the tomato purée with a little water and stir into the stew with the cabbage and celery leaves. Cook for a further 20 minutes. Serve with bread or polenta, or with baked potatoes.

Pizzoccheri della Valtellina

Buckwheat pasta with cabbage, beans and cheese

Pizzoccheri is a type of short, wide tagliatelle made from a mixture of buckwheat flour and wheat flour. It originates from Teglio in the Valtellina, the valley north of Milan where the famous bresaola (air-dried beef), Bitto cheese and lots of very good wines come from. The use of _grano saraceno_ (buckwheat) was widespread in ancient times, as it was a grain that could grow almost anywhere. This rustic, rich pasta bake is a favourite in Lombardy.

SERVES 4–6

200 g potato, peeled and diced
150 g green beans, topped, tailed and halved
300 g Savoy cabbage or spinach, shredded
salt and pepper
300 g _pizzoccheri_ pasta
150 g Bitto (or Asiago) cheese, cut into small cubes
100 g unsalted butter
3 garlic cloves, finely sliced
60 g Parmesan, freshly grated

Heat the oven to 200°C/Gas 6. Cook the potato, beans and cabbage together in boiling salted water until tender, about 15 minutes. Meanwhile cook the *pizzoccheri* in a separate pan of boiling salted water until *al dente*. Drain the vegetables and pasta.

Layer the pasta and vegetables in a shallow ovenproof dish, starting with the *pizzoccheri*, and interspersing the vegetables with the diced cheese. Melt the butter with the garlic in a small pan until it foams, then pour over the top of the layers. Scatter the grated Parmesan and pepper on top, and bake for 15 minutes. Mix everything together – it's a messy dish – and serve!

Risotto con Acetosa e Rane Sorrel and frog's leg risotto

Frog's legs are commonly eaten in the province of Pavia. While filming for TV in Italy, I tried adding them to my favourite sorrel risotto – the result was so good that I dedicated the dish to my niece Sophie Conran on the occasion of her wedding, which I was unable to attend. I rarely tinker with food that is good already, but in this case it worked a treat … I hope Sophie will think so too. Frozen frog's legs will do, unless you happen to live in Lombardy or France!

SERVES 6

6 tbsp olive oil
400 g fresh or frozen frog's legs
salt and pepper
4 tbsp dry white wine
1.2 litres chicken stock (page 250)
80 g butter
1 onion, finely sliced
350 g risotto rice
150 g trimmed wild or cultivated sorrel (cleaned weight, without stalks), chopped
60 g Parmesan, freshly grated

Heat 4 tbsp of the olive oil in a frying pan and very briefly fry the frog's legs with some salt and pepper, until cooked, about 4–5 minutes. Add the wine and let it evaporate, about 2–3 minutes. Allow to cool, then strip the frog meat from the bones.

Meanwhile, heat the stock, and keep it hot – at simmering point – on the hob.

Melt 20 g of the butter with the remaining olive oil in a medium pan and fry the onion until soft. Add the rice and stir for a minute, then start to add the hot stock, ladle by ladle. Avoid drowning the rice in stock, and wait until each ladleful is absorbed before you add the next.

After 10 minutes' cooking and stirring, add the chopped sorrel and the frog meat. Continue to cook and add stock in the same way until the rice is *al dente*, then add the rest of the butter and the grated Parmesan. Stir well and serve. The sorrel gives the risotto a distinctive bright green colour.

REGIONAL PRODUCTS

Lombardy is the bread basket of Italy, with a huge proportion of its acreage given over to grain production, primarily rice and wheat. Beef and pigs are the major livestock, their meat eaten both fresh and preserved, and the milk of course goes to make excellent cheeses. The wines of Lombardy are also very good.

MEAT PRODUCTS Lombardy is the source of many of Italy's finest cured meats and salami. Bresaola, the delicious cured raw fillet of beef, comes from Valtellina and is typically served thinly sliced as an antipasto. *Cotechino bianco*, a fresh pork sausage made with *cotica* (pork rind) comes from Valtellina too. Prosciutto and a good salami are produced in Brianza and the hills of Mantua. *Salame milano* is a very fine salami (also called *crespone*). *Salame varzi* comes from Pavia, and is pure pork with 30 per cent fat. *Salame d'oca* is made from goose in Mortara, a small town in the Lomellina. The *violino di Chiavenna* is a ham produced in Valtellina from the leg of a lamb or goat, then air-dried. It is called 'violin' because, to cut it, the ham is slung over one shoulder as you would while playing the violin. *Mortadella di fegato*, from Lago d'Orta, is a lesser-known version of the famous Bolognese mortadella, made with pig's liver. In Milan, the Bolognese form is so admired, they call it simply Bologna (corrupted in America to 'boloney' sausage).

CHEESES Some of Italy's most famous cheeses are produced in Lombardy (see page 35). Lombardian *formaggi* are mostly DOP (*denominazione origine protetta*) or in EU parlance, PDO, 'protected denomination of origin'. Lombardy's fresh cheeses esteemed locally, among them some wonderful *caprini* (goat's cheeses).

WINES Oltrepò Pavese is the largest of Lombardy's wine-growing areas (the name translates as 'across the Po from Pavia') and it is a small hilly triangle, covered with vines. Here red Bonardas and Barberas are produced, and many of the whites go to form the basis of much of Italy's fizz. Elsewhere the wines produced include Franciacorta, Valcalepio, Sforzato, Garda and Valtellina Superiore – all red and DOCG (or *Denominazione di Origine Controllata e Garantita*).

Codeghin in Camisa Sausage in chemise

This recipe originates from the Val Camonica, a source of many classic recipes. The idea is to make a pocket in a joint of veal and stuff it with the cooked pork sausage and sautéed porcini ... intriguing and delicious! The *cotechino* (cooking sausages) of this area are made of 75 per cent pork and the rest beef. If you can't find fresh *cotechino*, you can use pre-cooked ones.

SERVES 6

- **2 raw or cooked *cotechino* sausages, about 250 g each**
- **6 tbsp olive oil**
- **1 garlic clove, finely sliced**
- **500 g fresh porcini mushrooms, cleaned and sliced**
- **1 tbsp chopped flat-leaf parsley**
- **1 tbsp chopped basil**
- **1 boned breast or loin of veal joint, about 2.2 kg**
- **salt and pepper**
- **40 g butter**
- **150 ml chicken stock (page 250)**
- **200 ml white wine**

Put the *cotechino* sausages into a saucepan and cover with cold water. Bring to the boil, then lower the heat and simmer, allowing 3 hours if raw, 20 minutes if pre-cooked. Drain and cool slightly.

Heat 4 tbsp of the olive oil in a large sauté pan with the garlic. Add the porcini and sauté until softened and the juices have evaporated. Remove from the heat and mix in the herbs. Leave to cool for 10 minutes or so.

Heat the oven to 180°C/Gas 4. Using a sharp knife, cut a deep pocket in the veal from one side, between the layers of fat and meat. Season the inside of the pocket with salt and pepper, then stuff with the *cotechino*. Put the mushrooms into the pocket too, pushing them all around the sausage. Sew up the opening with kitchen string.

Heat the remaining olive oil and the butter in a flameproof casserole and brown the veal on all sides. Add the stock and wine, cover and braise in the oven for 1½ hours.

Skim off the fat from the surface of the liquor. Carve the veal into slices and serve with the liquor and potato purée or polenta.

FORMAGGI

Cheeses of Lombardy

Bagoss This is a cow's milk cheese produced in the Caffaro Valley in the province of Brescia. It can be eaten fresh, or matured for grating or grilling. Also known as Bagosso and Bagolino.

Bitto A half-fat cow's milk cheese from the province of Sondrio, and from Valtellina. Mainly used for grating, it can be eaten as a table cheese and is used in the making of *pizzoccheri* (see page 30).

Crescenza A full-fat soft cow's milk cheese, which can be enjoyed now all year round. Eaten as a dessert cheese, or for spreading – delicious in the Ligurian *focaccia al formaggio* (see page 84). Also known as certosino.

Dolcelatte This is a milder version of Gorgonzola, factory made in Pavia, and sold very young, after two months.

Gorgonzola This famous blue cheese began life as a *stracchino* or *stracchino verde*, made from the milk of cows *'stracche'* (tired) after the long spring or autumn trek to and from the Alpine pastures. Like most blue-veined cheeses it was originally aged in caves, the veining developing naturally from spores present inside. It was named Gorgonzola, after one of the few villages in which such cheeses were made. Nowadays it is made in other places throughout Lombardy, and the spores are mixed in with the curds. The veins are greenish-blue, in a white to pale yellow paste, and the cheese is aged from 3 to 6 months. It has a 48 per cent fat content.

Grana padano True Parmigiano Reggiano is allowed to be made only in the Po Valley of Emilia-Romagna, but grana padano – a hard cow's milk cheese which is very similar, but recognisably younger – can be made elsewhere in the Po Valley, notably in Lombardy. It is matured for 6 months, and has a fat content of about 30 per cent. It is used like Parmesan, mainly for grating, cooking, or eating raw.

Mascarpone Once only made in southern Lombardy, mascarpone is now produced all over Italy, although it cannot truly be classified as a cheese because rennet is not involved in the processing. It is produced from double cream coagulated with acid, and consists of 50 per cent fat and upwards! It is used as an ingredient for sweets and desserts (including the Venetian *tiramisù*).

Panerone This full-fat soft cheese from the Lodigiano area of Lombardy is also known as 'white Gorgonzola' because it has a similar flavour and shape. Also labelled Pannarone and Pannerone.

Quartirolo This full-fat soft cheese is made exclusively in Lombardy, from the milk of cows who have fed on the fragrant grass in the high peaks of the Quartirolo. It is made in a square shape, like Taleggio, and its fragrance, to me, is reminiscent of mushrooms!

Robiola This soft cow's milk cheese used to be a speciality of Lombardy, but is now made in Piedmont as well (see page 15).

Taleggio This famous Italian table cheese, said to have existed since the 11th century, was once made only in the Taleggio valley, in the Italian pre-Alps. Now it is made elsewhere in Lombardy, and indeed in Veneto. It is another *stracchino* (cow's milk cheese). It has a high fat content (48 per cent), is matured for up to 10 weeks, and is sold in squares.

Torta di San Gaudenzio One of several names for Gorgonzola layered with mascarpone.

Other typical regional dishes

Agnolini dei Gonzaga Small handmade egg pasta cushions, filled with boiled capon, oats, bone marrow, egg and cheese

Agoni all comasca Fish from Lake Como, fried and served with a dressing of olive oil, lemon juice and anchovy fillets

Câsonséi Pasta filled with salami, spinach, eggs, raisins, amaretti, grana padano and breadcrumbs, served with melted butter

Costoletta alla milanese Veal chops, formerly with the bone in, coated in egg and breadcrumbs, then fried in butter

Mondeghili An old Milanese dish made from the minced and fried leftovers of *bollito misto*

Nervitt Calf's feet boned, boiled, cut finely and flavoured with olive oil, capers and onions

Ossobuco Stewed veal shanks, traditionally served with *risotto alla milanese*, and topped with gremolata sauce

Pan de mei A sweet Lombardian bread, also called *pan meino*

Risotto alla milanese Risotto flavoured with saffron and bone marrow, the traditional accompaniment to *ossobuco* or sausages, also eaten on its own

Timballo di piccione A pigeon pie from Cremona

Tinca all lariana Fish from Lake Iseo, stuffed with breadcrumbs, grana padano and some spices, then baked in the oven

Trippa alla milanese Called *busecca* in Milan, tripe is stewed with aromatic vegetables, tomatoes, pancetta and large white beans

Valigini Savoy cabbage leaf parcels enclosing chicken and potatoes (or beef and spices)

Torta Paradiso con Mascarpone

Sponge cake with mascarpone

Rich, creamy mascarpone comes from southern Lombardy and it is the ideal filling for this wonderfully light sponge.

SERVES 4–6

250 g butter, just melted but not oily, plus extra to grease
250 g caster sugar
4 large eggs, beaten
1 tsp vanilla extract
225 g self-raising flour
25 g cornflour
1 tsp baking powder

To serve

300 g mascarpone cheese
50 g caster sugar
few drops of vanilla extract
3–4 tbsp raspberry jam
icing sugar to dust

Heat the oven to 180°C/Gas 4. Line a 25 cm shallow round cake tin with baking parchment and grease with a little butter.

Using a balloon whisk, whip the melted butter into the sugar until light and fluffy, then slowly beat in the eggs and vanilla. Gradually sift the flour, cornflour and baking powder together over the mixture, carefully folding it in with the balloon whisk. Pour into the prepared tin and bake for 20–25 minutes until golden and springy to the touch.

Turn out and cool on a wire rack, then cut horizontally into two layers. Beat the mascarpone with the caster sugar and vanilla extract until smooth. Spread the jam over the bottom cake layer, then cover with the mascarpone mixture. Top with the other cake layer, sprinkle with icing sugar and serve. A glass of Moscato or Malvasia di Pavia is the perfect complement.

Trentino-Alto Adige

This landlocked Alpine region in north-east Italy is bordered by Lombardy and Veneto to the south, and Austria and Switzerland to the north. Trentino and Alto Adige were once separate regions and they have retained some of their own culinary characteristics. The cooking of Trentino is similar to that of Veneto, while Alto Adige is more Austrian and Middle European in flavour.

Set in the Dolomites with the Alps to the north, this region is distinctly mountainous. Alto Adige was part of the Austrian Tyrol until it passed to Italy after World War I, and it is still known to the Germans and Austrians as Südtirol (*Tirolo del Sud* in Italian). As a consequence, in the north people speak German as much as they do Italian, the schools and road signs are bi-lingual, and the cuisine shows many Austrian and German influences. Gnocchi (or *knödel*) is served with *speck* (Austrian smoked ham), and other pork dishes, breads and sweets are decidedly Austrian in concept. In Trentino, fish, polenta and fungi are especially popular. While Trentino may lean towards the Veneto, it was once also part of the Austro-Hungarian Empire and in pockets throughout the region you will find people of Germanic origin, who speak a Germanic patois and cook dishes with a German flavour.

The region is bisected by the Adige River, which flows from the very north in the mountains, flanks Lake Garda, then flows on to the plain of Veneto, emerging into the Gulf of Venice just north of the mouth of the greater River Po. The whole region relies on forestry, tourism (both winter and summer, with mainly German and Austrian visitors), and agriculture, the latter dependent, of course, on terrain. In the mountainous north, it tends to be the fruits of the wild – mushrooms, berries and game of all kinds. In more southerly Trentino with its gentler slopes, it is olive oil, wine, grain, maize, vegetables and fruit. Orchards abound and some 50 per cent of Italy's apples are cultivated in Trentino.

CULINARY TRADITIONS & SPECIALITIES

In Alto Adige, the pig rules, and the main protagonist of the cuisine is *speck* (see page 44). This salted, air-dried and smoked shoulder ham is both farmhouse and factory produced, and is eaten alone like prosciutto, or cooked together with an array of other items. Other meats are preserved too: there are salami made from game, horse and donkey, and a bresaola – *mocetta rendenera*. A pork and turnip sausage is produced and eaten with sauerkraut, which is popular in homes throughout Alto Adige. Flavourings, such as horseradish and caraway seeds, are similar to those of Austria and are added to breads, meat and vegetable dishes.

Trout and game are popular, both being eaten fresh and smoked. *Gulasch* (meat stew), *knödel* (bread dumplings, *canederli* or gnocchi in Italian), *strudel* and *krapfen* (doughnuts) all feature in the cooking. Breads are dark, often made with rye, and some are so tough they have to be softened – usually in soups – to make them palatable; others are soft and light. Although the food is undeniably Tyrolean in influence, the Südtiroleners or Tirolesi don't claim to be either Austrian or Italian; they regard themselves as unique and independent.

As I have said, Trentino shares many culinary characteristics with its northern neighbour, filtered down through Alto Adige perhaps. Wild mushrooms are a passion, and in season if you visit some of the markets in Trentino, you will see a spectacular array – over 60 varieties at times. Collectors from all over the region bring in these mushrooms and experts are on hand to help differentiate between edible and inedible species. Chestnuts, cherries and soft fruits – including blueberries, wild strawberries and raspberries – come from the Valle Garina. If you are ever in the area, I recommend you visit the restaurant Al Borgo in Rovereto, south of Trento, which specialises in the local cuisine.

With nearly 300 lakes and rivers, Trentino has been called the 'Finland of Italy' and there is a splendid variety of freshwater fish. These are grilled, baked, smoked, cooked in risottos, and often served with polenta. Despite this bounty, like their neighbours in Veneto, the Trentini are equally fond of *stoccafisso* (dried cod) that they mistakenly call *baccalà*, which is salted and dried. *Stoccafisso* is so dried that it retains only about 15 per cent water, and is brittle. It has to be soaked before cooking, and is often beaten with a mallet to tenderise it, too. It can be combined

with raw potatoes, or even raw artichokes and baked with oil and milk, often with porcini added. I love this, but my wife says it tastes like cardboard!

Fish, meat and wild mushrooms are all accompanied by bread, usually the dark, tough rye or barley type, or by polenta. The latter is either golden or *polenta nera* (black polenta), when the maize is mixed with darker-hued *grano saraceno* (buckwheat). Surprisingly for Italy, there is little pasta in the region, although Trentino has a spinach-stuffed ravioli. Spaghetti dishes and pizzas may have crept in, but on the whole, both parts of the region have remained true to their culinary traditions.

Wine is important to both provinces and festivals are dedicated to wine growing – and drinking. In the Südtirol, men and women wear a *tracht*, a sort of uniform (the ladies with multicoloured shawls), and parade through the villages and towns in a military fashion, accompanied by bands playing traditional marching music. One of the most curious traditions reminds me of the Heurigen celebration of the new wine in Vienna and Burgenland. From around the end of October, in the various cellars of Trentino, the *neuen* wine is offered for tasting, together with roasted chestnuts and walnuts (also of the season). The resulting inebriation is measured in particular degrees, from *stiebr* (light), through *rieberle* (jolly), *tull* (a bit worrying), and *bissofen* (time for bed). The ultimate condition, *sbornia claustrale* (a colossal cloister drink), is supposedly a reference to the ways in which monks, nuns and others in cloisters would preserve and encourage the growing of vines – rather than an inference concerning the amount of wine drunk therein.

There are a number of *sagre* or festivals throughout the year. In Torbole, on the last Sunday of Carnevale, there is the festival of Sbigolata, at which *bigoli* (thick pasta) is served with a sauce made of olive oil and *aola* (salted fish). In the second half of July in San Martino di Castrozza, *salsiccie e polenta* is celebrated. Around the same time, there is a 'mushroom and butter village fair' in Predazzo, where roasted pig, sausage and polenta are served. This is repeated on the first Sunday of August in Bellamonte. During September, there is a grape and wine festival in Mezza Corona. And in Torgelen and Trentino in November, the wine cellars are opened for the tasting of the new wine.

Schwammerlsuppe Chanterelle soup

SERVES 4

As you may know I am passionate about wild mushrooms. This soup, also called *Zuppa di Finferli*, is from the Alto Adige, and it reminds me of Vienna, where I studied for two years.

250 g fresh chanterelles, cleaned
90 g butter
60 g plain flour
1.5 litres hot chicken stock (page 250)
1 small onion, finely chopped
1 garlic clove, finely chopped
salt and pepper
1 tbsp finely chopped flat-leaf parsley
4 tbsp double cream

Chop the fresh chanterelles, keeping a few whole for garnish.

To make the soup base, melt 50g of the butter in a pan, then add the flour and cook, stirring continuously, until the flour starts to change colour. Gradually add the chicken stock, a little at a time, continuing to stir to avoid lumps.

Melt the remaining butter in another pan and fry the onion and garlic until softened. Add all the chanterelles and fry for 6–7 minutes. Add some salt to taste, and the chopped parsley. Take out the whole chanterelles and set aside. Tip everything else into the soup base liquid and stir well. Taste and adjust the seasoning, then stir in the cream.

Serve in warm bowls, topped with the whole mushrooms and accompanied by lightly toasted crusty bread.

Gnocchi di Ricotta con Sugo di Porcini

Ricotta dumplings with porcini sauce

SERVES 4

Trentino is justifiably proud of its wild mushrooms, used here to make a flavourful sauce for ricotta dumplings, which are often eaten just with grated Parmesan and butter.

Dumplings
400 g fresh ricotta (preferably sheep's milk)
180 g plain flour
4 tbsp dry breadcrumbs, plus extra if needed
salt and pepper
freshly grated nutmeg

Sauce
20 g dried porcini mushrooms
70 g butter
1 garlic clove, crushed
200 g fresh porcini mushrooms, finely sliced
1 tbsp torn parsley leaves
2 tbsp dry white wine

To finish
50 g Parmesan, freshly grated

To make the dumplings, mix the ricotta, flour and breadcrumbs together, seasoning with salt, pepper and nutmeg to taste. To check that the mixture will stick together (there is no egg here), take a little pellet of the mixture and drop it into boiling salted water. If it falls apart, you need to add some more breadcrumbs to the mixture. When the consistency is right, roll the mixture into sausages, 2 cm in diameter, and cut into 2–3 cm lengths. Press the gnocchi gently on the tines of a fork to give them a rippled effect, rolling them off on to a clean tea-towel. Cover and rest for 30 minutes.

Meanwhile for the sauce, soak the porcini in hot water for 20 minutes. Drain and chop the soaked porcini, reserving the liquid. Melt the butter in a pan, add the garlic and fry until softened but not coloured. Immediately add the sliced fresh and dried porcini and sauté for 5–8 minutes. Season with salt and pepper, and add the parsley, wine and porcini liquid (leaving any sediment behind). Bring to the boil and reduce slightly.

Bring a very large pan of salted water to the boil, add the gnocchi and cook for a minute or two, scooping them out with a slotted spoon when they come to the surface. Add them to the porcini sauce and toss to mix. Serve hot, sprinkled with grated Parmesan.

REGIONAL PRODUCTS

SPECK This Austrian smoked ham shoulder features greatly in the cuisine of Alto Adige, yet it is a relatively recent introduction into the more southerly regions of Italy. In Alto Adige it is used in sauces, *ragùs*, stews and with vegetable dishes, and the real thing is still made at home. The boned shoulder is flattened and cured with saltpetre, garlic, bay leaves, juniper berries and pepper. Each family will add their 'secret ingredient' to the cure. After the initial marinating, the meat is put in a sloping container so that exuding juices can gather, to be poured back over the meat at intervals. The meat is then hung in a special smoking chimney, to be slowly dry-smoked over sweet wood and branches of juniper. *Speck* doesn't taste too salty, and is deliciously smoky. It is eaten in the same way as prosciutto, although it tastes quite different and is much cheaper.

CHEESES Trentino-Alto Adige cheeses are little known outside Italy. The most popular – and the cheese with the longest history – is probably Vezzena. It is made from cow's milk and is very similar to the Asiago of Veneto. Other cheeses are mostly produced in the area between Trento and Bolzano. Of these, Nostrano, Puzzone di Moena ('the stinker'), Spressa, Casolet, Salandro and Poina Enfumegado are worth trying if you are in the region.

WINES AND SPIRITS The DOC wines of Alto Adige are noticeably Austrian in flavour. They are produced from grapes grown on the mountains that descend to the Adige river and its tributary, the Isarco. Red grapes such as Lagrein, Schiava and Cabernet are planted lowest, with the French Chardonnay, Pinots Grigio and Bianco a little higher, and the German grapes such as Riesling and Sylvaner furthest up. Good sparkling wines are made from Chardonnay and the Pinots Bianco, Grigio and Nero.

Some of the DOC Trentino wines are similar to those of Alto Adige, while others are more typically Italian. There are 17 different varietal wines, the best of the local ones being Teroldego Rotaliano and Marzemino di Isera, both reds. There is also an interesting Vin Santo.

Fruit grappas and schnapps – usually from pears – are made in Alto Adige, and to counteract all that alcohol, the cool, fresh waters of the rivers running down from the Alps are sourced for bottling, among them Pejo.

Hering Hausfrauenart

Salt herring with soured cream, onion and apples

In my limited time in Austria, I learnt to appreciate various aspects of Germanic culture. Among other things, I become more punctual and more precise – as an Italian I needed to! Regarding food, I appreciated everything that tasted good. This recipe reminds me of Hamburg, but herrings are popular in Trentino and prepared in a similar way. For this you need a *schmaltz hering*: these are caught during the months when the fish are very fat and are then kept in salted brine for up to a year. You may be lucky enough to find some already filleted and kept in oil, as I have come across in London's Soho.

SERVES 4

8–12 small potatoes, peeled
salt
1 crisp, green dessert apple
fillets of 4 *schmaltz hering*, not too salty
1 onion, thinly sliced
8 tbsp soured cream

Cook the potatoes in boiling salted water until just tender, then drain. Thinly slice the apple.

Arrange the herring fillets on serving plates along with the apple and onion slices. Add the warm potatoes and drizzle the soured cream on top. Serve with a good glass of schnapps.

Krauti con Speck e Canederli Choucroûte garnie

This rather elaborate preparation, also called *schlachter platte mit knödeln*, is a great winter dish for ravenous appetites. Originally from Austria and Germany, the *schlachter platte* is made with fresh black pudding and smoked pork products. It is also eaten in Alsace (once German) and the French call it *choucroûte garnie*, not surprisingly as sauerkraut is the main ingredient. If prepared properly it is a delight, and for me it is a wonderful dish to enjoy in northern Italy. The accompanying *canederli* or *knödeln* are the rich Tyrolean type, which are often eaten in a tomato sauce. Should you prefer a leaner version, then omit the *speck* and salami.

SERVES 4

1 kg sauerkraut (from a jar)
100 ml apple juice
1 1/2 tsp caraway seeds
6 black peppercorns
160 g smoked belly pork (4 slices)
200 g *kasseler* (smoked pork cutlets) or 4 slices of pork loin
4 frankfurter sausages
4 little *blutwurst* (black pudding) sausages, or in slices (optional)
olive oil for frying (optional)

Canederli

350 g stale bread, crusts removed, cut into small cubes
200 ml milk
4 eggs, beaten
about 4–6 tbsp plain flour
50 g *speck*, finely cubed (optional)
100 g good salami, finely cubed (optional)
1 tbsp finely chopped flat-leaf parsley
1 tbsp finely chopped marjoram
freshly grated nutmeg
salt and pepper

For the *canederli*, put the bread cubes in a bowl with the milk and beaten eggs and leave to absorb for 1 hour.

Tip the sauerkraut into a pan and add the apple juice, 100 ml water, the caraway seeds and peppercorns. Cook slowly for 1 hour, adding water if necessary.

To make the *canederli*, add a third of the flour to the bread mixture, then the cubed meats and herbs. Mix well, seasoning with nutmeg, salt and pepper to taste. The mixture should be firm enough to shape into balls, if not mix in more of the flour. Shape into balls, each the size of a tangerine and dust with flour.

To cook the *canederli*, plunge them into a pan of boiling salted water, lower the heat and simmer for 20 minutes or until they come to the surface.

Meanwhile, steam the smoked pork belly, cutlets and frankfurter sausages in a steamer until hot and tender, about 15–20 minutes. Fry the black pudding slices in a little olive oil if using.

Put a portion of the sauerkraut in the middle of each plate. Arrange a slice of pork, a cutlet, a slice of fried black pudding if using, and a frankfurter on top. Drain the *canederli* and place two on each plate. Serve with mustard.

Gulasch con Spätzle Meat goulash with dumplings

Goulash originates from Hungary, while *spätzle* come from Stuttgart in Germany. How they came together in this part of Italy, I don't really know, but they combine well. In Trentino, as in Germany, a special perforated tool called a *spätzle* plate, which fits over a saucepan, is used to shape the *spätzle*, but I find the large-holed side of a cheese grater works fine. As an alternative, you could serve the goulash with boiled potatoes.

SERVES 6

1.1 kg leg of beef (*ossobuco* or shin of beef is the best)
80 g pork fat (lard), cut into small cubes, or bacon lardons
4 tbsp olive oil
400 g onions, coarsely sliced
1 bouquet garni (rosemary, oregano, bay leaves)
2 tbsp tomato purée
1 tbsp sweet Hungarian paprika (more if you prefer)
salt and pepper

Spätzle

300 g plain flour
150 ml milk
3 eggs
pinch of salt
50 g butter, melted

Trim the beef of all sinews and cut into cubes. Put the pork fat cubes and olive oil in a large saucepan over a medium heat and allow to sweat and brown. Add the onions and fry until softened, about 5–8 minutes. Now add the beef, bouquet garni, tomato purée diluted with a little water, paprika and 1 litre water. Bring to a simmer and cook gently, covered, for 1½ hours or longer until the meat is tender. Stir from time to time, and add a little more water if required.

Meanwhile, make the *spätzle*. Put the flour into a bowl and make a well in the centre. Add the milk, eggs and salt, then gradually incorporate into the flour and stir well to make a smooth, runny dough. Set aside for an hour or so, until little bubbles come to the surface.

When the goulash is ready, take out the bouquet garni and season with salt and pepper to taste. To cook the *spätzle*, bring a large pan of lightly salted water to the boil and position the *spätzle* plate if you have one. Cook the dough in batches, forcing it through the holes in the plate (or a large-holed grater) directly into the boiling water – they will rise to the surface almost immediately. Cook for another minute or so, then scoop them out on to a clean tea-towel to drain while you cook the rest.

Toss the *spätzle* with the melted butter in a pan over a medium heat to warm through. Serve the goulash with the *spätzle*.

Other typical regional dishes

Anguilla alla trentina Eels braised with butter, onions, wine, herbs and spices

Chifel Crisp breadstick coated in caraway seeds, eaten in the Südtirol with frankfurters

Eisacktaler weinsuppe A fine beef stock mixed with half its volume of Pinot Grigio, then whisked with cream and Parmesan; also called *zuppa di vino della Val d'Iscarco*

Gnocchi di ricotta Ricotta dumplings, served with melted butter and cheese

Kastanientorte Cake made of puréed chestnuts

Knödel Bread dumplings – plain or stuffed with *speck*, salami or liver – eaten in soups, stews, or as an accompaniment to roasted or boiled meats. Also called *canederli* or gnocchi

Krapfen Doughnuts filled with jam or cream

Misto di funghi Wild mushroom stew

Pestolato della val lagarina Leftover cheeses, mixed to a paste with grappa, white wine and pepper; eaten as a spread, on bread

Smacafam The buckwheat polenta of Trentino, typically mixed with *luganega* sausage and baked. It can also be sweet, with raisins instead of sausage

Strudel Flaky pastry with fruit, cream or cream cheese filling

Trota alla trentina Trout marinated in vinegar, then poached in a lemon and red wine sauce

Zelten Festive cake, based on rye in Alto Adige, wheat in Trentino, filled with dried fruit and nuts

Lamponi e More al Limone

Raspberries and blackberries with sugar and lemon

I have often said that Italians have a sweet tooth, but not necessarily after meals. Day-to-day, fresh, ripe seasonal fruit is the usual way to round off a meal. As a young boy, fruit became my responsibility and I became expert in monitoring farmers' fruit crops. During the autumn, I would obtain wonderful raspberries and pick wild blackberries to complement them. Use only perfectly ripe fruit for this dessert.

SERVES 4

300 g mixed raspberries and blackberries
juice of 1 lemon
100 g caster sugar
mascarpone to serve (optional)

Put the berries into a non-reactive bowl and sprinkle with the lemon juice and sugar. Mix very carefully and gently to amalgamate.

Serve the berries with mascarpone if you like.

Friuli-Venezia Giulia

Bordering Austria and the former Yugoslavia, this small region has been greatly influenced by its neighbours, and the cooking is rather like the melting pot of three cultures – Venetian, Austro-Hungarian and Yugoslav. Everyday ingredients, such as pulses, polenta and soup, are typical of a somewhat impoverished region, but one exceptional local product is the excellent *prosciutto di San Daniele.*

This Italian region was only formed in 1947 after centuries of rule by the Austrians and the Venetians, and its capital city, Trieste, was not incorporated until as late as 1954. Friuli is in the Alpine north, while Venezia Giulia occupies the coastal plain. Venezia Giulia is adjacent to Slovenia (once part of Yugoslavia) and many in the area speak Slovene rather than Italian. The Friuli province was founded by Julius Caesar and takes its name from *forum julii* (forum of Julius).

Geography dictates the nature of the region's agriculture and its cuisine. In the Alpine valleys, livestock are raised for meat and milk to produce cheeses; vines, orchards and vegetable gardens flourish on the lower slopes; while maize and other cereals are grown on the plains of southern Friuli. Here fields of golden maize stretch as far as the eye can see. Fish dishes are naturally common along the coast, and reminiscent of those in neighbouring Veneto. Fish stews and *risotti* – some of them *neri* (black) from cuttlefish ink – are popular, as indeed they are in Veneto and further south in Croatia.

Perhaps because of their multi-ethnic origins and the diverse nature of their terrain, the people of this region are pragmatic and always seem to get on with life, whatever befalls them. This was evident to me several years ago after a devastating earthquake hit northern Italy. The damage in Friuli was extensive, yet the Friulians were the first to start rebuilding houses, businesses, farms, roads and their lives. They are also very friendly people. Visit the *osterie*, *trattorie* and restaurants in the region and you will be greeted warmly and made to feel at home immediately. If you're not in need of a full meal, you can simply order a *tajut* (plate of titbits), along with one of the many excellent local wines. Further along the coast in Venice, restaurants cater mainly for tourists, but here in Friuli, tradition reigns supreme and there is not a fast food establishment in sight.

CULINARY TRADITIONS & SPECIALITIES

Mountainous Friuli lies in what is known as 'the polenta, bean and risotto belt' and, in particular, the region grows a lot of maize for polenta. The Friulians love it and eat it as often as other Italians might consume bread. As in Venice, polenta in Friuli is white and is eaten with game, wild mushrooms, pork and salami. Beans are grown in the Carnia Mountains in the north (the most earthquake-prone area); these are served with polenta and used in a variety of soups.

The best-known soup is *jota*, which is traditionally made with beans, polenta and *broade* (turnip relish). Modern versions, including that of Trieste, replace the polenta with potato purée and the *broade* with sauerkraut, and may include softened pork skin and *kasseler* (pickled smoked pork chops on the bone). More like a stew than a soup, *jota* is perfect for surviving the region's winters. The cold, dry *bora* wind affects coastal regions, with gusts of up to 100 miles per hour. In Trieste, rope railings are attached to buildings, so that you can hang on if necessary!

Broade, the traditional flavouring for *jota*, is a unique turnip relish. To make it, turnips are fermented in grape juice or eau-de-vie until acidic, then cut into strips and fried in pork fat with onion and parsley. *Broade* is also served with pork and other meat dishes such as *bollito misto*, though nowadays, sauerkraut or *krauti* – introduced from Germanic Austria – is often used instead. Sauerkraut is also eaten with a special Friulian spiced sausage called *musetto*, made with flesh from the pig's snout. Rye bread is eaten in this region, often flavoured with caraway or fennel seeds, a relic of the Venetian spice influence (as is the spicing of *musetto*). Meats – beef, pork, lamb, venison and a variety of other game – are served with unusual flavourings for Italy; lamb with horseradish, and ham with mustard, for example.

In Trieste and other cities, culinary influences merge. You can enjoy versions of Hungarian goulash (of both meat and fish), with sauerkraut in one of Trieste's *bierkellers*. (A word of advice here: when you drink in company, everyone buys a round – it's an obligation, and you have to drink!) *Knödeln* or gnocchi from Austria are also popular; the simplest of these are made from bread, milk, eggs, and a little flour, or from potato; more complex versions include little cubes of San Daniele ham or, more authentically, of *speck* (smoked Tyrolean shoulder ham). Known as *canederli* in Italian, these are boiled and eaten with meats and meaty sauces. Some can be sweet, with a filling of fruit (see page 58).

There is little pasta in the region, but one particular speciality is *cialzons*, a sweet pasta made in villages in the Carnia Mountains; this is closely related to the Lombardian *câsonséi* and Veneto's *casonziei*. Large, wavy-edged, half-moons of pasta dough enclose a filling of spinach, raisins, candied peel, cinnamon and chocolate. These are boiled, then served with melted butter, sugar and more ground cinnamon, but there are also savoury versions.

In Trieste, there are many Viennese-type coffee houses offering sweet delicacies with an Austro-Hungarian flavour. You can find a variety of strudels, an Italian version of *Kügelhupf* (a large sponge cake), and *gubana* – once an Easter speciality, but now eaten all year round. Made with puff pastry, this delicious strudel-type cake is filled with walnuts, dried figs, raisins, prunes, pine nuts, candied orange and citron, plus pieces of chocolate. In the *pasticcerie* of Udine and Gorizia, the custom is to slice the cake and serve it drizzled with local grappa. Cakes are also made with chestnuts in this region.

The region's festivities are mostly wine-related, but you can be sure that a great deal of good food and local specialities are prepared at the same time. Virtually every town and village has a *sagra* at some point throughout the year, from March to September.

Jota Triestina Bean and sauerkraut soup

Jota **is one of those *cucina povera* dishes developed in the country by hungry farmers with gourmet tastes, which has now been elevated to appear on posh restaurant menus. If you haven't the time to soak and cook dried beans, use two 400g cans instead: simply drain, rinse and cook with the potatoes, etc., for 30 minutes.**

SERVES 4

- **250 g dried cannellini beans, soaked in cold water overnight**
- **1 litre chicken or vegetable stock (pages 250–1)**
- **2 large potatoes, peeled and cubed**
- **2 garlic cloves, crushed**
- **salt and pepper**
- **250 g sauerkraut (from a jar)**
- **2 bay leaves**
- **6 tbsp olive oil**
- **150 g *speck*, from the fat side, sliced and diced**
- **1 tbsp plain flour**

Drain the soaked dried beans, then put them into a pan with the stock. Bring to the boil, lower the heat and simmer for 1½ hours. Add the potatoes, half the garlic, and salt and pepper to taste, and cook for a further 30 minutes.

Meanwhile, put the sauerkraut into another pan, add water to cover with the bay leaves and cook for 20–30 minutes. Drain well and add to the beans and potatoes.

Heat the olive oil in a pan and fry the *speck* with the remaining garlic for a few minutes. Stir in the flour, then mix in 2 tbsp of the liquor from the beans. Add to the sauerkraut and bean mixture and cook for a further 30 minutes. Scatter with plenty of freshly ground black pepper just before serving.

REGIONAL PRODUCTS

PROSCIUTTO DI SAN DANIELE Almost as famous as that of Parma, this DOP ham comes from the area around Udine, originating in the small hill town of San Daniele, where the atmosphere is said to be perfect for curing hams. The specially reared small black pigs of San Daniele produce smallish (not too plump) legs, and the salting is on the delicate side, which produces a redder flesh and sweeter flavour. The hams are cured for at least 12 months.

CHEESES The best-known cheese from this region is Montasio, a DOP semi-hard cheese, originating from the Montasio Massif in the Roccolone Valley. Dating back to the 13th century, it is made from the milk of special cows – Red Pezzatas and Alpine Browns. Montasio is creamy yellow and close-textured, but full of tiny holes; it can be eaten fresh, or pressed and ripened for 4–12 months. When fully matured, Montasio is slightly piquant and perfect for grating over Friulian polenta and other dishes. Anucia, a fresh ricotta that is salted and pressed over a few days, is something to enjoy when you are in the area.

MUSETTO This sausage is made from *muso* (the pig's snout), and is spiced with pepper, cloves, nutmeg, cinnamon, chilli and coriander. The meat is packed into a gut casing, and matured for a short while. It is then cooked and served like *cotechino*, but with sauerkraut or stewed red cabbage. The best *musettos* are said to be the ones made from San Daniele pigs.

WINES AND SPIRITS The wine area covers much of the southern half of Friuli, which is a flat, gravel plain (Grave del Friuli DOC identifies wines from the region). Here individual wines are named for their grape variety – Merlot and Tocai, for instance. The most admired wines come from the districts of Collio and Colli Orientali, in the hills beside the Slovene border. Most wines are white and fresh, using the Germanic Traminer and Riesling, along with the French Chardonnay and Sauvignon, and the native Verduzzo, Malvasia, Pinot Grigio and Pinot Bianco grapes. Traminer Aromatico DOC is a golden green wine, usually enjoyed as an aperitif, and is the forefather of Gewürztraminer. A Friulian version of the Yugoslav *slivovitz* is found in and near Trieste, and *grappa* is made all over the region.

Arrosto di Capriolo al Pino

Roast venison with pine needles

Pine needles are an unusual flavouring for a game marinade, but one that works very well. This is a typical Germanic dish, which may be served with *canederli* (page 46), *spätzle* (page 48), polenta or mashed potato.

SERVES 6

1 venison fillet (or boneless leg joint), about 1 kg
4 tbsp olive oil
50 g butter
6 tbsp soured cream

Marinade

1 litre strong red wine
500 ml chicken stock (page 250)
2 celery stalks
2 large carrots, peeled
1 bouquet garni (rosemary, bay leaves, marjoram, sage)
pinch of freshly grated nutmeg
pinch of freshly ground cinnamon
1 sprig fresh pine needles (from the end of a branch)
1 lemon, halved
salt and pepper

For the marinade, put the wine, stock, vegetables, bouquet garni, spices and pine needles into a saucepan. Squeeze the juice from the lemon and add to the pan with the spent halves and some salt and pepper. Bring to the boil and simmer for 5 minutes, then allow to cool. When cold, add the meat and leave to marinate in a cool place for 24 hours, turning from time to time.

Preheat the oven to 220°C/Gas 7. Drain the venison; strain and reserve the marinade. Put the olive oil in a roasting pan on the hob over a medium heat. Add the venison fillet and sear on all sides, about 8–10 minutes in total. Add 8 tbsp of the reserved marinade and the butter, stir, then put into the oven. Roast, basting from time to time with more marinade, for 20–25 minutes or longer, depending on the thickness of the fillet is and how pink you like your venison.

Transfer the venison to a warm platter and rest for about 15 minutes. Meanwhile, add the soured cream to the juices in the roasting pan, stir well and heat. Carve the venison and serve with the sauce. If you dare, garnish each plate with a little sprig of pine needles!

Seppiette o Calamari Ripieni di Granchio

Little cuttlefish or squid stuffed with crab

The Friulian cuisine is largely based on meat, game, beans and pork, but it is different on the coast, where fish is predominant. This tasty recipe from Grado is eaten locally with fried or grilled polenta.

SERVES 4

- **1 cooked medium crab, cleaned**
- **16 small cuttlefish or squid, cleaned but kept whole**
- **5 tbsp olive oil**
- **1 onion, finely chopped**
- **1 tbsp plain flour**
- **4 tbsp milk**
- **2 egg yolks**
- **50 g butter**
- **salt and pepper**
- **4 tbsp dry white wine**
- **1 tbsp finely chopped flat-leaf parsley**

Remove the meat from the crab and set aside. Rinse the cuttlefish or squid pouches and set aside with the tentacles. Heat the olive oil in a pan and fry the onion until soft, then stir in the flour. Add the milk and cuttlefish or squid and cook gently, allowing 10–12 minutes for small, 12–18 for larger ones.

Remove the cuttlefish or squid from the sauce. Chop the tentacles very finely and put them into a bowl with the crabmeat, egg yolks and butter. Mix well, seasoning with salt and pepper to taste. Use to stuff the cuttlefish or squid cavities.

Put the stuffed fish back in the sauce. Add the wine and a little water to obtain a thick sauce, and cook slowly for another 10 minutes. Adjust the seasoning and sprinkle with chopped parsley. Serve with polenta.

Gulasch di Pesce Fish goulash

Take the Hungarian influence from the border of Friuli and Austria, apply it to the abundant fish in the Adriatic and you have a rare fish goulash, which has become very popular in my London restaurant.

SERVES 4

500 g mixed filleted white fish (such as monkfish, sole, halibut)
200 g meaty fresh mussels
2 tbsp Italian '00' or plain flour
2 tbsp sweet Hungarian paprika
6 tbsp olive oil
200 g ripe tomatoes, diced
200 g flat small onions, peeled and diced
200 g red peppers, cored, deseeded and diced
salt and pepper
300 g fish stock (page 250)
20 g flat-leaf parsley, chopped
a little extra virgin olive oil to serve

Cut the white fish into large squares. Scrub the mussels, removing the beards, and discard any that are open and refuse to close when sharply tapped. Mix the flour and paprika together.

Dust the white fish in the spiced flour. Heat the olive oil in a frying pan and lightly fry the fish squares until coloured. Put into a large flameproof pot or casserole, then add the mussels, tomatoes, onions, red peppers and a little salt. Pour in the fish stock, bring to a simmer and cook very gently for 15 minutes or until the fish is cooked.

Check the seasoning and discard any unopened mussels. Scatter over the chopped parsley and drizzle with a little extra virgin olive oil to serve.

Other typical regional dishes

Broade Relish of white turnips, fermented in grape juice or eau-de-vie; also called *brovade*

Cevapcici Grilled little cylinders of minced pork, originating from Yugoslavia

Cialzons Strudel filled with spinach and sweet spices, fried or boiled

Frico Fried cheese with onion, pepper, lard and butter

Gubana Strudel-type cake made with puff pastry and filled with candied fruit and nuts

Knödeln Dumplings made from a flour or potato dough, savoury or sweet

Lasagna ai semi di papavero Broad noodles with meat, poppy seeds and sugar, also typical of Vienna

Liptauer condito Hungarian cheese, cooked with butter, spices, anchovy, leek and onion

Lumache alla friulana Snails in a garlic, parsley and red wine sauce

Paparot A thickish soup made from pulped spinach, butter, garlic and flour

Sanguinaccio alla boema Bohemian blood pudding, boiled then fried

Canederli con Prugne Dumplings with plums

This recipe, which comes from near the Slovene border, is in fact Austrian in origin. Ripe, fresh apricots can be used instead of plums; I have also had excellent results with prunes. Serve the dumplings as a dessert or sweet snack.

MAKES 8

8 ripe plums, about 500 g, pitted
8 sugar cubes
2 tbsp dried breadcrumbs
50 g butter
large pinch of ground cinnamon
icing sugar to dust

Sweet dumpling dough

500 g floury potatoes (unpeeled)
salt
4 tbsp caster sugar
100 g plain flour
1 egg yolk

To make the dough, boil the potatoes in salted water until tender, then drain and remove the skins. Pass through a sieve or potato ricer into a bowl. Add the sugar, flour, egg yolk and a pinch of salt to the potato purée and mix to a smooth, pliable dough.

Take a small handful of dough (enough to coat a plum), and flatten it in your hand. Place a plum in the middle, and put a sugar cube into the plum cavity. Fold the dough around the plum to enclose and form a dumpling, making sure it's sealed all around. Do the same with the remaining plums, sugar cubes and dough.

Cook the dumplings in 2 or 3 batches. Bring a large pan of water to the boil, plunge the dumplings in and cook for a few minutes, just until they rise to the surface. Scoop them out with a slotted spoon and keep warm while you cook the rest.

Fry the breadcrumbs in the butter until golden brown, then flavour with cinnamon to taste. Sprinkle this spicy mixture on top of the dumplings and serve hot, dusted with icing sugar.

Presniz Friulian pastry with rum-soaked fruit and nuts

This sweet pastry, filled with rum-soaked dried fruit and nuts is traditionally eaten during the Easter celebration and is believed to be of Yugoslav origin. It is easy to make, especially if you use bought puff pastry.

SERVES 6–8

100 g raisins
100 ml dark rum
40 g butter, diced and softened, plus extra to grease
140 g biscuits (such as digestives)
70 g pine nuts, toasted
70 g walnut halves, toasted
70 g blanched almonds, toasted
80 g quality dark chocolate, finely chopped
60 g candied orange and citron peel, diced
grated zest and juice of 1 lemon
1 egg, beaten
500 g ready-made puff pastry
flour to dust
3–4 tbsp icing sugar

Soak the raisins in the rum for 1–2 hours. Preheat the oven to 180°C/Gas 4 and lightly grease a baking tray. Drain the raisins, reserving the rum.

Crush the biscuits, using a pestle and mortar, then tip the crumbs into a bowl. Add the butter and mix until evenly combined. Add the raisins, pine nuts, walnuts, almonds, chocolate, candied peel and lemon zest and juice. Stir well, then mix in the beaten egg and some of the rum to make a moist filling.

Roll out the pastry on a lightly floured surface to a 60 x 40 cm rectangle, about 2 mm thick. Spoon the filling along the middle and brush the pastry edges with water. Fold one long side over the filling to enclose it and make a sausage, then press the edges together to seal. Coil into a circle and place on the greased baking tray. Bake in the oven for 50 minutes.

Carefully transfer the pastry to a wire rack to cool. Serve warm or cold, sprinkled generously with icing sugar. A good glass of Picolit or Torcolato wine alongside would do very nicely.

Veneto

The Veneto and its famous city, Venice, lie in the Po Valley, between the Adriatic Sea in the south, and the Dolomites to the north. Venice was once the most famous maritime trading city in the world, dominating the spice trade amongst others, and its cosmopolitan history is reflected in the cooking of the whole region. Indeed Veneto is regarded as one of the formative regions, along with Tuscany, responsible for Italian cuisine as we know it today.

Veneto is the largest of the three northern Italian regions known collectively as Le Tre Venezie (the three Venices), comprising Friuli-Venezia Giulia, Trentino-Alto Adige and Veneto. Venice, 'La Serenissima', is the heartbeat of Veneto. It is built on over 100 alluvial islands in the lagoon of Venice, mostly separated by narrow canals crossed by some 400 bridges. Venice may be in danger now from sinking and high water, but at one time it was virtually the most important city of Italy.

The city's origins can be traced back to the 5th century when Italians fleeing barbarian invasions sought refuge on the islands in the lagoon. Separated from the mainland by two or three miles of water, the early Venetians were protected from invaders and removed from mainland politics. Strategically placed between Europe and the East, Venice became an independent republic and a great commercial and maritime power. Although its role declined in the 16th century following the discovery of the Cape route to India, other influences were to emanate from the city, particularly during the Renaissance, when Venetian musicians, architects, painters and sculptors were pre-eminent. The refined Venetians introduced the rest of the world to the fork and table napkin, and glass made in Murano, one of the Lagoon islands, lent style and grace to their dining tables.

Venice, of course, is unique, but the Veneto has so much more to offer. The cultural city of Verona with its wealth of architecture, art and theatre is a wonderful place to visit – and you can eat at the fabulous 12 Apostoli restaurant, owned by my fellow mushroom enthusiast, Giorgio Gioco. The northern province of Vicenza is home to most of Veneto's Palladian villas, and you can eat well here too. The provinces of Belluno, Padova and Treviso are all interesting and, as with so many other parts of Italy, every province has its own traditions and specialities.

CULINARY TRADITIONS & SPECIALITIES

The Veneto forms part of 'the polenta, bean and rice belt', which runs across the north of Italy, and these are important ingredients in the regional cuisine. Not surprisingly, fish is highly popular too – particularly along the coast – and fish from the sea is supplemented by freshwater varieties from the many lakes and streams in the region. Land reclamation and clever irrigation have created fertile pastures, especially on the river plains in the south; here agriculture is intensive too. Fruits of the woods, such as mushrooms, truffles and chestnuts, and soft fruit are abundant throughout the region. A particularly distinctive characteristic of the cooking in Veneto is the use of spices, dating back to the spice trade and very little evident elsewhere in Italy.

Maize polenta was first popularised in the northern parts of Veneto (and Friuli). In earlier times, spelt, millet and chestnuts (and in leaner times, acorns) were ground to make flour for the basic porridge. In the north, polenta is often served with a *ragù* of small wild birds such as sparrows. In Venetian cooking, a special white form of maize is eaten with small lagoon shrimps, razor shell clams, and to accompany *baccalà*.

Risottos are common throughout the Veneto and there are numerous specialities. Venice is renowned for its fish risottos and *risi e bisi*, which is cooked to celebrate the new young peas from Lumignano. The risottos in Venice differ from elsewhere, in that they are more liquid, or *all'onda* (like a wave). They are also mounted with butter, *mantecare*, as in Lombardy. Vialone nano is the short, stubby rice used in all the best Venetian risottos. A typical risotto from Mantua is *alla pilota*, so called because it is dedicated to the 'pilot' or cultivator of rice. A speciality of Treviso, north of Venice, is *risotto al tajo* – made with a stock of eels and prawns.

Pasta isn't particularly popular anywhere in the Veneto, but a typical northern dish is *casonziei*, a pasta stuffed with pumpkin, spinach and ham (akin to the Lombardian *câsonséi*). A traditional Venetian dish is *bigoli in salsa* – fat wholewheat spaghetti extruded through an implement called a *bigolaro* and served with an anchovy sauce.

To appreciate the wonders of the fish caught in the Adriatic, all you have to do is visit the market by the Rialto Bridge in Venice. Stall after stall is laid out with the most fantastic seasonal array. There are baby monkfish no larger than a man's thumb, tiny cuttlefish, prawns, crabs, mussels and clams. Mussels – *muscoli* or *peoci* – are grown on ropes in the lagoon, and are made into a soup, or eaten with rice or pasta. The tiny cuttlefish – called *seppie* or *seppioline* – are used to make a variety of dishes characterised by the black colour from their ink: *polenta e seppie*, *tagliatelle al nero con seppie*, or the classic *risotto nero con seppie*. Fish are often served *in saor*, fried then marinated in a vinegar-based sauce, which is an Arabic custom. Sole are cooked with basil and pine nuts, another hint of the Arabic.

Bisato sul'Ara Eel baked with bay leaves

This typical Venetian recipe is traditionally eaten on Christmas Eve. It originates from the Comacchio Valley, south of Chioggia, where the eels are wonderful and fat. This recipe calls for chunks from a large eel and bay leaves only. Oven baking does the rest, as it regulates the amount of fat and cooks the eels perfectly. I suggest you accompany the dish with a beetroot salad.

SERVES 4

20–30 bay leaves
8 large chunks of fresh eel, about 110 g each, cleaned with skin
salt and pepper
lemon wedges to serve

Preheat the oven to 200°C/Gas 6. Lay the bay leaves over the bottom of a shallow baking dish, then place the chunks of eel on top. Bake in the oven for 30–35 minutes, or until the eel is tender. The fat in the eels and the bay leaves will be enough to flavour the dish.

Season the eels with salt and pepper to taste and serve, with lemon wedges.

To sample these Venetian specialities, visit some of the little bars that are everywhere in the city. Order an *ombra*, a glass of white wine, and some of the *cicheti* on offer (the Italian equivalent of *tapas*). I like to do this during La Festa del Redentore, the main Venetian festival, when the *seppioline* are usually eaten *alla brace*, charcoal-grilled. Another favourite of mine are *moleche*, soft-shell crabs. Cultivated in the lagoon, these crabs are used when they shed their shells in spring and autumn. They are soaked alive (thus drowned) in beaten egg, then deep-fried in olive oil. It sounds barbaric, I know, but they taste divine.

Meat dishes are less important, but *bollito misto* is popular (the stock reserved for *riso in brodo*), and offal dishes are numerous and varied throughout the Veneto. *Carpaccio* (dressed wafer-thin slices of raw beef), was created by Arrigo Cipriani of Harry's Bar in Venice. Less to the taste of non-Italians are *nervetti* – made from veal and pork trotters, and served as *cicheti*. I ordered some one morning at about 10 o'clock, and my wife Priscilla had to beat a hasty retreat!

Game is a feature throughout the Veneto. A famous dish of the charming walled town of Treviso is *sopa coada*, a thick, slow-cooked pigeon soup. Many game birds, particularly guinea fowl, are served with a pepper sauce, *peverada*, a reminder of the Veneto's spicy past. In Arqua Petrarca, in Padova, once home of the poet Petrarch, you can sample *torresano allo spiedo* (pigeon raised in tower-lofts) in the restaurant, La Montanella.

Salami are made all over the Veneto, from both pork and horsemeat, and *coppa* is popular too. *Sfilacci* is a speciality of Padova made from salted, dried and smoked horsemeat, while *bondole* is a smoked pork and fat sausage, ideal for cooking. One of the local meat dishes from Badia Polesine that horrifies many visitors is *stracotto d'asino* (braised donkey), which is eaten with polenta.

Sheep are raised in Rovigo, the most northerly province, and some pecorino is produced from their milk. The cow's milk cheese, Asiago, comes from the high plains in Vicenza; it is available both as a hard grating cheese and as a softer table cheese. Local cheeses in the northern province of Belluno are *nostrano di malga*, *comelico*, *carnia dolce*, and *puira*, a smoked ricotta; if you are in the area, try them with *la puccia*, an interesting local bread made with rye flour, wheat grains and caraway seeds.

Fruit and vegetables are grown all over the Veneto. Radicchio is highly prized – notably the long raddichio from Treviso and the striped variety from Castelfranco; the familiar round red variety comes from Chioggia (south of Venice). Radicchio features strongly in local dishes – risottos, salads, soups, even with fresh-water fish; you can sample these in the many *trattorie* and *osterie*, especially around Montello near Castelfranco. In the northern province of Belluno, the beans of Lamon are well known, and cooked to accompany the prolific game from the woods or brown trout from the rivers. Mushrooms and truffles abound throughout the Veneto, especially in Padova and Vicenza, which is also famous for its fat white asparagus centred around Bassano. In Padova, excellent peaches are grown near Monselice and, although I haven't tried them, the figs of Teolo are reputed to be out of this world.

The northern towns of Conegliano and Belluno are known for their ice-cream and some enterprising locals travel to other parts of Europe to open ice-cream parlours for the summer, returning home to their families at the end of the season. The well-known pudding, *tiramisù* was invented in Treviso some 35 years ago, by Alfredo Beltrame, the owner of El Toulá restaurant.

If you visit Treviso, be sure to try a glass of *fragolino*, an exquisite wine produced with grapes that taste of strawberries. I happen to have a single vine of these grapes in my West London garden, which produces around 100 kg of fruit every year. The best-known Italian spirit, grappa comes from Bassano in Vicenza, while in Treviso – in Valdobbiadene and Conegliano – the grapes are grown for Prosecco, the sparkling white wine so characteristic of Venetian *caffè* life.

The prime celebration in the Veneto is, of course, Carnevale, the Biennale in Venice, in March, when the city is in festive mode for days. Verona hosts a trade wine fair in April, and grape and wine festivals are held in towns and villages all over the Veneto throughout the year. Food *sagre* are too numerous to mention individually, celebrating the region's finest produce and dishes, including peaches, strawberries, cherries, chestnuts, gnocchi, risottos, fish, snails and duck.

Pesce in Saor Sweet and sour fish

Venetians adore fish, and this special way of cooking – frying and then marinating – is also applied inland to freshwater fish. It is a good way to preserve a bumper crop of fish, and a lovely antipasto dish. Sardines and sole are typically used, and freshwater fish such as trout. Prepare a day in advance to allow time for the marinade to flavour the fish.

SERVES 6

800 g fresh sardines, scaled and cleaned
flour to dust
olive oil for shallow-frying
500 g onions, sliced
50 g pine nuts
50 g sultanas
50 g caster sugar
50 ml white wine vinegar
freshly ground black pepper

Dust the cleaned fish with flour, then shallow-fry in olive oil until crisp and brown on both sides. Drain well on kitchen paper, then arrange in a single layer in a shallow dish.

Gently fry the onion in the same pan, adding a little more oil if necessary, until soft, then add the pine nuts, sultanas and sugar. Stir well, then add the wine vinegar and allow to evaporate a little.

Pour the sweet and sour mixture over the fish and leave to cool, then refrigerate for at least 24 hours. Eat cold, sprinkled with pepper.

Baccalà Mantecato Dried cod Vicenza style

This dish is typical of Vicenza, but you will find it all over Veneto. Here *stoccafisso* is confusingly called *baccalà* though it describes dried cod, not the salted and dried cod that we know as *baccalà*. This dish is eaten with polenta (often white in Venice). I still find it interesting that with all the abundance of fresh fish from lakes, rivers and sea, preserved cod from Norway is considered a delicacy in many parts of Italy.

SERVES 6

1 *stoccafisso* (dried cod), about 1 kg
$1\frac{1}{2}$ tsp freshly grated nutmeg
salt and pepper
300 ml extra virgin olive oil
1 tbsp very finely chopped parsley

Quick polenta

300 g instant polenta
pinch of salt
50 g butter
50 g Parmesan, freshly grated

Beat the dried cod vigorously with a mallet to break up the fibres, then soak in cold water to cover for 48 hours.

Drain the fish and put into a pan. Add water to cover, bring to the boil and cook for 10 minutes. Drain, then remove the skin and reserve. Take off all the bones and fins. Break the flesh into filaments with a fork, then put into a steamer together with the skin and steam for $1\frac{1}{2}$ hours.

Push the gelatinous skin through a sieve into a bowl. Flake the fish and add to the bowl. Add the nutmeg, salt and pepper, and start to beat with a wooden spoon. Continue to beat and stir, adding a little stream of olive oil from time to time, as if making mayonnaise. As you beat, the mixture will swell and become whitish in colour.

Meanwhile, make the polenta (get a helper to do this if possible, while you beat the *baccalà!*). Put the polenta, salt and 1.5 litres water in a pan and heat, stirring, until thickened and cooked (following the packet instructions). Stir in the butter and Parmesan.

When all the oil is incorporated into the *baccalà*, return to the pan and heat through, stirring, for a couple of minutes, then add the parsley. Eat with the freshly made polenta.

Other typical regional dishes

Anatra col pien lessa Boned stuffed duck poached whole for 2 hours. The stock and giblets are used for *bigoli co' l'anara* (see below). Both dishes are served for the celebration of the Madonna del Rosario on 7th October

Baccalà alla vicentina Cooked and puréed dried cod, mixed with olive oil, garlic and milk, then baked

Bigoli co' l'anara Pasta cooked in duck stock, then tossed in a sauce of duck livers (see *anatra col pien lessa*, above)

Bigoli in salsa Thick spaghetti served with an onion and anchovy sauce, a speciality of Venice

Carpaccio Prime raw beef fillet, very thinly sliced and dressed with a little mayonnaise, seasoned and flavoured with a little lemon juice and Tabasco

Faraona con la peverada Roast guinea fowl in a heavily peppered sauce

Moleche alla muranese Soft-shell crabs, dipped in beaten egg and flour, and fried

Nervetti Veal and pork cartilage, mostly from the foot, which is boiled, sliced, dressed and served as a snack

Polenta e osei Small wild birds skewered with interspersing slices of *lardo* (pork fat), grilled slowly and served with polenta

Pridole sulla grena Grilled lamb cutlets

Risi e bisi Wet risotto of rice, bacon, onion and peas

Tiramisù Popular dessert of sponge fingers soaked in brandy and coffee, layered with a mascarpone cream, and topped with chocolate

Pasta e Fagioli Pasta and bean soup

This is the best-known peasant dish in Italy. Every region has a version, but the Veneti, Trentini and Tirolesi have elevated it to a dish smart enough for posh restaurant menus. For me, it is the benchmark of a good chef – because it is so simple, it must be perfect.

SERVES 6

300 g fresh borlotti beans, or 200 g dried beans soaked in cold water overnight and drained
6 tbsp olive oil
1 onion, finely chopped
2 basil leaves
1 rosemary sprig
1 litre chicken or vegetable stock (pages 250–1)
1 red chilli, chopped (optional)
1 tbsp tomato purée
salt and pepper
150 g tubetti pasta (little tubes)
4 tbsp extra virgin olive oil to serve

Put the beans into a heatproof earthenware pot or large pan and cover with cold water. Bring to the boil and cook gently, allowing 1 hour if using fresh beans, 1½–2 hours if using dried. Don't salt the water or the skins will remain tough. When soft, drain and purée half of the beans in a blender or food processor, then mix together with the whole beans.

Heat the olive oil in a saucepan, add the onion and fry until softened. Add the basil, rosemary, stock, chilli if using, tomato purée, beans, and salt and pepper to taste. Bring to the boil, then add the pasta and cook for 7–8 minutes or until the pasta is *al dente*.

Leave to stand for 30 minutes before serving to allow the flavours to mingle. Reheat if you like, but in Italy soups are more often served warm rather than hot, even cold in summer. Top each portion with a drizzle of extra virgin olive oil to serve.

Risotto Primavera Spring vegetable risotto

I had always assumed that Lombardy was the birthplace of risotto, but it is Veneto. There are hundreds of risottos in Venice and Veneto, many more than in Lombardy. One featuring the radicchio of Treviso is a favourite, but this risotto is made with spring vegetables, as its name suggests, which gives it the flavour of new life.

SERVES 4

1 onion, finely chopped
4 young carrots, finely diced
2 celery stalks, finely diced
50 g podded fresh peas
100 g green beans, cut into pieces
2 artichoke hearts, finely diced
12 asparagus tips
50 g hop shoots (*bruscandoli*), optional
2 litres boiling chicken or vegetable stock (pages 250–1)
100 g butter
400 g risotto rice
salt and pepper
60 g Parmesan, freshly grated

Have all the vegetables ready. Bring the stock to the boil in a pan and keep it at a low simmer.

Melt 50 g of the butter in a large pan and fry the onion until soft. Add the carrots and celery and cook for 5 minutes, then add the peas, green beans and artichokes. Stir over the heat briefly, then add the rice and stir to coat with the butter.

Ladle by ladle, add the boiling stock, allowing each addition to be absorbed before you add the next. After 10 minutes, add the asparagus and the hop shoots if using. Carry on adding stock and stirring, until the rice is *al dente*, about 20 minutes. When the rice is cooked, everything else will be.

Remove from the heat and season with salt and pepper to taste. Add the rest of the butter and the Parmesan. Stir briskly and serve warm.

REGIONAL PRODUCTS

WINE Almost 20 per cent of Italy's wine is produced in Veneto (see opposite) and vineyards cover a fair proportion of the land, in a broad strip heading north-west towards Lake Garda and a vast area straddling the River Piave to the north and east of Venice.

MEAT PRODUCTS Several good salami are made in Veneto. *Soppressa*, a large salami, originally from Valpolicella, is now produced all over the region. It is made from very coarsely ground pork taken from the shoulder, neck and upper thigh, and up to 35 per cent fat. *Bondiola* is a large round sausage from Polesine, an area in south Veneto. It is a mixture of coarsely ground pork and beef, seasoned with red wine and variously encased in ox intestine, pig's bladder or turkey crop (not dissimilar to the Scottish haggis). A lot of *cotechino* and *luganega* are made in the region and typically eaten with lentils, though *cotechino* also features in *bollito misto* (page 12). *Coppa* is made here as well.

GRAPPA This is the Italian equivalent of French marc, primarily found in the Veneto and Piedmont. After the grapes (usually Muscat) have been crushed to produce wine, the leftover pulp and mash are distilled to make grappa. It can be spiced up, have herbs added, made bitter with radicchio root, or indeed sweetened with honey, and there are many different varieties to try. A particularly macho version includes a small snake or scorpion in the bottle, believe it or not! Grappa is not just drunk after meals, but often during the day as a pick-me-up. It is perhaps at its restorative best in a cup of black coffee – a *caffè corretto*.

Wines of the Veneto

Amarone della Valpolicella The same grapes that are used for Valpolicella (Corvina Veronese, Rondinella and Molinara) are left to dry and shrivel, then fermented very slowly to make this wine. This makes for a strong flavour, promising sweetness, but delivering a bitter-dry (*amaro* means bitter) taste. Older vintages are labelled with the wine's former name, Recioto della Valpolicella Amarone. Recioto della Valpolicella Amabile is a sweet version, made the same way.

Bardolino DOC This is made from the same variety of grapes as Valpolicella, although often with a little Negrara added. The vines for Bardolino are grown on the slopes on the eastern side of Lake Garda. The wine is light ruby-red in colour, light in flavour and should be drunk young. Bardolino Chiaretto is a rosé version.

Bianco di Custoza DOC Produced next door to Bardolino, near Lake Garda, this white wine is considered by many to be better than Soave. It is made from the same grapes as Soave (Garganega and Trebbiano), but Tocai, Malvasia or Riesling grapes are often added to liven up the blend.

Gambellara DOC A white wine from an area neighbouring Soave, and made with the same blend of grapes (see right). There is also a Gambellara Recioto and a Vin Santo.

Prosecco di Conegliano/Valdobbiadene DOC The vines for this most popular sparkling wine are cultivated in the hills of the Conegliano-Valdobbiadene area, between the towns of Treviso and Belluno. The Prosecco grape is the one that produces the 'fizz' – for the *frizzante* or *spumante* – but it also produces a still wine. All styles can be sweet or dry. Prosecco's gentle fizz is the basis for Bellini (with fresh peach juice) invented in Harry's Bar, Venice, but it can also be used in a Tintoretto (with pomegranate juice), a Rossini (with crushed strawberries) or a Mimosa (with orange juice). There is also a popular sparkling demi-sec wine, called Cartize.

Soave DOC The area where this famous white wine is made abuts Valpolicella, and is small despite the large volume produced. The wine blends Garganega and Trebbiano grapes, and at best is crisp and bright. Like Valpolicella, it is generally made from grapes grown on flat land, but the best wines – the Classicos – are produced from grapes grown on hillsides.

Recioto di Soave DOC A fine, honeyed sweet white wine, produced by drying Soave grapes, either on the vine or in controlled conditions (the *passito* process) to intensify and concentrate the natural sugars in the fruit.

Valpolicella DOC This well-known wine from the province of Verona is made in 19 communes from Corvina Veronese, Rondinella and Molinara grapes. Ruby-red with a faint almond taste, it is an easy wine to drink, especially when young, and goes well with dark meats. The best is Valpolicella Classico, produced on hillsides near Lake Garda.

Pollo alla Buranea Chicken Burano style

This simple recipe honours the little island of Burano, in the lagoon of Venice. While the fishermen are at sea, their wives are busy making special embroideries called *merletti*, which they sell to tourists. Their houses are painted in wild colours, supposedly because when the fishermen have been drinking with friends they are more likely to recognise the colour than the house number! If you ever get to Burano, don't forget to eat at Trattoria dei Pescatori, where a real *mamma* is still at the stove.

SERVES 6

1 free-range chicken, about 1.5 kg
100 g *luganega* sausage (fresh sausage in skin)
50 g lard (or pork fat), cut into small pieces
2 tbsp olive oil
1 onion, finely chopped
2 celery stalks, diced
2 carrots, diced
1 garlic clove, sliced
1 small rosemary sprig
finely grated zest and juice of 1 lemon
about 20 large green olives
50 ml dry white wine
about 100 ml chicken stock (page 250)
salt and pepper
2 tbsp grappa

Cut the chicken into 12 meaty chunks. Remove the skin from the sausage and pinch the sausagemeat into pieces. Melt the lard with the olive oil in a casserole. Add the chicken, sausage, vegetables, garlic, rosemary and lemon zest, and fry, stirring, for a few minutes until the chicken is lightly coloured.

Add the olives, wine, stock and some salt and pepper. Cover and cook very gently on the hob for 1 hour, or until the chicken is tender. Add more stock or water during cooking if needed.

Just before serving, add the lemon juice and grappa. Accompany either with boiled potatoes or *spätzle* borrowed from Trentino (page 48).

Fegato alla Veneziana Calf's liver with onions

This classic Venetian dish features on Italian restaurant menus around the world, and I feel duty bound to include it here!

SERVES 4

6 tbsp olive oil
350 g white onions, finely sliced
600 g calf's liver, trimmed and finely sliced
flour to dust
50 g butter
2 tbsp white wine vinegar
salt and pepper

Heat the olive oil in a pan, add the onions and fry gently over a very low heat for 20 minutes or so, until soft; don't let them brown.

Dust the liver slices with flour. Heat the butter in a large frying pan and fry the liver slices very briefly, about 1 minute on each side, until cooked to your liking. Place on top of the onions and keep warm.

Deglaze the frying pan with the wine vinegar, then pour over the onion and liver mixture. Toss to mix and season with salt and pepper to taste. Serve with potato purée or boiled potatoes and spinach.

Lingua in Salsa Tongue in a piquant dressing

You may find this popular Venetian dish served as *cicheti* (Italian-style tapas), in the little bars of Venice.

SERVES 4–6

1 calf's tongue, about 700–800 g
salt and pepper
2 bay leaves
handful of parsley stalks
4 sage leaves
flour to dust
3 tbsp olive oil
30 g butter
6 anchovy fillets in oil
2 tbsp salted capers, rinsed and chopped
100 ml dry white wine

Put the tongue in a saucepan with lightly salted water to cover and the herbs, bring to a simmer and cook for 30–40 minutes. Remove from the water and allow to cool a little, then peel off the skin.

Cut the tongue into 1 cm slices and dust with flour. Heat the olive oil and butter in a frying pan and fry the tongue slices in batches until golden on both sides. Drain on kitchen paper and arrange on a serving plate.

Add the anchovies, capers and wine to the juices left in the frying pan. Stir over a low heat until warmed through to develop the flavours, then check the seasoning. Pour the warm dressing over the tongue and serve hot or cold.

Liguria

Squeezed into a narrow arc between the Apennines and the Tyrrhenian Sea, and stretching from Ventimiglia near the French border down to La Spezia and Tuscany, Liguria is a beautiful region but it doesn't have a lot of acreage for agriculture. As a result, the Ligurians have become adept at maximising the potential of their land, and they have acquired a hard-working reputation.

Ligurians are often portrayed as being a little stingy, but in my view it is the geography of the region that has shaped this attribute and encouraged them to be prudent with limited resources. Historically, they were great sailors. Christopher Columbus – perhaps the most famous sailor of all – came from Genoa, the capital of the region. This city was one of the four marine republics of Italy during the fourteenth century (the others being Pisa, Amalfi and Venice), and Ligurians ventured far and wide, connecting and trading with the rest of the world. Those that stayed at home were equally, if not more, industrious.

To cultivate crops on the steep terrain, terraces needed to be built – some along the coast almost overhanging the sea like balconies! The work involved must have been immense, but shows great determination. The best example of this terrace culture is in the Cinqueterre, five picturesque villages in the hills just north of La Spezia. Originally this remarkable topographical feature was approachable only by sea, but now a road has been built. Here grape vines and olives are cultivated without the help of agricultural machinery, as the terrain is only accessible on foot.

Summer is the time to visit Liguria – especially the sunny, colourful coastline in the west, known as the *Riviera dei fiori* (of flowers). It is a holiday playground, home to some of Italy's most famous resorts, such as San Remo. To appreciate the coastal views, travel on the minor roads and you will also find charming places where you can stop at local *trattorie* and sample the local food and wine. And, if you are in Genoa, don't forget to go to Zeffirino, a well-established restaurant, where my friend Gianpaolo Belloni will take care of you.

Liguria hasn't been immune to outside influences, but because the Apennines formed an almost impenetrable barrier at one time, most of the acquired traditions and specialities have come from more southerly parts of Italy and the Mediterranean, rather than from the north. Ingredients imported from other regions include pecorino from Sardinia, and pine nuts from Pisa, to make the famous pesto. There are Arab influences, evident in the names of certain ingredients and dishes, like the pasta squares, *manilli de sea*, from the Arab for 'silk handkerchief'. The proximity of France has had its effect too, and indeed Liguria was once part of the French kingdom of Savoy. The famous pesto of Genoa is similar to the Provençal *pistou* – which came first is a constant source of argument! And the Ligurian *minestrone con pesto*, is echoed by the Provençal *soupe au pistou*. Also very alike are focaccia and *fougasse* (flat breads), and *panissa* and *socca* (chickpea flour crêpes). A focaccia covered with anchovies and onions, known variously as *pissaladeira*, *pissalandrea* or *pissadella*, is virtually indistinguishable from the Provençal *pissaladière*.

In the forests and woods, there is a wealth of wild mushrooms. In between the vines and olives on the hills, and on the narrow coastal plain, herbs and greens are prolific – both wild and cultivated – and these play a major part in Ligurian cuisine. In addition to the celebrated basil, you'll find borage, chard, spinach and dandelion among others, known locally as *erbette*. A local speciality, *pansôti al preboggion* (a curled ravioli) has a filling of these local wild greens mixed with Parmesan. And, of course, the wonderful fragrant Ligurian basil – grown on every balcony and windowsill – is pounded with olive oil, pine nuts, garlic and Parmesan or pecorino cheese to make the famous *pesto alla genovese*.

Polpette di Borraggine Borage fritters

To do justice to the various wild greens of Liguria, here is a simple but delicious fritter recipe, based on borage and sweetbreads. I love this combination of flavours and textures. You could use *cavolo nero* (black cabbage) instead of borage, cooking the leaves for 10–12 minutes.

MAKES 12 FRITTERS

300 g calf's sweetbreads, cleaned
salt and pepper
400 g borage leaves
olive oil for frying
4 eggs
50 g pecorino cheese (not old), freshly grated
100 g fresh breadcrumbs
freshly grated nutmeg
flour to dust
lemon wedges to serve

Blanch the sweetbreads in boiling salted water for 10 minutes. Meanwhile, cook the borage leaves in another pan of boiling salted water for 8–10 minutes until tender. Drain the borage very well, squeezing out all liquid, then chop.

Drain the sweetbreads thoroughly, cut into small pieces and season with salt and pepper. Sauté them in a little olive oil for a few minutes.

Beat 3 eggs in a bowl, then add the borage, sautéed sweetbreads and cheese. Bind with the breadcrumbs, and season with nutmeg and salt and pepper to taste. Shape the mixture into 12 balls with your hands, then flatten into large ovals or rounds. Beat the other egg in a bowl.

Heat a frying pan containing a good depth of olive oil for shallow-frying. Dip the fritters first into the flour, then in the egg to coat, then fry them in the hot oil for a few minutes until golden and crisp. Drain on kitchen paper and serve hot with lemon wedges.

The four major provinces of Liguria – Imperia, Savona, Genova and La Spezia – each have their own culinary characteristics, mainly dictated by local produce. Even the classic pesto is subject to variation away from its home province. In La Spezia and the east, for example, it is rendered milder with the addition of *prescinsoeua* (a sort of junket). Of course, pesto is typically tossed with pasta – normally *trenette*, similar to *linguine*, and Liguria is quite famous for its pasta. The art of pasta-making dates back to ancient times when Genoa held the monopoly of the grain trade in the Mediterranean. Ligurian pastas include *agnolotti* (ravioli), *corzetti* (handmade coin-shaped pasta), *trofie* (hand-rolled spirals), *piccagge* (1 cm wide ribbons) and *manilli de sea* (large 12 cm squares).

The region has a long coastline, but the Ligurians seem to prefer preserved fish to fresh, and *baccalà* and *stoccafisso* (dried cod) feature in quite a few recipes. However, there is a typical *cacciucco* (fish soup), and mussels are cultivated. The latter are delicious stuffed (as my friend, Pinuccia, serves them in the San Giovanni Restaurant in Casarza Ligure). Many other shellfish were once found in the Gulf of La Spezia, including the famous sea dates (*datteri di mare*), which are no longer fished for ecological reasons (they over-did it in the past). Anchovies are eaten, although many more are exported to Piedmont where they are especially popular.

Liguria is not one of Italy's main wine-producing regions, because the rugged terrain isn't particularly conducive to vine-growing. The few Ligurian wines that are known beyond the region include Pigato DOC (the typical white), Vermentino, Rossese di Dolceacqua and Dolcetto. In the Cinqueterre, you will find the DOC Cinqueterre whites and the Cinqueterre Sciacchetra' (dessert wine) and many other good local wines to accompany regional food.

Summer is the time to enjoy the many local festivals in Liguria. In May there is a *sagra del pesce* in Camogli, where tons of fish are fried in hundreds of litres of oil in a huge frying pan. In the same month there is a *sagra dell'acciuga* (anchovy feast) in Deiva Marina near La Spezia, a *sagra della focaccia* in Recco near Genoa, and a *sagra* of salami and broad beans in Mioglia, in the province of Savona. In June you can taste strawberries in Morialdo, where a feast dedicated to this fruit takes place. And in July there is a *sagra dell'olio* (feast of the oil) in Arnasco, Savona, and the *Polentata di Sant'Anna* (a polenta feast) in Cantone, Genova.

Manilli de Sea Silk handkerchief pasta sheets with pesto

Before I knew of this recipe, I made *stracci*, which is pasta torn from a big sheet of dough, to go with pesto. Here the pieces are larger, quite like a handkerchief, and very thin and silky. The pasta must be made at home and rolled with a pasta machine to make the thinnest sheets possible, to be cut into 15–20 cm lengths. The sauce is the classic Genovese pesto.

SERVES 4

350 g very thin fresh pasta sheets (page 251), 1 mm thick and (15–20 cm long
salt
a little olive oil (optional)
Pesto
80 g basil leaves
2 garlic cloves
30 g pine nuts
60 g Parmesan, freshly grated
10 g coarse sea salt
100 ml olive oil

To make the pesto, pound the basil, garlic, pine nuts, Parmesan and salt together, using a pestle and mortar, to a smooth paste. Slowly add the olive oil, stirring all the time.

Add the pasta sheets, one by one, to a large pan of boiling salted water, with a little olive oil to avoid sticking if you like, and cook until *al dente*. Being so fresh and thin, the pasta cooks quickly, within 2–3 minutes.

Scoop the pasta sheets out of the boiling water, drain well and divide between warm plates. Gently mix each pile of pasta with a quarter of the pesto and serve at once.

Insalata di Gianchetti Newborn fish salad

It seems sinful to eat such small fish as newborn sardines, anchovies or elvers, but they are popular in many coastal regions of Italy. They are known as *cehe* in Tuscany and *neonato* in Sicily. Serve the fish as a little appetiser, or in a frittata.

SERVES 6

300 g *gianchetti*
salt and pepper
juice of 1/2 lemon
3 tbsp olive oil
1 tbsp finely chopped chives
lemon wedges to serve

Wash and drain the *gianchetti*. Plunge into a pot of slightly salted boiling water for 1 minute or less and drain well.

While still warm, mix with the lemon juice and olive oil. Season with salt and pepper to taste, and add the chives. Serve with lemon wedges and accompany with toasted bread.

Other typical regional dishes

Antipasti di mare Antipasto of mixed fish and seafood

Boghe in scabecio Fish marinated in vinegar, garlic, onions and olive oil, then fried

Cappon magro Mixed cooked vegetables on a bread base, with anchovy sauce

Coniglio in umido Braised rabbit with black olives, pine nuts and rosemary

Fricassea d'agnello e carciofi Lamb stewed with artichokes, enriched with an egg yolk mixed with lemon juice at the end; a dish of Greek origin

Frisceu Little fish fritters

Minestrone alla genovese Minestrone with fresh pesto

Pansôti al preboggion Ravioli stuffed with wild herbs and Parmesan, usually served with a walnut sauce

Picagge tagliatelle Pasta served with meat or porcini sauce

Ravioli di Genova/San Remo Ravioli served with a *tocco di carne* or *ragù* of meat

Riso e preboggion Cooked wild greens mixed with boiled rice, olive oil and pesto

Stocco alla genovese Stockfish stew with Taggiasca olives

Torta pasqualina A savoury Easter tart using local wild greens, including borage or artichokes

Trenette/trofie al pesto Pasta with pesto – a must in Liguria

Funghi al Funghetto Sautéed mushrooms

The wooded hills behind the Ligurian coastline boast a wonderful array of wild mushrooms. Locals collect them regularly and prepare this dish, known as *funzi al funzetto* in Liguria. The equivalent can be found all over Italy, wherever fresh porcini are collected. The Tuscans flavour it with *nepitella*, a minty wild herb, while the Piedmontese use parsley rather than oregano, which is typical in Liguria. The mushrooms can be eaten with bread or on *crostini* as a snack or starter, or served as an accompaniment to a main course – fish or meat.

SERVES 4

600 g fresh porcini or other wild mushrooms, cleaned
8 tbsp olive oil
2 garlic cloves, finely chopped
salt and pepper
2 tbsp chopped oregano
squeeze of lemon juice

Slice the mushrooms. Heat the olive oil in a sauté pan and sauté the mushrooms over a high heat with the garlic until softened, seasoning them with some salt and pepper.

Add the oregano, with a squeeze of lemon juice, and serve immediately.

Frittata di Carciofi e Funghi

Frittata with artichokes and mushrooms

I love utter simplicity in food, and this easy dish tastes wonderful. There may not be much growing space in Liguria, but virtually everything is grown, from artichokes to *zucchini*, and wild mushrooms are plentiful in season. A wedge of this frittata with a little salad makes a wonderful springtime meal.

SERVES 4–6

20 g dried porcini mushrooms
1 fresh bread roll
a little milk
50 ml olive oil
8 fresh small artichoke hearts, thinly sliced
300 g button mushrooms, thinly sliced
2 garlic cloves, very finely chopped
salt and pepper
10 eggs
1 tbsp finely chopped marjoram
1 tbsp finely chopped oregano
60 g Parmesan, freshly grated

Soak the dried porcini in hot water for 20 minutes, then drain and chop. Dip the bread roll in the milk, then squeeze dry and crumble to make breadcrumbs.

Heat half the olive oil in a large non-stick frying pan. Add the artichokes, button mushrooms and garlic, and sauté until soft. Season with salt and pepper to taste.

Beat the eggs in a bowl and add the herbs, breadcrumbs and Parmesan. Mix well, then stir in the soaked porcini and the mushroom and artichoke mixture.

Heat the remaining olive oil in the frying pan, then pour in the egg mixture. Cook on a low heat for about 8–9 minutes until set, then carefully slide the frittata out on to a plate or large flat lid and invert back into the pan. Cook the other side gently as well, for about 7–8 minutes. Slide the frittata out of the pan on to a board. Serve cut into wedges.

REGIONAL PRODUCTS

Liguria has been called the small vegetable garden of Europe. Its main specialities are olive oil, herbs and vegetables, notably the white beans of Pigna and Conio in Imperia, but also artichokes and many others. Fruit and nuts are important too, particularly peaches, chestnuts and walnuts. Liguria also has mushrooms and truffles, some choice pork products including salami, and a few cheeses.

OLIVE OIL Ligurian olive oil is considered by many to be the best in the Mediterranean. Popular throughout Italy and elsewhere, the extra virgin olive oil is very light and delicate, and less fruity than that produced in neighbouring Tuscany – perhaps because the olives are grown so high up on the terraces. It is ideal for making mayonnaise, where a lighter taste is required, and to flavour fish and seafood dishes. And of course, it also goes to make the region's famous pesto. Ligurian oil is made from the small, sweet Taggiasca olives, which are cultivated all over the region, but mainly in Taggia near Imperia. These olives are also grown for consumption, which is relatively unusual in Italy as olives are generally grown either for eating or their oil, but not both.

BASIL There are two types of basil grown in Italy, one with large leaves and one with small leaves. The small-leaved basil of Liguria is soft, delicate and very fragrant, with an almost minty aroma. It is famously grown in Prà, predominantly for the making of pesto, which has become a thriving business in the region, with a worldwide demand.

CHEESES These are less numerous than in other parts of Italy, though a reasonable quantity is produced in the Polcevera Valley and there is a good *formaggio di Santo Stefano d'Aveto* made near Rezzoaglio, above Chiavari. As in Piedmont, small goat's cheeses and other cheeses are immersed in vinegar and oil, sometimes with added chilli, and tomino is produced in Liguria as well as in Piedmont. Indeed there is a Ligurian pecorino used in the making of pesto, although most pecorino is still imported from Sardinia, and the Lombardian crescenza cheese is used in a wonderful focaccia (see below).

BREADS AND BAKED GOODS Focaccia, Liguria's famous flat bread – made and topped with good olive oil and/or coarse salt and rosemary – is now popular throughout Europe. Topped with anchovies and onions, focaccia is transformed into the Ligurian version of pizza (see page 76). I particularly love *focaccia al formaggio*, a speciality of Camogli, a fisherman's village near Genoa. It is stuffed with crescenza cheese and eaten in the morning, fresh from the oven. *Farinata*, a speciality of Liguria, as well as Piedmont, is a crêpe made with chickpea flour, baked with olive oil and rosemary. *Pandolce genovese* is the equivalent of *panettone milanese*; the Ligurian version is made with lots of butter and is therefore richer – perfect with a glass of Spumante.

Pandolce Genovese Sweet bread from Genoa

This is the Ligurian equivalent of *panettone*, the traditional Christmas yeast cake of Milan. It is more substantial and keeps better than *panettone*, which dries quite quickly. *Pandolce* is usually served with Moscato Spumante, a sweet sparkling wine from Piedmont, or with one of Liguria's own sweet wines, such as the Moscadello of Ventimiglia, or a *passito* wine (made from late-harvested, semi-dried grapes). It is easy to make and quite delicious.

SERVES 6

- **125 g butter, melted, plus extra to grease**
- **50 g fresh yeast**
- **500 g Italian '00' flour**
- **2 tbsp milk**
- **150 g caster sugar**
- **pinch of salt**
- **25 g candied orange peel, finely diced**
- **25 g candied lemon peel, finely diced**
- **50 g sultanas**
- **50 g raisins**
- **150 g pine nuts**
- **25 g fennel seeds**
- **2 tbsp Marsala**
- **200 ml orange flower water**

Grease a 20 cm round, deep cake tin with butter. Crumble the yeast into a cup and add 50 g of the flour and the milk. Stir until the yeast has dissolved, then leave at room temperature for about 30–40 minutes until frothy.

Put the remaining flour in a mound on a board and make a well in the middle. Pour in the melted butter, and add the sugar, salt, candied fruit, sultanas, raisins, pine nuts and fennel seeds, followed by the frothy yeast mixture. Mix the ingredients in the well together and add the Marsala and orange flower water.

Gradually work in the flour until the mixture is smooth and knead until you have a soft, elastic dough – about half an hour, I'm afraid! You might need to add a little water if the mixture is too dry. Shape the dough into a round and place in the prepared tin. Cover loosely with a cloth and leave to rise in a warm place for about 2 hours until doubled in size.

Heat the oven to 180°C/Gas 4. Remove the cloth and cut a deep cross on top of the dough with a very sharp knife. Bake for 40 minutes, then lower the oven setting to 150°C/Gas 2 and bake for a further 20 minutes. Allow to cool in the tin. Serve cut into slices.

Emilia-Romagna

From Emilia in the north-west to Romagna on the Adriatic, this area is part mountainous, part the plain of the Po River, and the cooking is robust, rich and full of flavour. The region is famous for its wonderful prosciutto and parmigiano, as well as the aged balsamic vinegar of Modena, and Emilians claim to be Italy's primary pasta-makers. Many renowned Italian dishes and products come from the capital, Bologna, and other towns, including *mortadella*, *zampone*, *coppa* and pancetta.

I've been to Emilia-Romagna many times and I know this part of Italy well, but I always discover so much more on every visit. Last year, I drove with Alastair, the photographer, from Liguria over the Apennines into Emilia-Romagna, to be greeted by a sign announcing that we were entering the famous *strada dei funghi*. You can imagine how delighted I was – the area around Borgotaro is a mushroom paradise. We drove on to Soragna and Busseto, where some of the best Italian musicians come from, among them Giuseppe Verdi, Luciano Pavarotti and Carlo Bergonzi.

Driving through the wonderful flat country towards the city of Parma itself, the fields on either side of the road are interspersed with mulberry trees (grown for a once thriving silkworm industry). Pretty farms, large and small, are set off the road with patches of cultivated vegetables still tended, I like to imagine, by grandpa or grandma. In Italy grandparents often live with the family, and are probably the only ones with time enough for such pursuits. We met one such grandpa (photographed here) who proudly showed us his cellar, stocked with wonderful local produce – including salami, ham, *culatello* and *coppa*, Parmesan and wines, plus a multitude of homemade preserves.

In the past, Emilia-Romagna was two separate regions. Emilia, to the north, sits in the rich alluvial plain of the Po and has always been the wealthier of the two. Romagna possesses a long Adriatic coastline, but much of the land is hilly, rising up into the Apennines. The Romagnards are (or certainly were) poorer and more fiery than Emilians, leaning towards their southern neighbours in Marche. Differences are reflected in the food too, with Emilian cooking being subtle, rich and smooth, while the Romagnard is more peasant-like, strongly flavoured and uses olive oil rather than butter – a dividing factor between north and south. Today, Emilia-Romagna boasts a wealth of ingredients and is truly a major contributor to the Italian cuisine, and economy as a whole.

Emilia-Romagna is home to many of Italy's most famous foods, not least Parma ham and Parmesan cheese (see page 97). The products are linked, because the pigs for the hams are fed on the whey from the cheese (and often on acorns as well), giving that unique Parma flavour. So-called 'cathedrals' punctuate the whole province of Parma and within these the hams are hung to dry and the huge cheeses are matured. Up to 50,000 hams can be ageing in one 'cathedral' at a time, and the cheeses are turned every other day (to avoid salt depositing on one side only). In Langhirano, there are special ham warehouses with large windows that open in the morning and close in the evening, helping the curing process in a more controlled way. Dishes labelled *parmigiano* obviously originate from Parma.

Emilia-Romagna is renowned for other pork products (see page 95) besides Parma ham. Bologna is home to mortadella, known as 'boloney' (a corruption of the city's name) in America. *Zampone* is a speciality of Modena, made from pig's trotters, typically eaten with sauerkraut or lentils, and with *salsa verde* and a local *mostarda*. The town of Piacenza has some fine meat products such as salami, *coppa* and pancetta.

Zampone di Capodanno Stuffed pig's trotters

This celebration dish is eaten, with variations, all over Italy. You can prepare it in advance and just warm it up for the big occasion. Serve it with with *cren* (horseradish) or *mostarda di Cremona* (the crystallised fruit relish), and mashed potato if you like.

SERVES 6

2 *zampone* (stuffed pig's trotters), about 800 g each, fresh or pre-cooked
200 g dried cannellini beans, soaked in cold water overnight
8 tbsp olive oil
1 carrot, diced
1 celery stalk, diced
2 garlic cloves, sliced
1 tomato, diced
250 g Castelluccio lentils
2 tbsp tomato purée
500 ml chicken stock or vegetable stock (pages 250–1)
salt and pepper
1 small, tender rosemary sprig, leaves only
600 g spinach, washed
75 g butter

If using fresh *zampone*, cook in boiling water to cover for 3 hours. If using the pre-cooked variety, boil for about 20 minutes only.

Drain the cannellini beans and cook in plenty of water (without salt) for 1½ hours until tender.

Heat 6 tbsp olive oil in a pan and gently fry the carrot, celery, garlic and tomato until soft. Add the lentils, tomato purée and the stock. Bring to a simmer and cook until all the stock is absorbed and the lentils are tender, about 20 minutes. Check the seasoning; keep warm.

Drain the cooked cannellini beans and dress with the remaining 2 tbsp olive oil, the rosemary leaves, and salt and pepper to taste; keep warm. When the *zampone* is ready, drain and remove the skin. Cook the spinach briefly in the tiniest amount of salted water until just wilted, then drain very well and toss with the butter.

Cut the *zampone* into thick slices. Put a pile of lentils on each warm serving plate with a spoonful of beans, a mound of spinach and two slices of *zampone*.

VERDI

Bologna, the principal city of the region, is famous for its fresh egg pasta – for everything from stuffed tortellini, *cappelletti*, *anolini* and ravioli, to handmade tagliatelle, lasagne and cannelloni. Dishes appended with *alla bolognese* originate from here, among them *ragù di carne alla bolognese*. Regional specialities can be sampled at Biagi alla Grada or Paulo Atti e Figli, both famous Bolognan restaurants. A pasta speciality from Ferrara is *pasticcio alla ferrarese* (pasta pie). *Tortelli di zucca* (pumpkin ravioli) are associated with Lombardy, but they are also delicious in Reggio Emilia, filled with crumbled amaretti and a sharp *mostarda* as well as pumpkin. *Mostarda* is a fruit relish variously made with apples, pears, peaches, plums, etc., and a grape must, and it flavours a number of the region's dishes. The *mostarda* illustrated left is made of apples. In Forli e Cesana, handmade tagliatelle is served with a game, wild boar or veal sauce. Another speciality here is *passatelli*, which reminds me of the German *spätzle*; Parmesan-flavoured dough is passed through a special slotted plate, or a large-holed grater, into boiling broth. Parma is a centre for the tomato industry, as well as pasta's essential partner – Parmesan.

Freshwater fish of all kinds are found in the many rivers of Emilia-Romagna, and local dishes feature trout, tench, carp and eels. South of the Po estuary there are endless streams, lakes and salt marshes, and the town of Comacchio is actually built on a little group of islands connected by bridges. Here the local cuisine includes specialities based on freshwater fish, eels and frogs. Seafood rules the cuisine of Rimini on the Adriatic and the *brodetto di pesce* (fish soup/stew), which you find all around Italy's coastline, is particularly good here. Many years ago I had an oyster session with friends in Rimini and to everyone's amazement, I managed to eat 126 of them in one sitting! I hasten to add that they were very small (and did not have any of their notorious aphrodisiac effects). In ports such as Cattolica, grilled fish are wrapped in *piadina* for a quick snack. (Taste these at Zanni or Casa delle Aie or Fratelli Bonanni.) And don't forget to visit the little Republic of San Marino while in Rimini; Righi La Taverna is a good place to eat here.

Reggio Emilia is the land of *arrosti* – roasts of veal, beef and pork – the veal coming from the Razza Bianca Romagnola, a local, very tender mature breed of calf. Other meats appreciated throughout the region include turkey, chicken and rabbit, and in Romagna lamb is popular. In Ferrara, Jewish dishes such as smoked goose (*prosciutto d'oca*) and turkey loaf (*polpettone di tacchino*), are reminders of a once significant Jewish population in this area.

Above all, Emilia-Romagna is a wonderfully fertile region. The mountains and hills are rich in fungi, truffles, asparagus, chestnuts, game and soft fruit – notably peaches, apricots, plums, cherries and grapes. Almost every little town in the Bolognesi and Modenesi hills boasts precious white truffles and a host of wild mushrooms, while in Forli e Cesena the truffles are more likely to be black. In the town of Borgotaro in Parma, which is virtually synonymous with mushrooms, there is a huge industry involved in picking, pickling and drying. In Bobbio, the 'town of snails', in Piacenza, you can taste a local speciality, *bracettone*, which is an amalgam of snails and white truffle, served with a potato purée. You will also come across some wonderful local cheeses in the hills, such as robiola piccante, a fresh cheese of Castel Giocondo.

Trippa alla Parmigiana Tripe with Parmesan

Tripe is not to everyone's taste, but I love it and dedicate this recipe to those who like it too. I first tasted this dish in La Buca Trattoria in Zibello; it was simple and delicious. You will come across it in different guises all over Italy, but I prefer this version with Parmesan.

SERVES 4

1 kg very clean (but not bleached) tripe (*millefoglie* and/or *reticulo* (honeycomb)
2 litres chicken stock (page 250)
50 g lard
50 g butter
1 carrot, very finely diced
1 onion, very finely chopped
6 bay leaves
6 sage leaves
1 tbsp tomato purée
1 tbsp very finely chopped parsley
salt and pepper
60 g Parmesan, freshly grated

Cut the tripe into small strips. Bring the stock to the boil in a large pan. Add the tripe and simmer gently for 2 hours, or until it is soft. Drain, reserving about 150 ml of the stock.

Melt the lard and butter in a pan, then add the carrot, onion, bay and sage leaves, and fry briefly to soften the vegetables. Add the reserved stock and tomato purée, bring to the boil and add the tripe. Cover and cook for a further 15 minutes over a low heat.

Add the chopped parsley, adjust the seasoning, and serve scattered with the freshly grated Parmesan.

Vegetables and fruits of all kinds are cultivated in the plains, including onions, carrots, greens, beans and tomatoes. In Bettola in Piacenza, there is an unusual gnocchi dish made with carrots flavoured with basil, and served with a walnut sauce. The Borrettana is a special type of onion (flat, small and very tasty) from Reggio Emilia, while in Castelguelfo in Bologna, the local onion – *cipolla di medicina* – has been valued for its flavour and health-giving properties since the Middle Ages. Modena is noted for its cherries (of Vignola), melons, watermelons, wild mushrooms, and legendary local snails.

Throughout the region you will come across crusty wheat rolls named *coppiette*, because their shape resembles a coupled set of horns. Romagna is proud of its *piadina*, an unleavened flat and round bread reminiscent of the Jewish *pane azzimo*. A local poet once called this 'the national dish' of the Romagnans, and it is sold – wrapped round fillings such as local fresh cheeses or pork products – from roadside stands. In Bologna thicker focaccia-style bread is flavoured with pork fat or salt pork. You can sample a typical version, *la torta con i ciccioli*, in the Osteria del Morasole in San Giovanni di Persiceto.

Modena is the birthplace of Italy's famous *aceto balsamico* (see page 97), and I shall never forget visiting the *acetiera* in Nanantola of Signora Giacobazzi. She tended her barrels daily, stroking them affectionately to ensure that her precious balsamic vinegar fermented calmly.

Nocino is another famous product of Modena, and although this walnut liqueur is made elsewhere in Italy, the walnuts from here are very special. They are gathered on or around 23 June, San Giovanni's day. The liqueur is made commercially, but many Modenesi still make it at home. There is a club of nocino makers in Modena, and every year they exhibit their products, with a prize for the best. I was once a judge at the annual competition – a role that would make anyone happy!

Towards the hills, vines are everywhere, and these produce the grapes for Lambrusco. A number of other notable wines (see page 97) come from the region, especially near the border with Piedmont and Lombardy.

All over Emilia-Romagna, there are numerous festivals and *sagre* during the year, mostly to celebrate wine. In May there is a celebration of *bruschetta* on the second Sunday of May at Predappio Alta, in Forli. On the first Sunday of July in Medolla in Modena, there is an exhibition of wines (Lambrusco especially), and in September, in Sasso Morelli in Bologna, there are wine-pressing competitions. The culmination of wine celebrations comes in November, when there is a huge *bacchanale* of tastings (both wine and food), in Imola, near Bologna.

Other typical regional dishes

Brodetto di pesce A fish soup-stew containing at least four different types of fish and tomatoes

Cannelloni Pasta sheets wrapped round a filling and baked with tomatoes, béchamel and Parmesan

Erbazzone Frittata made with eggs and greens

Fritto misto Mixed fried meat and vegetables

Funghi sott'olio Preserved mushrooms in oil

La torta con i ciccioli Focaccia-style bread with pork scratchings

Lasagne Baked pasta, with meat or vegetables

Mistigriglia Mixed grilled meats

Passatelli Small Parmesan dumplings in broth

Piadina An unleavened bread, filled with prosciutto, cheese or salad and eaten as a snack

Schiacciata Flat bread, similar to focaccia

Stracotto alla parmigiana Extra long, slow-cooked pork, eaten warm or cold

Tigella Unleavened bread, roasted and usually filled with a flavoured paste of Parma ham fat

Tortelli alle erbette Herb flavoured ravioli

Tortelli di zucca Pumpkin ravioli flavoured with crumbled amaretti and *mostarda*

Tortellini al ragù Stuffed pasta with meat sauce

Zuppa inglese Italian trifle

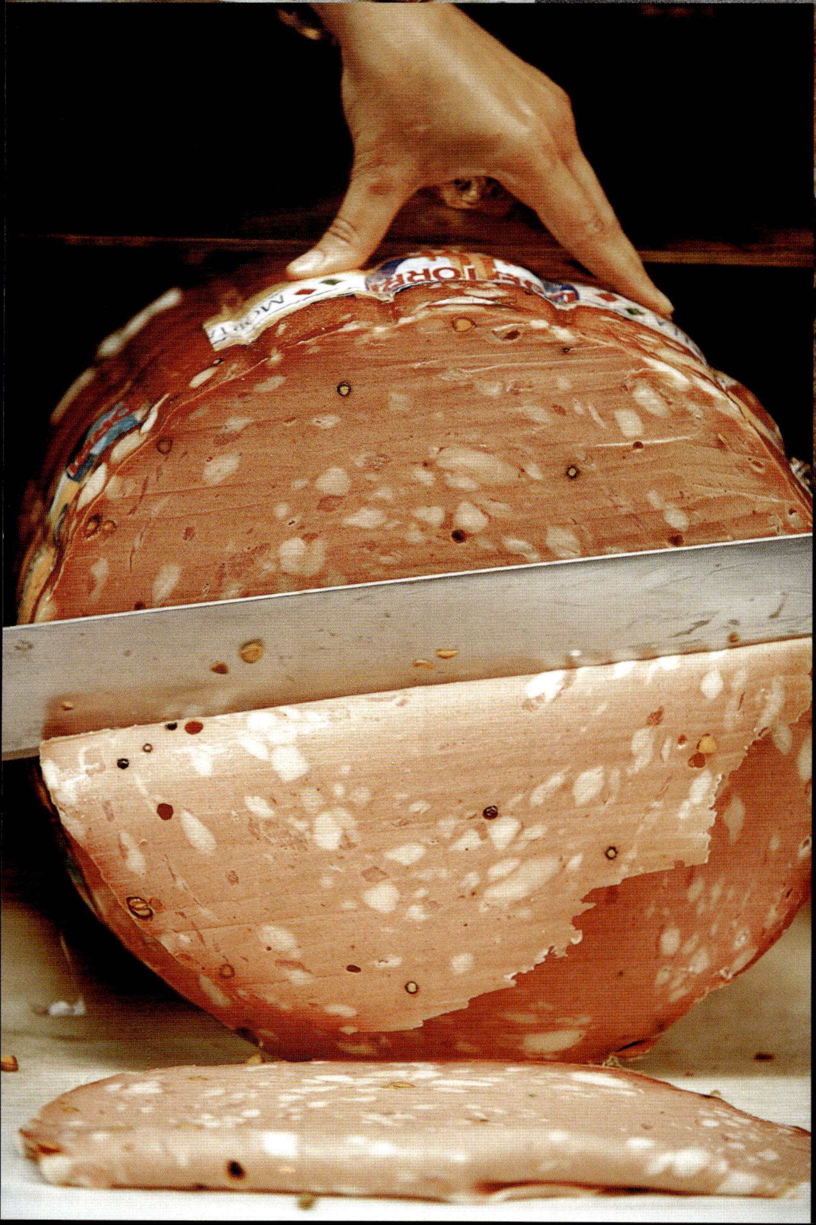

Pork Products of Emilia-Romagna

Coppa A speciality of Piacenza, this is made from the neck or shoulder end of pork, which is brined, bound and air-dried for at least 6 months. The large pieces of fat within *coppa* make it look like a sausage, though the fat content is only about 40 per cent. It is eaten thinly sliced as an antipasto.

Cotechino These pork sausages are made all over the country, but some very good versions are found in Emilia-Romagna. They are usually served with lentils or sauerkraut. *Cotechino* take 3 hours to cook, but you can buy pre-cooked *cotechino* in foil packets (ready in 20 minutes).

Culatello This is a speciality of Zibello, near Modena, the name meaning 'little arse'. A round or pear-shaped piece is cut from the heart of the ham, soaked in brine, then wrapped in a natural skin and hung for 18 months. During drying, it loses up to 40 per cent weight but keeps a sweet flavour. A horse bone, a pointed piece of tibia, is inserted into the ham to see if it is ready – the smell rather than the taste indicating maturity. (The same is done with Parma hams.) *Culatello* is eaten thinly sliced by itself, or in antipasti.

Felino Traditionally made with offcuts from Parma-ham making and spices, this is a superb salami. It is cured for 3 months, irregular in shape, and best cut into thicker slices.

Mortadella This is the largest of the Italian sausages, weighing between 5 and 15 kg. The best mortadellas are now made of finely minced pork cooked with spices such as coriander seeds and peppercorns, and pistachio nuts. To bring out the flavour, mortadella must be sliced very thinly, on a machine.

Pancetta This cured belly of pork, the Italian version of streaky bacon, is made all over Italy, not least in this region with its abundant ham-producing pigs. Although pancetta is generally unsmoked, it can also be smoked, and may be rolled with spices to be sliced like a salami.

Prosciutto di Parma This cured raw ham, *prosciutto crudo*, made from the hind legs of the pig, is famous the world over. The hams are rubbed daily with salt for a month, then hung in an airy place for up to 16 months, during which time the ham loses at least 30 per cent of its weight. The pigs for Parma ham are fed in a particular way (supplemented by whey from the making of Parmesan cheese), and the hams are only permitted to be made in Emilia-Romagna.

Salama da sugo This cured sausage is an ancient speciality of Ferrara. Pork tongue and liver are minced with a unique blend of spices (different in every town), and bound and dried in a pig's bladder (much like haggis) for up to 6 months. It requires lengthy cooking and is traditionally served with potato purée, or it may be cooked in a tomato sauce to make a tasty sauce for pasta, after which the sausage is eaten. Also known simply as *salama* or *salamina*.

Zampone This is a speciality of Modena. Pig's trotters are cooked, boned out and filled with a spiced mixture of pork (meat, skin and part of the cheek). *Zampone* takes 2 or 3 hours to cook, although you can buy vacuum-packed pre-cooked *zampone* that's ready in 20 minutes.

Bomba di Riso con Tartufo Rice bomb with truffle

This is a speciality of Piacenza, and one of the few rice dishes in Emilia, where pasta is so popular. You can find similar dishes elsewhere, notably the *sartù* of Naples. It is an ideal dish for grand occasions – quite rich and time-consuming, but well worth the effort.

SERVES 6–8 OR MORE

20 g dried porcini mushrooms
2 large pigeons or 6 large quail, cleaned, plus flour to dust
50 g butter
50 ml olive oil
1 onion, finely chopped
2 tbsp finely chopped parsley
few sage leaves
1 small rosemary sprig
salt and pepper
freshly grated nutmeg
few juniper berries
about 100 ml chicken or beef stock (page 250)
2 tbsp *saba* (see page 100)
1 tsp truffle oil

Rice mixture

800 g carnaroli risotto rice
100 g butter
150 g Parmesan, freshly grated
2–3 tbsp milk
6 eggs, beaten
½ tsp freshly grated nutmeg

To finish

100 g butter
dried breadcrumbs to coat
50 g Parmesan, freshly grated
20 g fresh truffle, finely sliced

Soak the dried porcini in hot water for 20 minutes. Drain, reserving the liquid, and finely chop the mushrooms.

Dust the pigeons with flour. Heat the butter and olive oil in a large pan and brown the pigeons on each side. Add the onion, parsley, sage and rosemary, and cook until the onion has softened. Add some salt, pepper and nutmeg, the juniper berries, chopped porcini and enough stock just to cover. Cover and cook gently for about 20 minutes until the meat is cooked, adding some strained porcini liquid if necessary. Set aside to cool.

Bone the birds and put the meat back into the pan, discarding the rosemary and sage leaves. Warm through and add the *saba* and a few drops of truffle oil. Cook to let the flavours develop and reduce the sauce slightly, until it becomes quite dense, about 10 minutes.

Cook the rice in plenty of salted water. Meanwhile, heat the oven to 200°C/Gas 6. When the rice is cooked, drain thoroughly and mix in the butter and Parmesan while still warm. Add the milk, beaten eggs and nutmeg, and mix well.

Grease a 25 cm ovenproof pudding basin with 20 g of the butter and dust all around with breadcrumbs. Put two-thirds of the rice into the bowl, and press on to the base and against the sides, leaving a large well in the centre. Pour the pigeon mixture into this well, add the sliced truffle, then cover with the rest of the rice. Sprinkle with more breadcrumbs and dot with the remaining butter and Parmesan. Bake in the oven for 20 minutes.

Leave to rest for 10 minutes before serving. With a knife, loosen the sides, turn upside down on to a large serving plate and remove the bowl. In my opinion, a green salad dressed with balsamic vinegar complements this dish magnificently. *Buon appetito*!

Emilia-Romagna's most highly prized products – Prosciutto di Parma and Parmigiano reggiano – are famous the world over. The region is also esteemed for its other pork products (see page 95), aged balsamic vinegar and walnut liqueur.

PARMIGIANO REGGIANO This 'true Parmesan' is the most familiar hard cheese in the world. It is only allowed to be made in Emilia, although regions such as Piedmont, Lombardy, Veneto, Trentino and some parts of Romagna are permitted to produce its closest rival, grana padano. Parmigiano reggiano was originally made in Reggio Emilia, near Parma, hence the name. It is aged for up to 2 years (although you can find some vintage ones, aged for up to 5 years). Parmesan is so hard that it has to be split with a special knife rather than cut. As a table cheese, it is particularly good served with pears and walnuts, though it is most often grated on to pasta and other dishes.

OTHER CHEESES These include grana padano, robbiola piccante, pecorino dell' Apennino Reggiano, a sheep's milk cheese, and provolone valpadana DOP, a semi-hard cow's milk cheese that can be mild or strong.

ACETO BALSAMICO This is the best of all vinegars and originates from Modena. Worldwide demand has introduced a commercial approach to production, but some 30 to 40 families still produce the real thing at home. It is made in a succession of wooden barrels, which diminish in size as the original quantity of vinegar evaporates. These barrels, made of cherry, mulberry, apple, oak or walnut wood, are treasured family possessions, handed down from generation to generation. They are filled with initial grape must or *saba* from Trebbiano grapes and left under the eaves of houses to mature in the heat of the summer and the cold of the winter. The barrels 'breathe' and the must evaporates and concentrates, while the vinegar 'mother' present in the barrels changes the must into vinegar very slowly. The barrels become smaller every year – the process is known as *solera*, like that for sherry – until the black gold of the finest balsamic vinegar becomes treacle-like (and very expensive). The best balsamics are aged for 20 years, or longer. Nanantola and Spilimbergo are noted for their *aceto tradizionale* (balsamics without that '*tradizionale*' are not the real thing).

WINES AND SPIRITS Lambrusco is the most familiar of the wine types, producing DOC wines and *vini di tavola*. It is made in Emilia around Modena and Reggio Emilia. Romagna also grows vines, and produces wines from grape varieties with 'di Romagna' appended – Albana, Sangiovese and Trebbiano. From the Colli Piacentini on the Piedmont-Lombardy border come big reds such as Bonarda and Barbera.

Modena is famous for nocino, a walnut liqueur, made from unripe or green walnuts, usually collected in June. These are macerated in alcohol with cinnamon and left in the sun for up to 40 days. Once diluted with water and sweetened with sugar, the dark brown liqueur is 30 to 40 per cent proof. It is still made in Modena homes, as well as produced on a commercial basis.

Antipasto di Culatello e Prosciutto

Cured meats with pickles and fried dumplings

***Culatello*, an air-dried, cured cut from the leg of pork, is the pride of the areas of Busseto, San Giocondo and Zibello. It is often served with *giardiniera* (pickled vegetables) as an antipasto, but note that it should be freshly and very thinly sliced (by machine) shortly before serving. This dish is a must in the *trattorie* of Emilia-Romagna.**

SERVES 4

8 thin slices *culatello*
8 slices Parma ham
60 g cold butter, made into curls
Pickled vegetables
selection of vegetables (such as pearl onions, red pepper strips, cauliflower florets, baby carrots)
300 ml white wine vinegar
1 tbsp sugar
Gnocchi
250 g plain flour, plus extra to dust
15 g fresh yeast
30 ml milk
1 tsp olive oil
lard for shallow-frying

To pickle the vegetables, cook them in the wine vinegar with the sugar added and enough water to cover for about 20 minutes. Leave to cool in the liquor.

To make the gnocchi dough. Put the flour in a bowl and crumble in the yeast, then add the milk and olive oil and mix in enough tepid water (about 3 tbsp) to obtain a fairly soft dough. Leave to rise in a warm place for about an hour.

On a lightly floured surface, flatten the gnocchi dough with a rolling pin to a 2 mm thickness, then cut into 5 cm squares.

Arrange the *culatello* and Parma ham slices on serving plates and put the pickled vegetables and some butter curls alongside.

Heat the lard in a large frying pan and fry the gnocchi for about 3 minutes until puffed. Drain on kitchen paper and serve hot with the cold meats and pickled vegetables.

Anolini in Brodo Small tortellini in broth

Every respectable Emilian housewife (and some male cooks), knows how to turn pasta on the little finger to make tortellini. For this classic regional dish, the filling for the mini tortellini is simply freshly grated Parmesan and special breadcrumbs – flavoured with the deglazed juices from a pork or beef roast. You can buy freshly made, good quality tortellini (*anolini*) from delicatessens, but have in mind that sometimes *anolini* are little flat round ravioli.

SERVES 4

4–5 tbsp deglazed juices from a pork or beef roast
200 g soft dry breadcrumbs
50 g Parmesan, freshly grated, plus extra to sprinkle
2 egg yolks
salt and pepper
freshly grated nutmeg
200 g egg pasta dough (page 251)
1 litre very good beef stock, or a mixture of beef and chicken stock (page 250)

Collect the deglazed juices (from the bottom of the dish in which you have roasted some pork or beef). Put the breadcrumbs into a bowl and mix in enough of the meat juices to moisten. Add the Parmesan, egg yolks, and salt, pepper and nutmeg to taste.

Now make the tortellini. Roll out the pasta dough very thinly and cut out little circles. Place a teaspoonful of the filling to one side of each circle, then fold the opposite sides over to make half-moon shapes. Press the edges together to seal well, then curl the two ends round to meet, and pinch together. This isn't difficult, but it is fiddly as the circles are very small. If you lose patience, then make little flat round ravioli.

Bring the stock to the boil in a large pan. Add the *anolini* and cook until *al dente*, about 3–4 minutes. Ladle the soup into warm bowls and sprinkle with Parmesan to serve.

Tagliatelle al Ragù di Coniglio

Tagliatelle with rabbit sauce

It is customary to have a *ragù bolognese* with tagliatelle, and in Emilia-Romagna rabbit often features in the *ragù*. This recipe comes from a local family in Parma. Farmed rabbit is very good, but the sauce tastes even better with a wild one.

SERVES 4

600 g egg tagliatelle (page 251)

Sauce

20 g dried porcini mushrooms
1 large onion, finely sliced
60 g Parma ham fat, in little cubes
40 g butter
500 g boneless rabbit, minced
200 ml dry white wine
3 tbsp tomato purée
salt and pepper

To serve

60 g Parmesan, freshly grated

To make the sauce, soak the dried porcini in hot water for 20 minutes. Drain the porcini, reserving the liquid, then chop and set aside.

Put the onion in a pan with the Parma ham fat and butter. Brown a little, then add the rabbit meat and fry, stirring, for 6–8 minutes. Add the wine and let bubble to evaporate the alcohol, then add the tomato purée diluted with a little water. Add the porcini to the pan with the reserved liquid (leaving the sediment behind). Now cook very slowly and gently for 2 hours. Season with salt and pepper to taste at the end of cooking.

Cook the pasta in plenty of boiling salted water until *al dente*, then drain well. Dress with the *ragù* and serve sprinkled with Parmesan. Delightful.

Fegato Grasso al Balsamico

Foie gras with balsamic sauce

This recipe is my contribution to the cooking of neighbouring Lombardy and Emilia-Romagna. It has been an incredible success in my Neal Street restaurant, impressing many French customers! The *fegato grasso* is produced in the area of Mortara in Lombardy, where many goose products come from. The sauce is ancient, dating back to Roman times. *Saba* is a strong reduction of cooked grape must, which, incidentally, is the first stage of the famous Emilian *aceto balsamico*; you will find it in good delicatessens.

SERVES 4

4 slices of fresh foie gras (goose or duck) without skin, each 2 cm thick and about 50 g each

Sauce

6 tbsp *saba*

1 tbsp balsamic vinegar

1 tsp brandy

salt and pepper

First make the sauce. Heat the *saba* and add the balsamic vinegar, brandy and some salt and pepper to taste.

Heat a non-stick frying pan until it is very hot, then fry the foie gras slices very briefly, searing each side, but leaving the insides almost pink.

Arrange the foie gras on hot plates and surround with the sauce. Serve immediately, with some freshly toasted bread.

TOSCANA

Tuscany marks the divide between the heavier, richer cooking of the north and the simpler, lighter, more Mediterranean style cooking of the south. Tuscan olive oil is a defining factor, and beef and chickens here are the best in Italy. Pasta is less important than elsewhere, and is replaced by good soups, including *ribollita* and *pappa al pomodoro*. Vegetables are exceptional, as is the seafood along the Mediterranean coast.

Tuscany consists primarily of mountains and hills to the west of the Appennine range, with coastal lowlands on the Tyrrhenian Sea. It is bordered to the north by Liguria and Emilia-Romagna, to the east by Marche and Umbria, and to the south by Lazio. The region is rich in history and culture. From the 8th to the 5th century BC, it was known as Etruria, and was the country of the Etruscans, until they were subdued by the empire-building Romans. Much later Tuscany was the cradle of the Renaissance, her beauty captured in the paintings of Fra Filippo Lippi, Botticelli, Uccello and other artists of the time. Florence or Firenze, the region's present capital, was once the most influential city in Italy, a trading centre to rival Venice and a city of ideas and intellect, of religion, banking and power, all mainly the prerogative of the ruling Florentine family, the Medici.

Catherine de Medici, a daughter of this famous house, was married off (by her uncle, the Pope) to Henry Duke of Orleans, later to be King Henry II of France. As a result of the marriage, Catherine settled in France, bringing with her around fifty chefs from Italy. They introduced some foods that were previously unknown in France, including artichokes, and Italians probably also taught the French how to make sorbets and ice-creams (learnt from the Arabs), and pastry. As a consequence, Tuscany can claim to have had a hand in the development of French *haute cuisine*, although the French hate the idea, and some Italians are sceptical. Certain sophistications of the Italian courts were initiated in France at the time, reputedly drinking glasses instead of goblets, table napkins, tablecloths and the fork – a Venetian invention – the French previously ate with their hands.

Tuscany is one of the most familiar regions of Italy, attracting foreigners for centuries. During the 1960s, lured by the sun, beauty, history, food and wine, many British bought second homes in Tuscany and the region became known as 'Chianti-shire'.

CULINARY TRADITIONS & SPECIALITIES

I spent my summer holiday in Tuscany last year, ensconced in a delightful setting. This is the only part of Italy where bread is made without salt, and it takes a bit of getting used to. The ubiquitous salt-free bread is known as *pan sciocco* (silly bread), so I rather facetiously asked the local baker whether he had some 'intelligent' bread. I must admit, however, that it goes perfectly with the salty salami and other pork and wild boar products of the region. When it is toasted as *bruschetta* or *fettunta*, or indeed *crostini* (a Tuscan invention), it balances the spiciness of pâtés, tomato spreads or the peppery local olive oil. Tuscany is recognised for other savoury and sweet breads, biscuits and confections (see page 113), notably *cantucci* and *panforte di Siena*.

Bread is more important than pasta, although there are a few traditional Tuscan pastas, notably *pappardelle*, wide noodles (reminiscent of the Roman *laganum*), which are invariably served with a game *ragù*, usually of hare, wild boar or duck. A speciality of the province of Siena, is *pinci* or *pici*, a hand-rolled spaghetti served with a tomato and meat or sausage *ragù* (see page 114). There are also *tortelli* or *tordelli*, stuffed with ricotta and spinach, acquired from Emilia-Romagna. Pasticcio, a pasta pie made by Renaissance chefs, may have originated in Tuscany, but similar *'timbale'* and *'pasta al forno'* are now found in southern regions.

Bread also features in Tuscany's famous soups, used as a *crostone* in the bottom of a soup bowl, or as a basic constituent as in *pappa al pomodoro* (see page 112). In a sense, Tuscan soups replace pasta at the beginning of a meal, and some of them are so substantial that they serve as a complete meal. Beans are a prime ingredient in soups, and a product of the region. Cannellini beans, for instance, originated here, but are now grown all over Italy. Tuscans also cultivate borlotti beans, black-eyed beans and chickpeas, and *insalata di fagioli* (bean salad) is very popular. A curious ancient recipe is *fagioli al fiasco*: beans slowly cooked with Tuscan olive oil, garlic, sage and water, inside a Chianti flask over embers.

Olive oil features in the majority of Tuscan dishes (see page 113): in cooking and as a final flavouring added to many dishes, such as soups, *bruschette* and steaks. It is also an important part of a Tuscan antipasto, *pinzimonio* (see page 112). Tuscany is a meaty region, and is famous for its beef cattle. The Razza Chianina breed is raised in the Val di Chiana, the Tiber Valley and the Val d'Arno in the province of Arezzo. These cows produce T-bone steaks of gigantic proportions (weighing at least half a kilo), and these feature in the speciality of Florence, *bistecca alla fiorentina*. The meat is grilled, then seasoned and generously drizzled with olive oil to serve. Another beef speciality of Arezzo is *tagliata di manzo*, which is roasted fillet, sliced and served swimming in olive oil, with lots of green peppercorns and fresh rosemary. Vitellone Bianco and Vitellone Razza Maremma cattle are also bred in Tuscany.

Pork and lamb are less significant, though Tuscany has some delicious pork products, and sheep's milk is used for cheese (see page 113). Above all, the Tuscans love chickens, and they breed two very esteemed varieties. The first is the black-feathered Val d'Arno with dark feet, and the other is a white-feathered chicken with yellow feet called Livornese. Chicken is cooked in all manner of ways, often

stuffed (*in porchetta*), and flavoured with olives, fungi, or anything else available. A special dish of chicken offal, *cibreo* (meaning 'confusion' or a 'mixture of various things'), is made with chicken livers, hearts, kidneys, gizzard and sometimes cockscombs. The other popular meat is wild boar, and here in Tuscany it is really wild, rather than being raised by man in a controlled 'wild' habitat. A Tuscan friend, Alvaro Maccioni, told me that sex discrimination is usual in wild boar dishes. The meat of the sow is roasted, grilled or stewed, while the boar is turned almost exclusively into *ragùs* (for *pappardelle*). This is because boar meat tends to have a rank tang, which can only be disguised by the use of wine and spices in the sauce!

Boar are not the only wild treasure of the Tuscan hills. In season there is a wealth of wild mushrooms, and here they are very enthusiastically sought. You can find porcini, *ovoli*, chanterelles, *chiodini* and *famigliole*, and many of them are sold at the side of the road. Unlike those in markets or shops, these roadside mushrooms are unlikely to have been checked by an expert, so be careful – mistakes can be lethal. Truffles are here too – mainly black – and they are incorporated into dishes in season, for example with pheasant in Arezzo (see below). The Tuscans also eat their wild fungi with the wild mints *nepitella* or *mentuccia*, and with lemon balm, something I am not keen on. Indeed, a lot of spices and herbs are used in Tuscan dishes. This is partly due to the influence of Pisa, once a port for the spice traders, bringing in saffron, cloves, cinnamon, nutmeg and other spices from afar.

Fagiano Tartufato Truffled pheasant

This is something the Tuscans eat during the hunting season, and it would make a wonderful festive dish. Considering it is finished with a little cream, it may be one of those dishes returned to Italy from France. Ask your butcher to bone the pheasants ... he will be delighted!

SERVES 4–6

2 cock pheasants, boned, leaving the legs and wings
80 g black truffle
200 g Parma ham (on the fatty side), finely chopped
1 tbsp coarsely chopped flat-leaf parsley
salt and pepper
8 slices pancetta (or streaky bacon)
olive oil to brush
50 g butter
150 ml double cream
3 tbsp brandy
few drops of truffle oil (optional)

Heat the oven to 200°C/Gas 6. Have the boned pheasants ready. For the stuffing, grate 30 g of the truffle and mix with the Parma ham, parsley, and some salt and pepper. Put the pheasants flat on their backs, spread the stuffing on top and roll to enclose. Wrap 4 pancetta slices around each bird and tie with kitchen string, to form sausage shapes.

Brush the birds with olive oil. Heat a frying pan, then add the birds and brown for 2 minutes on each side. Take out the pheasants, wrap in foil and bake in the oven for 20 minutes. Put the frying pan to one side.

Slice the remaining truffle, then cut into tiny strips. Put into the frying pan with the butter, cream, brandy and a few drops of truffle oil if using. Add salt and plenty of pepper, heat gently and allow to reduce a little.

Take the pheasants out of the foil. Cut into slices, discarding the string, and arrange on warm plates. Pour the truffle sauce over the meat and serve. Braised Savoy cabbage and buttered turnips would go very well here. *Buon Natale!*

Even fish dishes, popular all along the coastline, are spiced, particularly the famous *cacciucco* of Livorno, which is a fish soup spiked with chilli. It is found elsewhere in Italy, but in Tuscany it should contain at least five different varieties of fish, one for every 'c' in its name! Fish is de rigueur, and most dishes are styled *alla livornese* – the most famous being the *triglie*, red mullet (see recipe opposite). In Grosseto, prawn tails are cooked with porcini (*coda di gamberi con porcini*). Further north in Pisa, tiny elvers are caught in the estuary of the Arno and Serchio rivers; these *cehe* or *cieche* are fried in olive oil with sage, and served with a little tomato sauce.

Tuscany is a fertile region, offering an impressive array of vegetables and fruit, especially asparagus, artichokes, courgettes, cabbages and chard. In the Garfagnana in the north, wheat and its ancient form – *farro* or spelt – are grown. Farro was known to the Etruscans and Romans, who used it to make bread and porridge; today it is used in soups, and sometimes ground to make pasta. Here too, in this wild part, you can find vines, olives and chestnuts (once used in polenta, now in a delicious chestnut cake), and even saffron near the Etruscan towered town of San Gimignano. To the east in Arezzo there are fields and fields of sunflowers grown for oil. In the south, *corbezzolo*, a delightful wild fruit (like a yellow crab apple with an uneven skin), grows in bushes all over the hills and is made into a delectable jam.

Tuscany is a magnificent region, and there is wonderful food to be had at local fairs, markets and selected restaurants. At the San Lorenzo market in Florence you will see virtually everything in season, similarly at the Piazza delle Vettovaglie in Pisa. For me, these markets are the best Italy, or any country, can offer. Go to Siena at the time of the Palio in mid-August, when different factions in the city race each other on horseback, without saddles, around the spectacular Piazza del Campo. Or visit the wild boar festival in Chianciano (Florence) in April, or the olive and olive oil *sagra* called Oleum in late autumn. The celebrations are legion, too many to list here, so contact the *proloco* of the area, or the regional tourist board before you visit.

Enjoy the festivals, the produce, the beauty, the history – and the food. But be wary when you are in more popular places. Florence, Venice and Rome are for me on the same culinary level: they can be sublime, but they can be awful as well – you just have to know and understand where and what to eat and drink. In the San Lorenzo market in Florence, for instance, you need to bypass the fast food tourist traps and seek out true Florentine specialities, such as the *zuppa di trippa* – a delicious tripe soup, once made for the poor who came to the market. I always go to the smaller *trattorie*, such as Coco Lezzone, where I can relax and be sure of quality and authenticity, rather than starred restaurants where the genuine has often been replaced by avant-gardism of a dubious taste and extortionate price.

Zuppa di Carciofi, Patate e Topinambour

Soup of two artichokes and potatoes

I don't want to change history by altering the ingredients of this classic Tuscan soup, but it came to me that I could reinforce the taste of the artichokes by replacing some of the potato with Jerusalem artichokes (*topinambour*). This root isn't actually in the normal repertoire of Tuscan vegetables. Well, it is now...

SERVES 4–6

4 small very tender artichoke hearts
300 g potatoes, peeled and diced
1.5 litres chicken or vegetable stock (pages 250–1)
400 g Jerusalem artichokes
2 garlic cloves, peeled
salt and pepper
2 tbsp coarsely chopped flat-leaf parsley
1 tbsp coarsely chopped marjoram
extra virgin olive oil to serve

Croûtons

3 slices Tuscan bread or ciabatta, toasted
1 garlic clove, halved
4 tbsp olive oil

Thinly slice the artichoke hearts and put into a pan with the potatoes and stock. Bring to a simmer and cook for 15 minutes. Meanwhile, peel and thinly slice the Jerusalem artichokes. Add to the pan with the whole garlic cloves and cook for a further 10 minutes.

Meanwhile, make some croûtons. Rub the toasted bread slices with the garlic, then cut into 3 cm squares. Heat the olive oil in a frying pan and fry the bread cubes until golden. Drain well on kitchen paper.

Add salt and pepper to the soup, then purée in a blender or push through a sieve. Add the parsley and marjoram, and check the seasoning. Serve hot, topped with a generous drizzle of olive oil and accompanied by the croûtons.

Triglie alla Livornese Red mullet Livorno style

An extremely simple dish, which relies on the freshest red mullet you can find.

SERVES 4

8 red mullet fillets, about 80 g each; or 4 small whole fish, about 180 g each, cleaned
salt and pepper

Sauce

1 garlic clove, finely chopped
6 tbsp olive oil
2 tbsp coarsely chopped flat-leaf parsley
2 tbsp coarsely chopped celery leaves
400 g *polpa di pomodoro* or chunky passata

To prepare the sauce, fry the garlic in the olive oil until softened, then add the parsley, celery leaves and tomato. Bring to a simmer and allow to reduce gently for a few minutes.

Add the red mullet fillets, with some salt and pepper, and cook gently for about 5 minutes. Serve with boiled potatoes or a little rice.

Fritto Misto alla Fiorentina Florentine fritto misto

Thanks to the abundance of olive oil and fresh raw ingredients, the Tuscans love a good 'fry-up'. This is a very popular dish, which can be changed according to whatever is available in any season and to your taste.

SERVES 4

150 g calf's brains
150 g calf's sweetbreads
100 g calf's liver, thinly sliced
4 small lamb cutlets, trimmed
4 young artichoke hearts, halved
200 g courgettes, thickly sliced
Potato croquettes
300 g plain boiled potatoes
freshly grated nutmeg
2 eggs, beaten
30 g pecorino cheese, grated
To cook and serve
light olive oil for deep-frying
flour to dust
salt and pepper
4 eggs, beaten
lemon wedges to serve

First make the potato croquettes. Mash the potatoes in a bowl and add some nutmeg to taste, the beaten eggs and cheese. Mix well, then dust your hands with flour and shape the mixture into 8 croquettes.

Cut both the calf's brains and sweetbreads into 8 chunks and blanch them in a pan of boiling water for 6–8 minutes; drain well and cut away the sinews and veins. Have all the other foods ready. Heat the olive oil for deep-frying in a suitable pan until it is hot. Season the flour with salt and pepper.

Cook the *fritto misto* in batches. Dip the prepared ingredients into seasoned flour first, then in the beaten egg and immediately into the hot olive oil. Fry until golden, turning once. Drain well on kitchen paper and keep warm while you fry the remaining ingredients. Serve immediately, with lemon wedges.

Fegatelli alla Cortonese con Funghi

Pig's liver Cortona style with mushrooms

Cortona is a lovely medieval town in the south of the province of Arezzo. It is of Etruscan origin, and the Cortonese keep gastronomy on top of the local agenda with plenty of food festivals. For this local dish, slices of pig's liver are wrapped in caul fat and baked with fennel and bay flavours, then served with garlicky mushrooms – *funghi al tegame*.

MAKES 8

100 g caul fat (ask your butcher)
8 medium slices pig's liver, about 650 g in total
salt and pepper
4 tbsp fresh breadcrumbs
1 tbsp fennel seeds
8 short twigs of bay leaves
600 g firm, fresh porcini mushrooms, cleaned
2 garlic cloves, crushed
6 tbsp olive oil
chopped *nepitella* or wild mint

Heat the oven to 200°C/Gas 6. Put the caul fat in slightly warm water to become soft, then remove and cut into eight 15 cm square pieces.

Season each slice of liver with salt and pepper, then sprinkle with the breadcrumbs and fennel seeds, and roll up. Wrap each roll in a piece of the caul, and secure with a bay twig (or you could use cocktail sticks). Place in a shallow baking tin.

Slice the mushrooms and put into a pan with the garlic, olive oil and about 100 ml water. Cook on a low heat for 30 minutes, stirring occasionally. Flavour with *nepitella* or wild mint to taste.

Meanwhile, bake the *fegatelli* (liver rolls) in the oven for 25 minutes. Serve as soon as they are ready, with the mushrooms.

Other typical regional dishes

Acquacotta Literally 'cooked water', this soup can be flavoured with various ingredients, such as mushrooms or even *baccalà* (dried cod), sometimes with the addition of beaten egg or cheese

Anguille alla fiorentina Eel pieces, fried in oil to render excess fat, then breadcrumbed and cooked in the oven with red wine

Arista di maiale Boned loin of pork roasted with garlic, rosemary, fennel and pepper, eaten hot or cold

Bistecca alla fiorentina T-bone steak simply grilled and eaten with *fagioli all'uccelletto*, a stew of cannellini beans with tomatoes

Cacciucco A Livornese fish soup, one of the many along Italy's extensive coastline

Castagnaccio Tuscan cake made from chestnut flour and flavoured with sultanas, pine nuts, walnuts and fennel seeds

Cenci Sweet egg dough noodles, flavoured with Vin Santo and spices, deep-fried until puffy then sprinkled with icing sugar and eaten straightaway. *Cenci* means 'rags', which they resemble

Crostini alla toscana Small pieces of toast with various toppings, such as chicken livers, tomatoes, meat *ragù* or salami, usually served as an antipasto

Lenticchie e fagiano Tuscan lentil soup enriched with pheasant

Lepre in agrodolce Sweet-sour hare, cooked with chocolate, similar to the Roman method of cooking wild boar

Minestrone livornese Version of minestrone from Livorno, featuring beans, Savoy cabbage and rice, with some prosciutto for flavour

Panzanella Salad of stale bread softened with vinegar and water, and dressed with tomatoes, onions, anchovies, olives and basil

Pappa al pomodoro Popular tomato and bread soup, flavoured with garlic, basil and olive oil

Pappardelle con l'anatra/cinghiale/lepre Broad noodles with duck, wild boar or hare *ragù*

Pinzimonio Springtime *trattorie* dish of the new season's peppery olive oil served in bowls with the first tender vegetables – spring onions, artichokes, fennel, celery, carrots, etc.

Ribollita Famous Tuscan soup based on *cavolo nero* (black cabbage) and beans, designed to soak up the bread, which replaces pasta. It is best made ahead and reheated, the literal meaning of *ribollita*

Riso e fagioli Simple, delicious soup of rice and beans

Zuccotto Sponge cake moistened with liqueur, topped with whipped flavoured cream and dusted with cocoa and icing sugar

REGIONAL PRODUCTS

BREAD AND BAKED GOODS *Pan sciocco* is common to the whole region, as are various *bruschette* and *crostini*. The southern province of Grosseto is known for its *pagnotta maremmana* – a delicious, round sourdough bread, weighing up to a kilo! *Schiacciata* is a flat bread made throughout the region, sometimes flavoured with rosemary, though fruit versions are also popular. Other Tuscan sweeter breads include *pane di ramerino* (with rosemary, eaten at Easter), and *pane dolce con l'uva* (with raisins). Siena is famous for its *panforte*, a flat cake dating back to the Middle Ages, rich with spices, nuts and dried fruit. Its predecessor, *panpepato* (a honeyed and peppered bread), is still made. In Lucca you will come across *castagnaccio* (chestnut cake) and *buccellato lucchese*, a simple bread-like cake, which is eaten for breakfast, dipped in milk. Biscuits are very popular in Tuscany, eaten after meals, often dipped into a glass of the local Vin Santo. They include *cantucci* (hard baked biscuits from Prato near Florence) and *ricciarelli* (soft macaroons from Siena).

OLIVE OIL The olive oil from this region is rather special and Tuscans will tell you it is the best in the world. The trees are grown mostly on hillsides – the best around Lucca – to be as near the sun as possible. Two varieties of olives are grown: the Muraiolo and Leccino. The olives are harvested before they are fully ripe, which makes for a bright green and very peppery oil. It is expensive because of its low yield (more mature fruit would produce more oil), and is used in a multitude of ways, even in cake making.

CHEESES This region does not produce many cheeses, but its pecorino is excellent – notably that from the Chianti areas of Casentino and Pienza. Pecorino toscano is milder than romano or sardo. A speciality of Siena and Arezzo is the marzolino, which is pecorino made in March when the grass is newly grown. It is eaten fresh, or left to mature and become more piquant, when it can be grated. In May marzolino is eaten with new raw broad beans – one of those rare annual treats. Some pecorinos in Tuscany are made from mixed milks, so you should look for the words *tutto di latte di pecora* or *latte pecora completo*, indicating that only sheep's milk has been used. Pecorino senese is a Tuscan pecorino whose rind has been rubbed with tomato purée, to give a pinkish tinge (instead of, say, oil and wood ash as in Lazio, for pecorino romano).

MEAT PRODUCTS Tuscany produces a *prosciutto toscano*, which is slightly saltier than Parma ham, but wild boar hams are more common, as are wild boar *salsiccie* and salami. *Mazzafegato* is a salami borrowed from Umbria, but more familiar is the *finocchiona*, a large salami flavoured with fennel seeds. Other products are *salame toscano* or *nostrano, salsiccia toscana* (a fresh cooking sausage), and *cotenne sott'aceto* (pickled pork skin, a delicacy). A particular speciality is *lardo di Colonnata*, made in the marble hills near Carrara by layering slabs of fat from specially fattened pigs in marble 'coffins' with salt and spices, and maturing for up to a year.

WINE Good wines have been produced in Tuscany for nearly 3,000 years, and central, not just geographically, is Chianti. But wine in Tuscany means much more than just Chianti (see page 117) and deserves a better reputation.

Pici o Pinci al Ragù di Maiale

Tuscan pasta with pork sauce

Pici **is possibly the only original Tuscan handmade pasta. It is made by pulling on a piece of dough made of durum wheat flour and water (usually no egg) until you have a lengthy string the size of a** ***bucatino*** **without the holes. It's similar to the Venetian** ***bigolo*****, so quite substantial. In Tuscany, it is regularly eaten with a** ***ragù*** **of wild boar, hare, rabbit or pork.**

SERVES 6

400 g *pici* or *pinci* (or the largest spaghetti as possible)
80 g pecorino cheese or Parmesan, freshly grated

Pork ragù

6 tbsp olive oil
1 small onion, finely chopped
1 celery stalk, finely diced
1 carrot, finely diced
400 g pork mince (not too fatty)
100 ml dry red wine
500 g *polpa di pomodoro* or chunky passata
5–6 bay leaves
salt and pepper

To make the *ragù*, heat the olive oil in a pan, add the onion, celery and carrot, and fry gently until soft. Add the meat and stir to brown a little, then add the wine and let the alcohol evaporate. Stir in the tomato pulp and add the bay leaves and some seasoning. Cook very slowly for 2 hours.

Cook the pasta in plenty of boiling salted water until *al dente*, about 15–17 minutes. Toss with the sauce and serve with grated cheese.

Panforte di Siena Spiced fruit and nut cake

This is perhaps one of the oldest sweets in Italy, dating back through the centuries to the introduction of new spices from afar, via the naval port of Pisa. *Panforte* is sticky but irresistible, and is normally eaten in winter, perhaps with coffee and liqueurs after a meal. A small piece is sufficient to tell you about the complexity of the spices used at that time.

SERVES 10

240 g figs or pitted dates
50 g honey
100 g soft brown sugar
1/2 tsp each of ground cinnamon, cardamom, cloves, nutmeg and black pepper
250 g candied fruit, such as cherries, citron, lemon and orange rind
50 g blanched almonds
50 g pine nuts
50 g shelled hazelnuts, toasted
3–4 tbsp plain flour, sifted
50 ml Vin Santo
icing sugar to dust

Heat the oven to 150°C/Gas 2. Line a shallow 25 cm round cake tin, or a 20 cm square tin, with rice paper.

Mince the figs or dates and put them in a pan with enough water just to cover. Add the honey, brown sugar and all the spices. Cook gently for about 10 minutes, then tip into a bowl. The mixture should be soft and sticky, but not wet.

Add the candied fruit and nuts and mix well, then add the flour and Vin Santo and mix to a sticky mass. Spoon the mixture into the prepared tin and bake in the oven for 30–40 minutes.

Take out of the oven and leave to cool in the tin. Sprinkle generously with icing sugar and serve cut into thin wedges.

Wines of Tuscany

Chianti Covering most of central Tuscany, the Chianti region is divided into 7 sub-districts of which Chianti Classico DOCG (between Florence and Siena) and Chianti Rufina DOCG (east of Florence, centred on Pontassieve) are the best. Most of these reds are Sangiovese based, though occasionally blended with some Cabernet. Chiantis have come a long way from the wines first introduced to the rest of Europe, in the familiar straw-covered bottle, aptly named a *fiasco*. These days, most Chianti estates produce a *vino da tavola*; some of these uncategorised simple wines are very good indeed – and expensive.

Brunello di Montalcino DOCG In the south, this wonderful red is made exclusively in and around the hilltop town of Montalcino. The wine's name is derived from the name of the grape Brunello (it is brownish when ripe), a clone of Sangiovese. Another good red, Rosso di Montalcino DOC, is a less intense and cheaper version of Brunello.

Vino Nobile di Montepulciano DOCG This deep, dense red from the province of Siena has been likened to a cross between Brunello and a good Chianti. It is made in the hilltop village of Montepulciano from the Prugnolo grape, a clone of Sangiovese, and not from the Montepulciano grape. Rosso di Montepulciano is a less intense, fruitier version of the Vino Nobile.

Sassicaia This is a wonderful red *vino da tavola*, first made in 1968 from the Cabernet Sauvignon grape under the patronage of the Marquis Piero Antinori. This marked the renaissance of Italian wines, which are now able to compete with the best in the world. In the province of Livorno, where Sassicaia comes from, there is a Strada della Costa degli Etruschi, a 'wine road' consisting of some 50 wine producers.

Morellino di Scansano DOC A fresh red made from a Sangiovese clone, Morellino.

Montecarlo DOC Red and white wines made near the olive oil town of Lucca, the reds from Sangiovese (and other) grapes, the whites from Trebbiano, Sémillon, Pinot Grigio (and other) grapes.

Tignanello A great red *vino da tavola*, made from Sangiovese with 20 per cent Cabernet Sauvignon.

Vernaccia di San Gimignano DOC This delicious white is made from the grape of the same name, in the 'town of towers', south-west of Florence. Good with antipasti or fish, or drunk as an aperitif.

Vin Santo del Chianti White *vino da tavola* into which Tuscans dip their *cantucci di Prato*. It is usually made from a Malvasia/Trebbiano blend of dried or semi-dried grapes (*passito*). Vin Santo means 'holy wine', possibly because it is usually made around Easter, but the name may be derived from that of the Greek island of Xantos, where the vine originally came from.

Umbria

Landlocked and one of the smallest regions of Italy, Umbria is naturally beautiful and full of antiquities. It is known for its meat and game, especially pork (fed on chestnuts and acorns), lamb, beef, goat, wild boar and pigeon, and these are typically either grilled or char-grilled. Legendary black truffles come from Norcia, tiny lentils from Castelluccio, and Umbria's capital, Perugia, is famous for its chocolate.

Umbria is bordered to the north by Marche, to the north-west by Tuscany, and the south by Lazio and Abruzzi. Although landlocked, it certainly does not lack for water. There is the famous Lago Trasimeno and a multitude of rivers and streams, including the Tiber (or Tevere in Italian), which rises in Tuscany and flows through Umbria on its way to Rome. This green and tranquil region has many qualities, not least its weather. As in most of central Italy, it is hot in summer, warm in spring, mild in autumn and relatively cold in winter.

Umbria is rich in history, art and culture. Etruscan and Roman arches, tombs and other remains are everywhere, and almost every town boasts wonderful architecture and art treasures. The region is known as *Terra Santa*, or 'Holy Land', because at least four of the most popular Italian saints come from here. San Francesco, founder of the Franciscan order, who was famously from Assisi; Santa Chiara (or Clare) of Assisi; Santa Rita of Cascia; and San Benedetto (or Benedict), the founder of the Benedictine order. There are many churches throughout the region, dedicated to these and other local saints, and there are pilgrimages and festivals in their honour throughout the year.

Umbria is not only attractive to foreigners, it is also very welcoming, especially to those who make an effort to understand the language and culture, and appreciate the cooking. I fully expect this beautiful region to become the new choice destination for British sun-seekers and third-home aspirants – following the saturation of Tuscany (or 'Chianti-shire').

CULINARY TRADITIONS & SPECIALITIES

In the same way as the land seems to have changed little over the centuries, neither has the food, and because of the rich terrain and its plethora of products, the eating is very good indeed. As in neighbouring regions, the hills provide soft fruits, chestnuts, mushrooms, black and white truffles, and olive oil. Umbrian meats include beef, lamb, goat, wild boar and other game and, of course, pork.

Umbrian pork products (see page 125) are renowned. Their manufacture is centred around the town of Norcia, which is famous for its pig butchery. Throughout Italy, a *norcino* is someone who is an expert in butchering pigs and making salami, and shops selling pork products are called *norcinerie* in Umbria and neighbouring Tuscany and Lazio. Several years ago, while filming for a TV series in Norcia, I came across a wonderful deli – the Boutique del Pecoraro (shepherds' boutique). The owner, Marco, was especially proud of his *coglioni di mulo* (mule's testicles), an odd name for a salami made with minced pork! Fresh pork dishes include *porchetta* (roasted, stuffed piglet), which is said to have originated in Umbria.

The beef in this region is Vitellone Bianco dell'Apennino, the white cattle also seen in Marche, Emilia-Romagna and Tuscany. From these cows comes the *tagliata* of Perugia, a huge T-bone steak. Wild boar is an ancient introduction, but it is now used in a variety of dishes. There is even a wild boar ham, which is distinguished from pork ham by the rather intimidating retention of some long black bristles! Game birds are popular, primarily pigeons, but pheasants, guinea fowl, quails and (sorry) thrushes feature as well. These birds are skewered and grilled over a dish containing red wine, seasonings, herbs, olives and sometimes the minced giblets. This mixture, *leccarda*, also the name of the dish – is basted over the bird as it cooks, and serves as a sauce for the finished dish. *Porchetta* is basted with *leccarda* as well. Hare is marinated in wine and herbs and stewed with olives. Snails, perhaps surprisingly, are served on *spiedini* (skewers) and charcoal-grilled.

A curious ancient recipe from Orvieto involves old chicken – and the older the better. In the 19th century, leaseholders had to give two chickens to the landlord on the day before Ascension. Inevitably, as neither the age nor sex were specified, the landlord would be offered the toughest, oldest birds, so some clever culinary skills were required. For *gallina ubriaca* (drunken chicken), pieces of an old bird are layered in an earthenware casserole with a flavouring *battuto* of ham fat, tomatoes, garlic and onion, then covered with dry white wine. The casserole is sealed with a tight-fitting lid and cooked slowly for 3 to 4 hours.

The freshwater fish of the area are excellent, particularly the trout and carp from Trasimeno and the River Nera. Trout are often served with truffles, and carp is traditionally stuffed with various herbs and baked to make the classic dish, *regina in porchetta* (literally 'stuffed queen'). Freshwater prawns are cooked simply, so that their flavour can be fully appreciated.

Umbria is renowned for its truffles and other wild fungi. Centred around Norcia, the truffle trade is important to Umbria, and indeed to the Italian economy. Truffles are used quite generously in Umbrian cuisine, with trout, in *ragùs* for pasta, on risottos, and with eggs in *frittate*. While filming in Norcia, I met one lady who had been cleaning black truffles for some 50 years. I presented her with a plate of *tagliolini* with white truffle, and her face lit up when she savoured the first morsel. In all that time, she had never tasted white truffles!

The lentils of Castelluccio (see page 125) are as famous now as those of Puy in France. Around Monteleone di Spoleto, the ancient grain known as *farro* is cultivated. A type of spelt used by the Romans for making bread and pasta, it is now mostly used in soups such as *imbrecciate di farro*. Pasta dishes in Umbria are not particularly noteworthy. The most characteristic are *ciriole*, *cirioline*, or *strengozzi*, which are large pasta strings stretched out by hand. These are typically served with truffles or mushrooms from Norcia, or a *ragù* of rabbit or wild boar, or giblets (*rigaglie*, a speciality of Perugia).

Crostini di Tartufo alla Spoletina

Truffle crostini Spoleto style

We are in black truffle territory, so be prepared. Truffles – especially the summer black variety – used to cost very little, but high demand has led to exorbitant prices. I suggest you use the black summer truffle here, with the addition of a few drops of truffle oil.

SERVES 6–8

4 slices bread

Truffle paste

50 g black truffle

few drops of truffle oil

100 g butter

70 g salted anchovies, rinsed and filleted

Put the ingredients for the truffle paste in a mortar and pound with a pestle to a smooth cream.

Toast the bread and cut into 12 small *crostini*. Spread with the truffle paste and serve with Prosecco, Champagne or a good glass of Torgiano (page 125).

An extra recipe for truffle hunters… Take a nice truffle, about 50–60 g, peel it thinly, and wrap in slices of pancetta. Wrap in foil (in Italy we would use damp 'straw' paper) and put under the ashes of a low fire to cook for about 30 minutes. Slice and eat with bread.

Olive trees are cultivated around Lago Trasimeno and in the hills of Assisi, Spoleto and Orvieto, for the very good oil used in local specialities. I remember once being invited by the Bartolini family to watch the olive pressing in Arrone. One woman brought in her olives and sat through the entire process, from the first grinding of the press to the bottling of her 100 litres or so of olive oil. Those bottles would have represented her family's consumption for the following year. Whenever you visit an olive oil press – or if you go to the Ercole Olivario, a competition for the best Italian olive oil – you will be offered a characteristic Umbrian *bruschetta* – a slice of toasted bread, rubbed with garlic and drizzled with their extra virgin oil.

Umbria has wonderfully fertile earth, and there are a number of other special vegetables. The red onions of Cannara, not dissimilar to those of Tropea, are sweet enough to eat raw in salads.

Trevi is known for its unusual black celery, and potatoes are grown in Colfiorito and Campitello. Cardoons are also cultivated here and used to make a dish called *cardi alla grifo* (see page 129).

Umbria is famous for its fine sheep's milk cheeses, especially pecorino, a product of the rich pastures. Sweet things are delicious in the region too, not least the chocolate *baci* or kisses, a speciality of Perugia, and *pinocchiate*, a Christmas pine nut confection from the 15th century.

There are many *sagre* and festivals. Highlights include the music and arts festival of Due Mondi in Spoleto, where you can taste Umbrian specialities. On the day before Palm Sunday, the Ercole Olivario or olive oil competition takes place. In May, there's a *porchetta* festival in Monte Saula Maria Tiberiana, with a similar event in September in Bastia. In Norcia from September to January a great truffle celebration takes place, and in November, Narni hosts a festival of chestnuts and wine.

Gamberi in Salsa Crayfish in green sauce

To celebrate the very good fish from the lakes and rivers of Umbria, especially the Nera River, here is a traditional recipe, which uses the local crayfish. In Sweden and other parts of the world, including Britain, there are impressive-looking crayfish with very sweet flesh, but I find they are often not meaty enough. I suggest you use scampi instead, which have a different taste but at least they have some meat to eat. This is a wonderful summer starter.

SERVES 4

4–6 crayfish or scampi per person (depending on size)
salt

Sauce

3 tbsp chopped mint
4 tbsp chopped flat-leaf parsley
finely grated zest and juice of 1/2 lemon
1/2 garlic clove, crushed
1 tbsp white wine vinegar
6 tbsp extra virgin olive oil (ideally a light oil from Liguria)

To serve

lemon wedges

To make the sauce, put the herbs, lemon zest and juice, garlic and wine vinegar in a mortar and pound together, gradually adding the olive oil to make a textured sauce. (You could use a blender here, but I prefer the sauce with a little texture.)

Cook the crayfish or scampi in lightly salted water for 8 minutes. Drain and shell them, keeping the head and tail attached to the meat.

Serve the freshly boiled scampi or crayfish on a portion of the sauce, with lemon wedges.

REGIONAL PRODUCTS

PORK PRODUCTS *Barbozza* is the Umbrian equivalent of what is known as *guanciale* in Lazio – pork cheek cured in salt then air-dried. It is used like pancetta in a *battuto*, or it can be finely sliced for an antipasto. *Prosciutto di Norcia* is a fragrant, non-salty ham produced in the towns of Cascia, Norcia, Monteleone di Spoleto, Poggiodano and Preci – all of which are about 450 metres (1500 feet) above sea level – ideal for air-drying. *Corallina* is a large salami, similar to *milano*, made of very finely minced shoulder pork with an 'eye' of lard through the middle. It is smoked lightly with juniper berries for a superb flavour. *Mazzafegato* is an unusual sausage in Gubbio, Spoleto, Norcia and Orvieto. A mixture of fat and lean pork, minced with liver and flavoured with pine nuts, it has a wonderfully intense flavour.

CASTELLUCCIO LENTILS These small, dark lentils have been grown on the volcanic plains of Monti Sibillini above Castelluccio, since before the time of the Ancient Romans. They cook in about 20 minutes without pre-soaking and are tender with a nutty flavour. These lentils often accompany sausages.

WINE Umbria's best-known wine is the white Orvieto, from the lovely town of the same name, near the border with Lazio. It has been made for some 2,000 years, and famously lubricated many of the most important Renaissance artists! It comes dry (*secco*) or semi-sweet (*abboccato*). Most other wines of the region, red and white, are prefixed with '*colli*' (hills), to echo the nature of the terrain, among them Amerini, del Trasimeno, Altotiberini (from the slopes of the Upper Tiber), Assisi, Montani and Perugini. The best two, though, are the red Torgiano Rosso Riserva and the Montefalco Sagrantino, both DOCG.

Lenticchie e Salsicce di Cinghiale

Castelluccio lentils and wild boar sausage

This is one of the tastiest of the peasant dishes that have been revived in modern *trattorie*. The Umbrian lentils from Castelluccio are wonderful, and cook in a short time without pre-soaking. Wild boar sausages are now widely available and are tastier than their pork counterpart. Simplicity is the essence of this dish – you just put everything in one pot and wait for it to cook.

SERVES 6

600 g or 12 wild boar sausages
50 g lean pancetta, diced
3 tbsp olive oil
1 small onion, very finely chopped
2 garlic cloves, finely chopped
10 sun-dried tomatoes, finely chopped
1 celery stalk, very finely diced
2 tbsp dry white wine
1 little rosemary sprig
5 sage leaves
5 basil leaves
250 g Castelluccio lentils
salt and pepper

Put the sausages and pancetta into a large pan or cooking pot with the olive oil and brown slightly. Add the onion, garlic, sun-dried tomatoes and celery, and fry gently to soften, then add the wine and let it evaporate a little.

Add the herbs, lentils and just enough water to cover. Bring to a simmer and cook for 20–30 minutes or until the lentils are soft, adding a little more water if it becomes too thick.

Season with salt and pepper to taste and serve.

La Costoletta del Curato Veal chop of the priest

In Italy, as we know, the clergy treat themselves proverbially well. You will find this recipe on the restaurant menus in Orvieto during May, when wild herbs are available in the fields. It was a challenge for me because the exact 'mixture' is apparently a secret. The only known fact is that there should be at least 18 herbs. Gather together as many as you can find, but go easy on the more pungent varieties.

SERVES 4

3–4 tbsp olive oil
4 veal cutlets, about 180 g each
Sauce
about 150 g mixed fresh herbs
4 tbsp extra virgin olive oil
50 g mild mustard
juice of 1/2 lemon
salt and pepper

To prepare the sauce, put the herbs in a mortar and pound with the pestle, dribbling in the extra virgin olive oil gradually, as you reduce the herbs to a paste. Add the mustard, lemon juice, and salt and pepper to taste; mix well.

Heat the olive oil in a large frying pan, add the veal cutlets and fry for about 6–8 minutes on each side until cooked. Spread the cold herb sauce on top of the cutlets and serve at once.

Strascinate di Cascia Pasta with pancetta and sausage

Marco, my friend from Norcia, told me that the famous *spaghetti carbonara* everyone associates with Rome really originated from this 15th century recipe of Cascia. It sounded fascinating to me, so I have included the recipe. Here, incidentally, *strascinate* means 'to drag the pasta on a board', or to make shapes with it.

SERVES 6

- **pasta made with 400 g Italian '00' flour, or 400 g tagliatelle**
- **3 tbsp olive oil**
- **100 g *guanciale*, *barbozzo*, or smoked pancetta, finely diced**
- **100 g fresh Italian sausage**
- **salt and pepper**
- **2 eggs**
- **3 egg yolks**
- **juice of 1 lemon**
- **freshly grated nutmeg**
- **aged pecorino cheese, freshly grated, to serve**

To make your own pasta in the traditional Cascian way, mix the flour with enough water to obtain a smooth, pliable dough. Roll it out to a sheet, 1.5 mm thick, and leave to rest for 15 minutes. Cut into strips, 3 cm wide and 6 cm long.

Heat the olive oil in a frying pan, add the *guanciale* or pancetta dice and fry for a few minutes. Pinch the sausage into pieces and add to the pan. Fry, turning from time to time, until the sausage is browned and cooked.

Meanwhile, cook the pasta in plenty of boiling salted water until *al dente*. In a bowl, beat the eggs, egg yolks and lemon juice together with a little nutmeg.

Drain the cooked pasta, add to the sausage pan (off the heat) and toss to mix. Pour in the egg and lemon mixture and toss well to coat the pasta. Allow to rest for a minute, then serve sprinkled with pecorino cheese.

Pollo all'Arrabbiata Chicken arrabbiata

***Arrabbiata* usually describes a pasta dish with tomato sauce that's spiked with chilli, but anything can be *arrabbiato*, or 'angry' (its literal meaning). The Umbrians like to do it with their wonderful free-range chicken. You could cook a good rabbit or even wood pigeon in a similar way.**

SERVES 4

- **1 free-range organic chicken, about 1.1 kg**
- **50 g lard**
- **4 tbsp olive oil**
- **1 medium onion, finely chopped**
- **8 garlic cloves, peeled**
- **150 ml dry red wine**
- **1–2 chillies, chopped**
- **600 g ripe tomatoes, finely chopped**
- **2 tbsp tomato purée**
- **salt**
- **2 tbsp finely chopped flat-leaf parsley**

Joint the chicken and cut into medium pieces. Heat the lard and olive oil in a flameproof casserole or large cooking pot. Add the chicken pieces with the onion and whole garlic cloves, and fry, turning the chicken pieces until they are brown on both sides.

Add the wine and allow to evaporate a little. Add the chilli, tomatoes, tomato purée and some salt, and bring to a simmer. Put the lid on and cook gently for 30–40 minutes, or until the chicken is cooked.

Check the seasoning, then scatter over the chopped parsley and serve. Polenta would be an excellent accompaniment.

Other typical regional dishes

Baci perugina Chocolate 'kisses', made industrially now, with a proverb tucked into in the wrapping

Bruschetta umbra Toasted bread rubbed with garlic and sprinkled with olive oil

Cardi alla grifo Fried cardoon pieces, layered with minced veal, chicken livers and tomato sauce, and baked

Ciriole alla ternana Large spaghetti with oil, garlic and chilli

Fagiano al tartufo di Norcia Braised pheasant with black truffle

Frittata alla tartufo Omelette flavoured with black truffles

Gallina ubriaca Boiling fowl pieces slowly casseroled with a flavouring *battuto* of ham fat, tomatoes, garlic and onion, in dry white wine

Lepre alle olive Hare braised with white wine and olives

Palombacci alla todina Stuffed pigeons, cooked on a spit

Porchetta Roast stuffed boned piglet, up to 40 kg, sliced and eaten in *panini*

Risotto alla norcina White risotto flavoured with black truffles

Tagliata Large grilled steak, sliced and served with olive oil, green peppers and rosemary

Trota al tartufo Fried Nera trout, served with black truffle

Zuppa di fagioli e porcini Thick soup of beans and mushrooms

Pinocchiate Pine nut toffee

This recipe is believed to date back to the 15th century in Perugia, where it is still made to celebrate Christmas as it has been through the centuries. Instead of pine nuts, you could use pistachios to add an Arabic note, or try almonds or hazelnuts.

MAKES 1KG

500 g caster sugar
1 tbsp *fécule* (potato starch)
400 g pine nuts
finely grated zest of 1 lemon or tangerine

Dissolve the sugar in 200 ml water in a heavy-based pan over a low heat, then increase the heat and boil to 110°C or the thread stage (when you lift a wooden spoon from the mixture, the syrup that falls from the spoon will form threads).

Immediately take the pan off the heat and as you stir with the wooden spoon, add the *fécule*, pine nuts and lemon zest, and mix well. Pour on to a dampened marble surface and flatten with a palette knife.

Cut the *pinocchiate* into small lozenges while still warm. Lift and put between leaves of rice paper, cool and keep wrapped until ready to eat. *Buon Natale!*

Marche

With a long coastline on the Adriatic, and more than two-thirds of the region formed by the foothills and rugged peaks of the Appennines, Marche is dominated by the fruits of the sea and rural countryside. The cuisine here is for gourmets who appreciate the essence of real Italian food – wonderful seafood and home-produced food, using farmyard animals like rabbit, chicken and duck, but also lamb and, of course, pigs.

Originally known as Piceno, the region takes its name from the word 'Marca', meaning small areas belonging for a while to invading German armies. Places like the Marca Camerinense (of Camerino) and Marca Ancontana (of Ancona) were united as the Marches or Marche when the entire territory was incorporated into the new Italian kingdom at the beginning of the 19th century.

With the exception of the coastline, which boasts wonderful stretches of golden sands, Marche is one of the least well-known areas of Italy. As a consequence, old traditions tend to be better preserved here than anywhere else, apart from Basilicata. The region is virtually self-sufficient in food, every citizen tending a plot of vegetables or raising animals, or fishing, or turning local produce into foods such as pasta, preserves, wine or cheese.

Although there are comparatively few visitors to inland Marche, those that do come are made very welcome and introduced with pride to the local specialities. I once had a memorable meal in a *trattoria* near Fabriano in the Appennine foothills. While *mamma* worked in the kitchen, helped by her four daughters, *papà* collected ingredients from the garden, orchard, field and wood (including wild mushrooms), to turn a simple repast into something special.

Apart from the gastronomy, there is much more to experience in Marche. The city of Urbino is famous for its art – the great artist Raphael was born here. And in the summer a music festival is held in Pesaro, dedicated to Gioacchino Rossini, who once lived there. I admire Rossini, not least for his music, but also because he was a gourmet – famously inventing *tournedos Rossini*! Indeed, the cooking of Marche is so renowned that many Marchigiani chefs have left to spread the word around the world, among them my friend Franco Taruschio, the inspired former owner of the Walnut Tree Inn in Abergavenny, Wales for more than 30 years.

CULINARY TRADITIONS & SPECIALITIES

Bordered by regions with strong culinary traditions: Emilia-Romagna to the north, Umbria to the west and Abruzzi to the south, Marche is inevitably influenced by its neighbours. In the south, for example, dishes are often spiked with chilli, a characteristic of Abruzzi. Marche also benefits from excellent ingredients, including the bounty from the Adriatic, which forms the eastern border. The cooking is similar throughout the region, although each of the four provinces – Pesaro Urbino, Ancona, Macerata and Ascoli Piceno – has its own specialities.

Seafood is dominant all along the coast from Pesaro in the north down to San Benedetto del Tronto in the south. Red mullet, sea bream, sole, turbot, lobster (a rarity in Italy), and crayfish (in the mountain streams and rivers), are caught and appreciated, not least in the numerous *brodetti* (main-course fish soups or stews). The capital city of the region, Ancona, specialises in fish and claims to have the best *brodetto di pesce* in the entire country. It is made from up to 12 varieties of fish and each family, *trattoria* and restaurant has its own version, with characteristic flavourings. A common feature, though, is a *crostone*, a slice of toasted bread in the bottom of each soup plate, which absorbs the flavours and is eaten at the end. Some of the region's fish dishes are served in rare combination with white truffles – a particular delight for me.

The clams and mussels of Pesaro are reputed to be the best in Italy, and *passatelli al sugo di vongole* (see page 138) is a delicious local dish. Mussels are also stuffed, topped with breadcrumbs and grilled. In the Fortino Napoleonico in Portonovo, near Ancona, I once enjoyed a very special shellfish, the *crocette*. The shell of this mollusc must be perforated with a special implement by the chef, to enable the diner to extract the succulent meat. I polished off four portions of these wonderful creatures, sucking the meat out of the shells and savouring every moment.

One oddity, common to other areas of Italy, is the liking for *stoccafisso* (dried cod), which is not a local ingredient at all. There are several popular recipes: *in umido* (with tomato, onion, carrot and celery), *in potacchio* (with rosemary and garlic) and *in teglia* (layered with potatoes). S*toccafisso* dishes are often eaten with polenta. Sweet and sour fish, or *scapece* is common here as well.

Inland, where the cooking becomes country cooking, the pig reigns supreme. The famous *porchetta*, common in many parts of Italy, is said to have originated here, in the province of Macerata. It is a boned suckling pig, weighing about 40 kg, stuffed with garlic, liver and heart, wild fennel and fennel seeds, and roasted on a spit. *Porchetta* is a celebratory dish, and often the centrepiece of a village *sagra* or Saint's Day.

Pork is also preserved throughout Marche (see page 140). Local sausages, hams and *coppa* are all produced in Macerata and washed down with the local Verdicchio (see page 140). San Leo, in the north, is famous for its prosciutto, which is served in *piadine* (unleavened bread), as it is in neighbouring Romagna. The ancient town of Fabriano, set amongst spectacular mountains in Ancona, is renowned for its excellent salami, and for paper-making. Here, at a price, you can still buy handmade paper, which is of extraordinary quality and beauty.

Beef is popular as well, and much of it comes from the Vitellone Bianco Appennino, a breed of cow common to all the regions of the Appennines. Good lambs, chickens, ducks and rabbits are bred, and horsemeat is eaten – usually from a breed called Catria. Often meat dishes are flavoured with sweet spices not usually associated with Italian cooking, such as cloves and cinnamon. Ancona is home to *vincisgrassi* (named after an Austrian general, Prince Windischgraetz, who came to regain the region from Napoleon in 1799). It is a lasagne, variously made with chicken livers, veal sweetbreads and other offal, mushrooms and spices. Shaved truffle is a traditional flavouring, although less expensive porcini are often substituted nowadays. Pasta is especially popular in Ancona. In Macerata, tagliatelle is often made from a mixture of pasta flour and broad bean flour.

I have always considered my home region, Piedmont, to be the prime place for truffles but, like Emilia-Romagna, Marche has a good trade in truffles, both white and black, although mainly the latter. Acqualagna is a thriving centre for the industry, and holds a large truffle celebration in February. And there are many wild mushrooms to be gathered in the hills and forests all over the region; these are used a lot, especially in '*alla cacciatora'* (hunter-style) dishes. Wild fungi are especially plentiful around Urbino, which is also famous for its snails.

Marche also produces a profusion of vegetables, such as broccoli, cauliflower (from Jesi, famous throughout Italy), leeks, artichokes (from Ascoli), fennel, broad beans, red potatoes (from Colfiorito), and white beans (from Tronto). Less familiar to us is the cardoon, a thistle-like plant, grown for its delicious stalks. The plants are bent over and covered with earth to 'blanch' them, which makes them tender, and accounts for their nickname *'gobbi'* (hunchbacks). Cardoon stalks are most often baked with Parmesan in this region.

Olives and grape vines are grown everywhere, taking over the lower slopes of the mountains, and their products are highly regarded. The delicate olive oil of Pesaro, for example, is considered to be one of the best in Italy. Ascoli in the south boasts the region's most renowned speciality – very large olives, grown to be eaten in the hand or *da tavola* (at the table), rather than to be made into oil. Pitted Ascoli olives are often stuffed, coated with breadcrumbs and deep-fried as an antipasto (see below). Other olives, including the Leccino and Frantoio, are used to make good extra virgin olive oils. Wonderful fruits too come from Marche, notably apricots from Macerata, pears from Serrungarina, peaches from the Aso Valley, and pink apples from Amandola.

There are a large number of food-related festivals in Marche, starting with the truffle in February (at Acqualagna) and ending with the same foodstuff in October (in San Agata). In between there are festivals for polenta (March, in San Constanzo), *porchetta*, artichokes and strawberries in May (in Monterado, Montelupone and Ostra respectively), and snails and seafood in July (in Monfortino and Porto San Giorgio). In August, roast meats are celebrated in Fiordimonte, and prosciutto in Ripatransone. There is also a *sagra* of nuts in Staffolo in September.

Olive Farcite all'Ascolana Deep-fried stuffed olives

MAKES 50

There are many variations of this recipe from Ascoli, but this is the original version.

50 Ascoli olives
olive oil for deep-frying
flour to coat
2 eggs, beaten
dried breadcrumbs to coat
Filling
3 tbsp olive oil
50 g butter
100 g lean pork, finely minced
100 g lean veal, finely minced
50 g boneless chicken, minced
salt and pepper
3 tbsp dry Marsala or sherry
1 small black truffle, diced
few drops of truffle oil
30 g Parma ham, finely chopped
3 tbsp finely chopped parsley
1/2 tsp freshly grated nutmeg
finely grated zest of 1 lemon
1 egg, beaten
50 g Parmesan, freshly grated
a little milk (if needed)

To make the filling, heat the olive oil and butter in a pan. Add the minced meats and fry, stirring, for 5–6 minutes until well browned. Season with salt and pepper, add the Marsala or sherry and let bubble to reduce down. Take off the heat and cool, then transfer to a food processor.

Add the truffle and truffle oil, the ham, parsley, nutmeg and lemon zest. Process briefly to mix, then add the egg and grated cheese, and whiz to combine. The mixture should be firm enough to use as a stuffing but not too dry; soften with a drop of milk if necessary. Taste for seasoning.

Starting from the top, cut each olive in a spiral fashion to reach and lose the stone inside, keeping the spiral intact. Take a little of the filling and enclose it in the olive spiral, pressing a little to regain the original shape.

Finish and cook the olives a few at a time. Heat the olive oil for deep-frying in a suitable pan. Dip the olives in a little flour, then into the beaten egg, and then roll them in the breadcrumbs. Deep-fry for 2–3 minutes until brown, then drain on kitchen paper. Serve hot as an antipasto, with little lemon wedges if you like.

Uccelletti di Mare allo Spiedo Seafood on a skewer

The literal translation of *uccelletti* is 'sparrows' but don't be alarmed, there are no birds here, just the very freshest morsels of seafood to grill at home, or on the barbecue. From Marche down towards the south, you will come across fresh breadcrumbs mixed with very finely chopped parsley, sprinkled on to foods for added flavour.

SERVES 4–6

800 g mixed fresh firm seafood (such as octopus, squid, large prawns, cuttlefish, shelled scallops)
150 g fresh fine white breadcrumbs
3 tbsp finely chopped parsley
salt and pepper
olive oil to brush
lemon juice to sprinkle

Pre-soak some wooden kebab skewers in water for around 30 minutes (to prevent them scorching during cooking). Clean the fish as necessary, peeling the prawns but leaving the tail shells intact. Cut the other seafood into chunks, roughly the size of an apricot. Thread these alternately on to double skewers to hold securely.

Mix the breadcrumbs with the parsley, and season with some salt and pepper. Brush the fish with olive oil, then dust with the savoury breadcrumbs on all sides.

Grill or barbecue the kebabs for 3–4 minutes, turning to colour on all sides, and basting with lemon juice and olive oil as they cook. Serve immediately.

Brodetto all'Anconetana Fish stew Ancona style

No other region produces as many different *brodetti* (somewhere between a fish soup and stew) as the Marche. This is hardly surprising as many fishing ports along the region's long eastern coastline have excellent fresh fish from the Adriatic every day – often more than a dozen varietes. Here they are partnered with other characteristic Marche ingredients – good olive oil and tomatoes. It's simplicity itself.

SERVES 4–6

1.2 kg mixed fresh fish, cleaned
500 g mixed fresh shellfish (clams, mussels, opened scallops, prawns)
5 tbsp olive oil
1 large onion, finely sliced
3 garlic cloves, finely chopped
3 tbsp tomato purée, or 4–5 fresh tomatoes, chopped
pinch of dried chilli
salt and pepper
3 tbsp coarsely chopped parsley
2 tbsp white wine vinegar

To serve

4–6 slices good bread, toasted
extra virgin olive oil to drizzle

Fillet the fish and cut into bite-sized pieces, or leave whole if small. Scrub the shellfish and clean as appropriate.

Heat the olive oil in a large pan, add the onion and garlic, and fry gently to soften. Add the tomato purée diluted with a little water, or the fresh tomatoes, and the chilli. Bring to a simmer and cook for 10 minutes, stirring occasionally. Season the sauce with salt and pepper to taste.

Start to add the large pieces of fish to the sauce first, followed by the shellfish and then by the small fish. Cook gently for 5–8 minutes, or until the fish is cooked and the mussels and clams have opened, then add the parsley and wine vinegar. Toss gently to mix.

Serve with toasted bread, which you either put at the bottom of the plate or offer separately. I always add a little stream of extra virgin olive oil on top for flavour.

Other typical regional dishes

Braciola alla urbinate Slice of beef rolled around an omelette, ham and cheese filling, then braised slowly, a speciality of Urbino

Bucatini alla marchigiana Large spaghetti, served with a slow-cooked sauce of onion, celery, carrot, pancetta, prosciutto, tomatoes and wine

Cappelletti alla pesarese Pasta 'hats' stuffed with roast pork, boiled capon, beef marrow, lemon zest, nutmeg and cheese, then cooked in chicken broth; traditional at Christmas

Coniglio in porchetta Roasted rabbit, typically stuffed with wild fennel, minced veal, pork, rabbit giblets and other flavourings

Fritto misto all'ascolana Lamb cutlets, stuffed olives, brains and artichokes, individually coated with egg and breadcrumbs, then deep-fried

Minestra col grasso *Tagliolini* (thin noodles), cooked in beef broth, then served with a sauce of onion, tomato and small cubes of prosciutto

Parmigiana di gobbi Blanched cardoons, crumb-coated and fried, then layered with béchamel and Parmesan and baked. Also known as *cardi al grifo*

Polenta alla carbonara Soft polenta layered with a *battuto* of olive oil, lard, garlic, parsley and lots of grated pecorino

Porchetta Spit-roasted, stuffed suckling pig

Potacchio From the French potage, to indicate not a soup but a thick sauce or *ragù*, which can be of pork, chicken or rabbit cooked with garlic, rosemary oil and wine. Even stockfish can be in *potacchio*

Seppie ripiene Cuttlefish stuffed with Parmesan, breadcrumbs and egg, then stewed in oil and wine

Torta nociata A walnut cake made with olive oil and flavoured with lemon and orange, a speciality of San Genesio

Trippa alla pignata Tripe slowly cooked in a terracotta pot, once sold at the roadside in Pesaro

Passatelli al Sugo di Vongole

Fresh egg pasta drops with clams

Passatelli are eaten in broth in neighbouring Emilia-Romagna, and you will also come across the German version, *spätzle*, in northerly parts of Italy, but the Marchigianio version – made with locally caught clams – is my favourite. You can buy a special gadget to make *passatelli* in Italy, but the same effect can be achieved using a grater with large holes.

SERVES 4

Passatelli

300 g plain flour
100 g dried breadcrumbs
2 eggs, plus 2 egg yolks
50 g Parmesan, freshly grated
salt and pepper
a little milk to mix

Clam sauce

5 tbsp olive oil
2 garlic cloves, finely chopped
1 small red chilli, chopped (optional)
600 g fresh clams, cleaned
100 ml dry white wine
3 tbsp coarsely chopped parsley

To make the *passatelli* dough, mix the flour and breadcrumbs with the eggs, egg yolks, Parmesan, a pinch of salt and enough milk to obtain a soft texture.

Bring a large pan of lightly salted water to the boil. To shape the *passatelli*, take a little of the mixture and press it through a large-holed grater, directly into the boiling water, using a spatula or your hand. Cook the *passatelli* for a couple of minutes, or until they rise to the surface. Scoop out with a slotted spoon, drain well, and keep warm while you cook the rest.

To make the clam sauce, heat the olive oil in another pan and briefly fry the garlic, with the chilli if using. Add the clams and wine, cover tightly and cook for 2–3 minutes, or until the clams open, exuding their precious juices. Add the parsley and taste for seasoning. Discard any unopened clams.

Toss the *passatelli* and clams together well, and serve hot in warm bowls as a starter.

Vincisgrassi 'Little lasagne'

The *vincisgrassi* made in the Marche is quite rich, based on offal such as brains, sweetbreads and livers. I decided to give you my own version, which you can make more easily at home. The best time to cook it is in autumn when fresh porcini are available. At other times, use oyster or shiitake mushrooms, plus 20 g soaked dried porcini.

SERVES 6

1 recipe egg pasta dough (page 251)
120 g butter
50 g plain flour
500 ml milk
salt and pepper
2 tbsp olive oil
500 g fresh porcini mushrooms, cleaned and sliced
2 tbsp chopped flat-leaf parsley
1 garlic clove, finely chopped
200 g Parmesan, freshly grated

Heat the oven to 200°C/Gas 6. Cut the pasta into 15 cm square sheets for lasagne.

Melt half the butter in a saucepan, stir in the flour and cook for 1 minute, then add the milk gradually, stirring all the time, to make a smooth sauce. Season with salt and pepper to taste.

To cook the fresh porcini, heat the remaining butter and the olive oil in a sauté pan, add the porcini with the garlic and parsley, and sauté until the mushrooms are softened and the juices have evaporated. Season with salt and pepper to taste.

Cook the pasta sheets in boiling salted water until *al dente*, about 4 minutes, then drain well.

Layer the *vincisgrassi* in 6 small individual baking dishes. Start with a thin layer of béchamel, cover with a layer of lasagne sheets, then spoon half the mushrooms over. Add another layer of béchamel and scatter plenty of Parmesan over. Repeat these layers, finishing with béchamel and cheese. Bake for 15 minutes until golden and bubbling, then serve.

REGIONAL PRODUCTS

PORK PRODUCTS A number of hams and salami are produced throughout the region. One distinctive product is *ciauscolo*, a soft salami made with spicy meat, to be spread on bread or toast. Made in Fabriano, Matelica and Amandola, it is similar to the Calabrese *'nduja*. The *prosciutto di San Leo*, from the town of the same name near the border with Romagna and Tuscany, has a particularly fine flavour. The prized salami of Fabriano is made from a mix of pork and beef (or pork alone), flavoured with whole peppercorns and a little garlic, and cured for at least 6 months. *Coppa* and salami are produced in Macerata.

CHEESES Few of Marche's cheeses are well known outside the region, although pecorino is made everywhere. In Cagli in Pesaro Urbino, and in San Leo pecorino cheeses are wrapped in chestnut leaves and left to ripen in terracotta jars. Formaggio di fossa from Talamello is a mature sheep's milk cheese, which is aged in sacks buried underground from mid-August to late November. It is very sought after locally, but a little over the top for my taste. Caciotta di Urbino is a renowned fresh cheese; ricotta is made too.

WINE AND OTHER DRINKS The wines of the Marche are all DOC. The most well known abroad are the Rosso Piceno and Rosso Conero, and the Verdicchio Castello di Jesi and Verdicchio Castello di Matelica. Montepulciano grapes grow abundantly on the Conero hills behind Ancona and go to make Rosso Conero – the best of the reds. Rosso Piceno is made all over Marche, from an admixture of Sangiovese and Montepulciano grapes, and a Superiore version is produced in Ascoli Piceno. The Verdicchio grape has been cultivated in this region since the 14th century and appropriately produces a white wine with a greenish tinge. That of Jesi, in Ancona, is sold in an amphora-shaped bottle and called locally, 'La Lollobrigida'; that of Matelica comes from further south. There is also a sparkling Verdicchio.

In Ascoli Piceno, there is a wine distillate called 'Mistra', made from a mixture of wines and local herbs, fruit and anise. Anise itself is often drunk here, probably a Greek influence, and the locally produced anisetta Meletti is common throughout the region.

Agnello alla Cacciatora Lamb cooked the hunter's way

This is a common recipe in the Marche. There are two versions: one uses lamb cut in pieces, while this recipe is made with 'olives' of sliced lamb stuffed with a little Parma ham fat, flavoured with rosemary and garlic.

SERVES 4

12 thin slices leg of lamb, about 10–13 cm square
salt and pepper
50 g lard
200 ml dry white wine
12 garlic cloves (unpeeled)
1 little rosemary sprig

Stuffing

100 g Parma ham fat, with a little lean meat, finely chopped
2 garlic cloves, very finely chopped
few tender rosemary leaves, finely chopped

Heat the oven to 200°C/Gas 6. Lay the lamb slices on a surface and season with salt and pepper. For the stuffing, scatter a little of the ham fat, chopped garlic and rosemary on top of each slice. Roll up and secure each 'lamb olive' with string.

Melt the lard in an ovenproof pan. Add the 'lamb olives' and brown well on all sides. Add the wine, garlic cloves and rosemary sprig, bring to a simmer and transfer to the oven. Bake for about 15–20 minutes until the meat is tender and the wine has evaporated.

Eat with bread, as everyone in Italy does.

LAZIO

The cooking of Lazio is usually defined in terms of its capital city, Rome. Emulating their forefathers, the Romans of today – at all levels of society – enjoy good food. Vegetables grow prolifically in the region's volcanic soil, notably the famous Roman artichokes. Dishes *alla romana* are light and flavourful – gnocchi, *stracciatella* and *saltimbocca*, for instance, and Lazio's pasta sauces, such as *carbonara* and *amatriciana,* are well known.

Lazio, in the middle of the west coast, is a huge area, bordered to the north by Tuscany and to the south by Campania. Rome, the 'Eternal City', dominates the region and three-quarters of Lazio's population is based here. The name of the region is usually followed by 'SPQR', or *Senatus Populusque Romanus* (the senate and people of Rome), and this says it all! Rome today, now the capital of the whole country (but only since 1861), is still as much the centre of the region in terms of power, culture and cooking as it was some 2,000 years ago. The remainder of the region serves as a 'larder' for Rome, supplying the raw ingredients for the hungry and demanding city.

The Romans throughout history have been empire builders and empire takers, and in cookery they are no different: many of the dishes on Roman menus have been commandeered from neighbours such as Tuscany, Abruzzi and Campania, and made part of the Roman way of life. The Jewish community in the capital has also influenced styles of cooking. You can sample traditional dishes in the city and outlying districts. Romans like to eat out, and they go to *trattorie* in the Castelli Romani outside the city where they eat at long tables under vine-draped pergolas until night falls.

On my last visit to Lazio, I ate some very special Roman food in Trastevere, in a restaurant called Sabatini, which I remembered from many years before. I was thrilled to find that it still had traditional dishes on the menu. Tripe wasn't on that day, but they found some in the fridge for me. I followed that with *osso di prosciutto con fagioli* (beans flavoured with a Parma ham bone), the inspiration for my recipe on page 157. Everything was fantastic, even though it was late on a Sunday night. And you will find many a *trattoria* like that in Rome, where the food may be based on offal, on cheaper cuts other nationalities would throw to the dogs, but it tastes wonderful. Even my brother-in-law, Terence Conran, came back from Rome enthusing about this sort of food.

CULINARY TRADITIONS & SPECIALITIES

Cooking in Rome in ancient times, as elicited from contemporary accounts, was elaborate and rich – or at least it was for the wealthy and the clergy. The poor, as in all other regions, had to make do with what they could get. Today the cooking in general is very much based on that *cucina povera*, and is simple, honest and true to the seasons. Prime cuts of meat, for instance, were the province of the rich, so the less privileged had to make do with offal. There are many famous offal dishes in traditional Roman cooking, including *coda alla vaccinara* (braised oxtail, see my version on page 154), *pajata* or *pagliata* (braised entrails of milk-fed lamb), and *coratella di abbacchio* (a *ragù* of lamb offal). Feet, heart, kidneys, head, tongue and sweetbreads are all eaten, as is *nervetti*, a salad made from strips of calf's feet. Trilussa, a satirical dialect poet of Rome in the early part of the last century, was not keen on eating brains: he said it would have been like eating their thoughts, *'Me pare de magnamme li pensieri'*!

Lamb is the primary meat, and milk-fed lamb is a particular speciality. Lamb is eaten in many ways in Rome – baked, braised, grilled, fried and *brodettato*. The latter is a stew, in which the sauce is enriched with egg yolks and lemon juice, a leaning towards Greece, and a dish that is eaten by the Romans at Easter. Sheep's milk is used to make cheese, pecorino romano, and its by-product ricotta (see page 152). Beef and veal feature too, of course, but to a lesser extent. Calf's offal is popular, but the most famous Roman veal dish must be *saltimbocca alla romana* (see page 149).

Romans are very fond of pork. In the 16th century, everyone kept a pig and the animals were allowed to roam freely. They were such a hazard to transport that the Pope issued an edict stating that anyone finding a pig on the road could take it home. The problem was solved! *Porchetta*, the roast piglet found in southern regions, has become particularly associated with Lazio and Rome. Wild boar is eaten in the north, as are game birds and animals. There are also some good salami and other preserved meats (see page 152). One of my favourite cured meats of Lazio is *coppiette*, which is traditionally sold by vendors moving from table to table in the *trattorias*. Chicken is eaten too, and is flavoured in a characteristic Roman style, with herbs such as rosemary and mint.

Fresh fish was once a luxury for most people of Lazio – it, too, was the province of the wealthy and the clergy – so it doesn't feature strongly except, of course, along the coast. Red mullet are popular and shellfish abound, particularly clams. Seafood is often mixed in a *brodetto* (fish soup) or a *tiella* (baked seafood and pasta), a dish that is more typical of Abruzzi and Puglia. In past times, when Church laws demanded that fish be eaten, the poor would eat *arzella* (a sort of skate) cooked with broccoli, or *baccalà*, which is more popular still in Rome than fresh fish from the sea. In the north, around the Lago di Bolsena, freshwater fish are eaten, including tench, pike, perch and eels. A mature eel, *capitone*, is traditional fare at Christmas in Rome. On Lake Bracciano, smaller eels, called *ciriole*, are braised in oil, garlic, capers, anchovies, white wine and chilli. Off the coast of the province of Latina in the south, the little island of Ponza offers a huge array of Tyrrhenian fish dishes.

S.P.Q.R.

M

Some of the best pasta dishes in Italy come from Lazio and Rome. The most widely known is perhaps *bucatini all'amatriciana* (see page 149), named after the town of Amatrice that lies in the spur of Lazio, towards the east. The sauce is flavoured with *guanciale*, which is also used to make the most authentic *carbonara* sauce. Fettuccine, the Roman equivalent of Emilia-Romagna's tagliatelle (only a little narrower and thicker), is served with a variety of sauces. *Puttanesca* sauce (tomatoes, anchovies, capers, olives and chilli) is claimed by both Naples and Rome (the name coming from *puttana*, 'whore'). Other simple sauces include *cacio e pepe* (cheese and black pepper), *ajo e ojo* (olive oil and garlic) and *all'Alfredo* (cream and pepper).

But the Roman ability to make the most from the simplest ingredients is seen best in the famous *gnocchi alla romana*, which is an admixture of no more than semolina, milk and egg (see page 151). In a good Roman cook's hands, these 'dumplings' can be sublime. Some of Rome's famous soups are equally simplistic – and delicious. *Stracciatella* is simply a good broth with raw eggs stirred in and grated pecorino scattered over. Another soup is made from *farro*, the ancient wheat variety that is now being grown again in Lazio, Tuscany and Umbria. *Aquacotta* or 'cooked water', a simple soup borrowed from Tuscany, is found in Viterbo in the north.

Vegetables grow big and beautiful in the volcanic soil of Lazio, the best-known being the various types of globe artichoke. They are used in many ways, including *carciofi alla giudia* or 'Jewish artichoke' (see page 149) and *carciofi alla romana* (page 147). When I was filming in Rome, I met a gentle lady called Donatella Limentani Pavoncello, who told me that her family, established for more than 500 years in Rome, was responsible for the famous Jewish way of cooking artichokes. Most of the vegetables for Roman consumption are grown in the outlying provinces, primarily the reclaimed land that is the extension of the Tuscan Maremma or marshes in the north in Viterbo, and Latina in the south, where once malarial marshes have also been drained. Workers from Friuli-Venezia Giulia were brought here to work the fertile land. A myriad vegetables and fruit are grown, among them the famous Gaeta olives. But the principal 'servant' to

Maccaruni Ciociari Angel's hair with giblets

SERVES 4–6

Pasta
350 g Italian 'oo' flour, plus extra to dust
8–10 very fresh egg yolks
Sauce
25 g dried porcini mushrooms
350 g chicken giblets (livers, hearts and gizzards)
4 tbsp olive oil
1 onion, finely chopped
2 tbsp tomato purée
pinch of dried chilli (optional)
salt and pepper
To serve
40 g pecorino cheese, freshly grated

***Maccaruni ciociari* is a fine-cut, handmade pasta, resembling angels' hair. You'll find similar pasta in a few other regions, such as Piedmont and Abruzzi. This dish is made in Ciociaria, the southern part of Lazio, and uses humble chicken giblets. It's delicious.**

To make the pasta, mix the flour with the egg yolks and a little water if necessary to obtain a fairly soft dough. Knead until smooth, then cover with a cloth and leave to rest for 30 minutes. Meanwhile, soak the dried porcini for the sauce in hot water for 20 minutes.

Roll out the pasta using a pasta machine to make thin sheets, or roll out to a 1 mm thick sheet on a lightly floured surface using a rolling pin, and then cut into very fine ribbons. Dust with a little flour to prevent the strands sticking together and leave to dry a little on a cloth.

To make the sauce, chop the giblets very finely. Heat the olive oil in a pan and fry the onion until softened, then add the giblets and fry until tender, about 5–6 minutes. Drain the mushrooms, and dilute the tomato purée with the soaking water. Add the mushrooms and tomato liquid to the pan with the chilli if using. Cook gently for about 20 minutes. Season with salt and pepper to taste.

Cook the pasta in boiling salted water for 2 minutes, then drain and mix with the sauce. Serve sprinkled with grated pecorino.

Carciofi alla Romana Artichokes Roman style

SERVES 4

8 young Roman artichokes
1 egg, beaten
2 tbsp fresh breadcrumbs
1 garlic clove, very finely chopped
1 tbsp chopped mint
salt and pepper
2 tbsp olive oil, plus extra to cook the artichokes

The Romans adore artichokes, the best of which are cultivated near Ladispoli. These are violet in colour, oval not round, and much smaller than their French counterpart, which accounts for their tenderness. Serve this classic dish as a first course.

Trim the top 2 cm off the artichokes, pull away the tough outer leaves and cut the bottom 4 cm off the stem. With a sharp knife, trim the tougher tops of the leaves, leaving only the tender parts of the artichokes – you will have cup-like containers. Make an aperture in the centre of each artichoke and excavate the choke if this has already grown; if the artichoke is young, this may not be necessary.

Peel the reserved artichoke stems and chop finely. Mix with the beaten egg, breadcrumbs, garlic, mint, salt and pepper, and 2 tbsp olive oil. Spoon the stuffing into the centre of the artichokes.

Put the artichokes head-down in a pan, in which they fit quite tightly together, and cover with half water and half olive oil. Bring to a simmer and cook gently for 15–20 minutes, or until very tender. To check, pierce one with a fine skewer – it should feel perfectly soft. The artichokes can be eaten hot or cold.

Rome is the province of Ciociaria to the south-east. Broccoli, garlic, artichokes, beans, salad leaves (for *misticanza*), *broccoletti* (the Roman name for *cime di rapa*), lentils, hazelnuts, chestnuts, strawberries and pears come from here. And in the mountains there are wild fungi and truffles. The Romans make jokes about this province, but the Ciociari are focused on their high quality produce and don't pay any heed to Roman arrogance.

Perhaps the most famous Roman vegetable dish is *cazzimperio* (the same as the Tuscan *pinzimonio*), a peasant dish elevated to culinary heights: good local olive oil from Viterbo and Rieti, still new and peppery, is seasoned and served with *bruschette* and raw spring and summer vegetables such as fennel, artichokes, peppers and celery. To see the vegetable produce of Lazio at its best, go to the Campo dei Fiori, a well-known piazza in Rome, where a daily market is held. There you will see Roman housewives carefully looking, feeling, pressing, sniffing and choosing, never accepting anything less than the best. Cooking in Rome is all about expert buying, then turning the ingredients into something special at home for the family. Deep-frying is a popular method of cooking, and there are many *fritto misto* recipes, of meat as well as vegetables.

If the Romans are keen on good ingredients and good food, they are also keen on any sort of celebration, especially if it involves food and wine. As throughout the rest of Italy, celebrations usually take place where something special is cultivated or raised. In Sermoneta in January, there is a festival of polenta. In Ladispoli in April, there is a *sagra* of artichokes. In June they celebrate strawberries in Grotte di Castro and Nemi, and cherries in Pastena. Garden produce is celebrated in Labico with a pea festival, and in San Lorenzo Nuovo with an onion, garlic and bean exhibition. July means *porchetta* in Ariccia, and at Castel Gandolfo, the papal residence, there is a peach *sagra*. August sees a gastronomic festival at Civitavecchia, and in Amatrice a festival celebrating *bucatini all'amatriciana*. Lake fish and eels are celebrated at Lake Bolsena, hazelnuts in Canteramo, and wine at Montefiascone. In September, in Lanuvio there is an exhibition and festival of table grapes, and in Roiate there is a festival of *abbacchio* (lamb). October celebrates mushrooms, chestnuts and the new oil, and there are festivals in Montelonico, Soriano del Cimino and Canino.

Anguille alla bisentina Chunks of eel fried in oil with the addition of bay leaves, salt, pepper and vinegar, as they are cooked in Bolsena

Animelle al prosciutto Lamb's sweetbreads briefly sautéed with thin slices of ham

Broccoletti strascinati Tender rape tops braised in their own juices with a little lard or oil and garlic

Bucatini all'amatriciana Large spaghetti with tomato, *guanciale*, lots of chilli and grated pecorino

Carciofi alla giudia Roman artichokes cooked the Jewish way, de-choked and gently fried with their leaves splayed until tender.

Coda alla vaccinara Oxtail braised in a *ragù* containing sultanas, pine nuts and even chocolate, the sauce of which is used to dress rigatoni pasta

Coratella di abbacchio Lamb's heart, liver, kidney and lung, stewed with a piece of the trachea, which adds 'texture'. Try it if you dare...

Crostata di ricotta A tart made from the local sheep's milk ricotta, sugar, egg and candied peel

Fave al guanciale Broad beans braised with onion, lard and pieces of *guanciale*

Fiori di zucca fritti Deep-fried courgette flowers stuffed with breadcrumbs, parsley and anchovies

Maritozzi Special soft buns stuffed with raisins, pine nuts and orange peel

Misticanza A salad of wild herbs and greens such as rocket, *cicoria*, *mâche* and little lettuce hearts; similar to the French *mesclun*

Pajata/pagliata Entrails of milk-fed lamb, braised in oil, garlic, parsley, tomatoes, chilli and white wine and served with rigatoni, or baked with potatoes, garlic, rosemary, oil and fennel seeds

Saltimbocca alla romana Pan-fried thin veal medallions, sandwiching a sage leaf and a slice of Parma ham, kept together with a cocktail stick

Spaghetti carbonara Pasta tossed with beaten egg, sautéed *guanciale* or pancetta, and pecorino

Trippe alla trasteverina Boiled tripe mixed with a tomato sauce flavoured with cloves, pecorino and mint leaves, and baked in the oven. Delicious...

Other typical regional dishes

Gnocchi alla Romana Roman semolina dumplings

Italians would eat this dish as a first course, but you could also serve it as a side dish to roast meat or a stew. Romans say this recipe was originally made with potatoes and flour rather than semolina, which is how normal gnocchi are made. They also claim that it was a man with poor teeth that developed the recipe. My teeth are OK, but I still like it!

SERVES 6–8

1 litre milk
salt and pepper
pinch of freshly grated nutmeg
300 g semolina flour
100 g Parmesan, freshly grated
150 g butter, softened, plus extra to grease
3 egg yolks
olive oil, to oil

Bring the milk to the boil in a large saucepan with a pinch of salt and nutmeg added. Add the semolina slowly, whisking constantly to avoid lumps forming. Cook for 6–7 minutes, then allow to cool slightly. Heat the oven to 200°C/Gas 6.

Fold half the Parmesan, 50 g of the butter and the egg yolks into the warm semolina, until evenly combined. Spread on an oiled cool marble or metal surface and flatten with a spatula to a 2 cm thickness. Leave to cool and set, then cut out rounds, using a 3–4 cm cutter.

Butter an ovenproof dish and lay the semolina rounds, overlapping, in the dish. Dot with the rest of the butter and sprinkle with the remaining Parmesan. Bake for about 15–20 minutes until browned on top. Serve sprinkled liberally with coarsely ground black pepper.

Pomodori Farciti al Forno Stuffed baked tomatoes

This is the time to use those large, sweet tomatoes, which are imported from Italy during the summer. When these are out of season, you can resort to hothouse tomatoes, as they will gain in flavour from the stuffing.

SERVES 4

4 large ripe tomatoes
50 g risotto rice
salt and pepper
2 tbsp coarsely chopped mint, plus extra leaves to garnish
8 anchovy fillets, finely chopped
4 tbsp olive oil
1 garlic clove, very finely chopped

Heat the oven to 180°C/Gas 4. Cut off the tops of the tomatoes, keeping the lids. Scoop out the seeds and liquid into a sieve over a bowl, to save the juice.

Cook the rice in salted water for 7 minutes, then drain and cool. Add to the tomato juice with the mint, anchovies, olive oil and garlic. Season the stuffing with salt and pepper to taste.

Spoon the stuffing into the tomato cavities and put the lids on top. Place the tomatoes on a baking tray. Bake for about 20 minutes, depending on size, until the skin have wrinkled and the tomatoes are soft. Serve garnished with mint leaves.

REGIONAL PRODUCTS

CHEESES The best known cheese of Lazio is pecorino romano, which is made from sheep's milk. By law, it can only be produced in the provinces of Rome, Frosinone, Latina and Viterbo but, oddly enough, romano-style pecorino is legitimately made in Sardinia. Buffalo mozzarella is also produced in Lazio, along with provatura, a version produced from a mix of cow's and sheep's milk. Ricotta romana is a by-product of pecorino making, and is used in desserts. Caciotta, a semi-soft cheese, is also made from cow's, sheep's or goat's milk, although it is best known in Tuscany.

MEAT PRODUCTS *Guanciale*, which is similar to the *barbozza* of Umbria, is pork cheek cured in salt and then air-dried, and is the meat used in genuine *carbonara* and *amatriciana* sauces. *Caporino* is an exciting little salami made of lean pork in the mountains of Rieti, near the border with Umbria. There are also *salsiccie* from Monte San Biagio, *mortadella* from Amatrice, *cojoni di mulo* (a salami with a square of fat through the middle), and *coppiette ciociare*, one of my favourites (illustrated left). Prepared from large strips of horse meat (or pork), cured with salt and chilli, *coppiette* is chewy and delicious, akin to South African biltong but fleshier and softer. *Porchetta*, stuffed and slow-roasted pig, is a speciality often sold on the roadside.

WINE It is on the hills to the south and east of Rome, the Castelli Romani, that many of the region's grape vines are found, and they mostly produce white wines. Frascati is the most famous (or infamous), made mainly from Trebbiano or Malvasia, or a mix of the two. Other whites are Marino, Velletri, Colli Albani, Orvieto (straying in from Umbria) and Est! Est! Est!!! The latter is from Montefiascone and was famously named when a bishop, sent to test the food and wine of the area before the coronation of King Henry V, gave an over-zealous triple sign of approval (the Latin word, *est* meaning 'OK' in this context). The wine still carries the name today. Reds are fewer, but some good ones are made, including Cerveteri Rosso (from Sangiovese and other grapes).

Frittata alla Menta Omelette with mint and pecorino

Romans like frittatas, and this one is said to be an aphrodisiac thanks to the mint! I love it for its fresh taste and simplicity. A frittata is a substantial omelette browned on both sides and not folded, as a French omelette would be.

SERVES 4–6

- **12 very fresh eggs**
- **200 g very fresh sheep's milk ricotta cheese**
- **4 tbsp coarsely chopped mint, plus extra leaves to garnish**
- **50 g pecorino cheese, freshly grated**
- **salt and pepper**
- **6 tbsp olive oil**

Beat the eggs in a large bowl, then add the ricotta and mix together until evenly blended. Add the mint, pecorino and salt and pepper to taste. Mix well.

Heat the olive oil in a non-stick pan, then pour in the frittata mixture. Cook over a medium heat, without stirring, for about 5 minutes until browned underneath. Then slide the frittata out on to a large plate and invert back into the pan and brown the other side.

Slide the frittata out on to a warm plate and garnish with a few mint leaves. Serve cut into wedges, as a snack, or a light main course accompanied by a tomato salad.

Coda di Bue all'Andrea Andrea's braised oxtail

This dish was created by my former head chef, Andrea Cavaliere, and it is one that he should be immensely proud of. Although it might require a little more work than usual, the result is stunning. Those wanting to suck and chew on the little bones will be disappointed because, to the delight of others, the oxtail is boned.

SERVES 4

2 large oxtails, boned into flat sheets (ask your butcher)
salt and pepper
2 tbsp finely chopped mixed sage, bay leaves and rosemary
flour to dust
6 tbsp olive oil
2 carrots, finely diced
1 small onion, finely diced
1 celery stalk, finely diced
1 litre red wine
3 cloves
2 bay leaves
1 cinnamon stick
4 black peppercorns
20 g butter

Heat the oven to 180ºC/Gas 4. Lay the oxtail sheets out flat on a work surface, and sprinkle with salt, pepper and the finely chopped herbs. Roll up each one to make a sausage shape and secure with string. Dust lightly with flour.

Heat 4 tbsp olive oil in a large frying pan and fry the oxtail rolls, turning until golden brown. Remove to a plate. Add the remaining olive oil to the pan and sauté the carrots, onion and celery until softened.

Transfer the vegetables to a fairly deep roasting pan and add the oxtail rolls. Pour on the wine to cover, then add the cloves, bay leaves, cinnamon and peppercorns, and some salt and pepper. Bake in the oven for at least 2 hours.

Once cooked, transfer the oxtail rolls to a plate and leave to cool, so they firm up. Meanwhile, skim the cooking liquor, boil to reduce by about half and then strain. Remove the string from the oxtail rolls, then cut into thick slices, about 4 cm thick. Warm through in the reduced cooking juices with the knob of butter added.

Serve the oxtail with the cooking juices spooned over. *Carciofi alla Romana* (page 147) make a delicious accompaniment.

Cinghiale in Agrodolce Sweet and sour wild boar

The Romans are partial to sweet and sour tastes, and they cook hare and ox tongue in the same way. This is rather a lengthy recipe, but the result is excellent – good enough for a celebration meal.

SERVES 6–8

1.2 kg piece lean leg or fillet of wild boar, well trimmed

Marinade

2 large carrots
1 large onion
2 celery stalks
4 garlic cloves
120 ml white wine vinegar
few thyme sprigs
2 tbsp chopped flat-leaf parsley
4 bay leaves

To cook

2 garlic cloves
2 celery stalks
1 onion
6 tbsp olive oil
100 ml dry white wine
50 g raisins
40 g pine nuts
60 g mixed candied lemon and orange peel, diced
2 tbsp caster sugar
2 tbsp white wine vinegar
60 g dark, bitter chocolate
salt and pepper

For the marinade, roughly chop the vegetables and garlic and put into a large pan with the wine vinegar, herbs and 120 ml water. Bring to a simmer and cook gently for 15–20 minutes. Set aside to cool.

Put the marinade in a suitable container, add the meat, cover and marinate in the fridge for 2 days, turning it from time to time.

Take the meat out of the marinade and pat dry, discarding the marinade. Roll up the meat and tie at intervals with string.

When ready to cook, finely chop the garlic, celery and onion. Heat the olive oil in a large pan and brown the meat lightly on all sides. Add the garlic, celery and onion, and brown a little. Add the white wine, then pour in enough hot water to cover the meat. Cover and cook on a low heat for 1½ hours. Test for tenderness with a fine skewer or fork – it should meet with little resistance.

Strain the liquor and return to the pan. Now add the raisins, pine nuts, citrus peel, sugar, wine vinegar and chocolate, broken into pieces. Heat gently until the chocolate has melted, then cook for a few more minutes. Add salt and pepper to taste.

Cut the meat into slices and arrange in a warm serving dish. Pour on the sauce and serve.

Fagioli con Osso di Prosciutto e Cotiche

Borlotti beans with prosciutto bone and skin

The Parma ham end of leg bone, with some meat, lends a superb depth of flavour to this dish. All of Italy loves pork skin, whether it is fresh or that of a Parma ham, cooked until soft.

SERVES 8

1 end of prosciutto bone, washed
200 g defatted pork skin
salt and pepper
600 g dried borlotti beans, soaked in cold water overnight
5 tbsp olive oil
2 celery stalks, diced
2 carrots, diced
1 onion, diced
15 g dried porcini mushrooms, finely chopped
1 large potato, diced
2 tbsp tomato purée
bouquet garni (sage, bay, thyme)
2–3 garlic cloves, halved
about 1 litre vegetable stock (page 251)
extra virgin olive oil to drizzle

Blanch the prosciutto bone in a large pan of boiling water for 1 minute, then drain. Return the bone to the pan, pour on fresh water and boil the prosciutto bone for 1 hour. In the meantime, cut the pork skin into 2 or 3 squares, season with salt and pepper, then roll up each square and secure with string. Cook the borlotti beans in a separate pan of water for 1 hour.

Add the pork skin rolls to the prosciutto pan and continue to boil for a further 1 hour, changing the water a couple of times. Remove the prosciutto bone and pork skin rolls from the pan, discarding the water.

Put the pork skin rolls and prosciutto bone in a large pan with the olive oil, celery, carrots, onion and dried porcini and fry gently to soften. Drain the borlotti beans and add to the pan with the potato, tomato purée, bouquet garni and garlic. Add enough stock to cover and cook slowly for at least 1½–2 hours, topping up with water occasionally if necessary.

Using a ladle, scoop out the potato cubes and a third of the beans and put into a blender with a little of the stock. Whiz until smooth and creamy, then stir back into the pan to thicken the liquor slightly. Lift out the pork skin rolls and cut into portions, then return to the pan.

Ladle the mixture into warm bowls. Drizzle with extra virgin olive oil and sprinkle with freshly ground black pepper to serve.

Bracioline di Abbacchio e Carciofi

Lamb cutlets and artichokes

This combination is well known from Liguria to Sicily. The *abbacchio*, milk-fed lamb from Rome, offers good flavour, despite its youth. In Rome, cutlets with the bone are called *braciole* or *bracioline*.

SERVES 4

12 young artichokes
50 g lard
2 tbsp olive oil
12 new season's lamb cutlets
1 garlic clove, finely chopped
1 small onion, finely chopped
2 tbsp coarsely chopped marjoram
100 ml dry white wine
150 ml chicken stock (page 250)
salt and pepper

Remove the tough outer leaves from the artichokes and trim the base of the stems. With a sharp knife, trim the tips of the leaves, leaving only the tender parts of the artichokes. Cut into quarters and remove any choke.

Heat the lard and olive oil in a large frying pan. Add the cutlets and brown on each side. Add the garlic, onion, marjoram and wine, and cook for 5 minutes.

Add the artichokes to the pan, then pour on the stock. Cover and cook for 10–12 minutes until the artichokes and lamb are tender. Season with salt and pepper to taste and serve.

ABRUZZi e MOLiSE

These two regions lie in the centre of Italy on the eastern side, bordering the Adriatic. The cooking style veers more towards that of southern Italy, and almost everything is flavoured with hot dried chilli. Inland from the long coastal plain, the terrain is mountainous and lamb, pork, other meats and cheeses are favoured, while seafood is predominant on the coast.

Abruzzi and Molise once belonged together politically and they were only divided into two regions in 1963. In a culinary sense, though, they can be considered as one, with the culture leaning towards the south. Historically the area has been vulnerable to invaders, among them the Greeks, but primarily the nearby Romans, and most of the villages were built on top of hills for security.

The entire east of the region lies on the Adriatic, from the border with Marche in the north to the border with Puglia in the south, and along the coast the cuisine is based on fish. This is the best-known stretch of Abruzzi and Molise, for the beaches and seaside towns are overrun with tourists in the summer. The lesser-known interior, where the coastal plain rises to the Appennino Abruzzese, is breathtakingly beautiful, green and lush, but it is probably less popular because it is the most earthquake-prone part of Italy. In the south is the densely forested Parco Nazionale d'Abruzzo. Further north is the highest mountain of the area, the Monte Carno Grande, almost 3,000 metres high. It is said that bears and wolves still roam through the Appennines in these parts – so don't go mushroom picking on your own…

My mother came from Pescara in Abruzzi, and some of her relations are still living there. At least I know now where my love of chilli came from, because Abruzzi and Molise vie with Calabria in the frequency of its use. In fact, being born on the Amalfi coast to a Campanian father (from Benevento), and an Abruzzan mother, then being brought up in Piedmont in the north, has made me enthusiastic about eating, cooking and talking about *all* Italian food. This isn't typical, as many Italians adhere to their sense of *campanilismo* ('to that which is near one's own church tower'), in other words a parochialism. I am a bit of a mongrel, but it has made me much more outward looking and I don't think that is a bad thing.

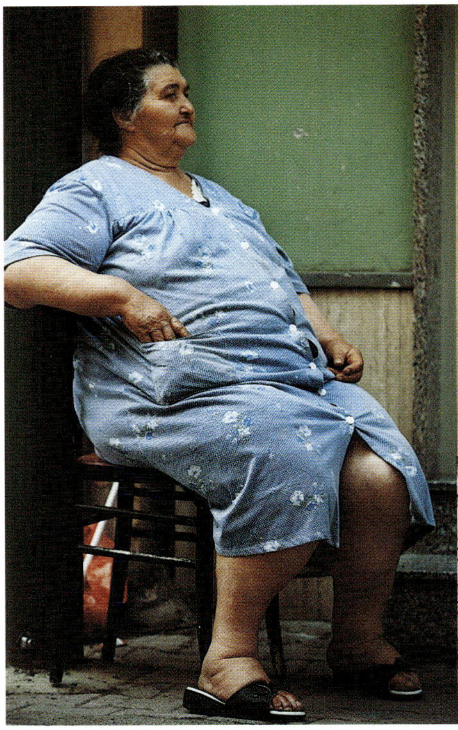

CULINARY TRADITIONS & SPECIALITIES

One of my childhood memories is of little sachets of saffron labelled with the name 'L'Aquila'. Rather romantically, I always imagined that an eagle had something to do with collecting the crocus stigmas, not knowing that L'Aquila, the capital of the region, is a major producer of the spice. Strangely, though, saffron is not much used in the local cuisine, most of the crop probably going to Milan in the north for the famous *risotto milanese*. There is, however, an annual festival in Prata d'Ansidonia, celebrated with a saffron risotto, and the spice occasionally turns up in the many *brodetti* (fish soups) along the coast. L'Aquila actually lies in the north of the region, where there are numerous vineyards growing the Montepulciano grape (see page 168).

In the mountains here and further south, the cooking is country cooking, based on meat. Lamb and pork are both eaten, and preserved pork and sheep's milk cheeses are characteristic of the whole region. The Abruzzans like to eat well, and they also like to eat a lot. *Panarda* is a prime example. This is a fantastic banquet, which used to consist of up to 50 courses – and they say guests couldn't leave the table until the last morsel had been eaten. It started with a soup of pulses, followed by several antipasti and pasta dishes, followed in turn by a variety of fish dishes and meat dishes, finishing with desserts and sweets. However much I love food, this sounds exhausting to me, and I'm glad to hear that the number of courses has been reduced in recent years (except, apparently, at local weddings).

Another Abruzzan feast – this time a single dish – is *Le Virtù* or *Il Minestrone delle Virtù* (the big soup of 'virtue'), which is served annually in May. Its 'virtue' is an intermingling of last year's leftover supply of dried foods, with the fresh products of the new season. Various dried pulses and an array of fresh vegetables, meat products (see page 168), pastas and cereals are all cooked together for several hours, to make a thick and extremely filling soup. Local wine accompanies the feasts – once pumped into the jugs of revellers from fountains that connected with underground wine cellars!

Meat dishes are popular in both Abruzzi and Molise, usually lamb or kid. Lamb is used in pasta *ragùs*, and is also cooked with egg and lemon. Lamb entrails and offal are bound together in little parcels to make *turcinelli arrostiti*. Tied together with gut, these are charcoal-grilled at the roadside for an instant snack. Similar tasty parcels are found in Puglia, Basilicata, Sicily and Calabria. *Cuccette al forno* is another interesting dish from the south, which wouldn't reach most of the tables of Italy – let alone abroad. This is the head of a lamb or kid (or even rabbit), cut in half and roasted in the oven with lots of spices; seemingly barbaric perhaps, but *la cucina povera* wastes nothing. *Porchetta* or roast piglet is common here as it is in the whole south of Italy, and there is a famous pork stew, known as *'ndocca 'ndocca*. Pork meats are preserved as well (see page 168).

These meat dishes and others – even fish – are characteristically given heat by the addition of chilli, variously called *peperoncino*, *lazzariello*, *cazzariello*, *saitti*, *pepento*, *diavolicchio* or *diavolillo*, depending on which town you are in. The degree of heat seems to increase as you descend from the mountains towards the sea, which is contrary to expectation. Dishes along the coastline are likely to be hot with chilli.

In the towns on the Adriatic, the fish dishes are similar to those along the rest of the coastline, particularly the ones in Marche. Specialities are the *pesce azzurro* (blue fish), such as sardines, anchovies, mackerel and bonito. In other words, any fish with a blue reflecting skin, although *triglie* (red mullet) is as popular here as it is in Tuscany. Fish and shellfish are served raw, prepared in soups, grilled, stewed, barbecued and fried – and all are flavoured with chilli. And although stuffed squid are popular everywhere in Italy, the version here is out of this world (see page 165).

The best-known pasta dish of Abruzzi and Molise is *maccheroni alla chitarra*. The *chitarra* or 'guitar' is a wooden frame across which wires are stretched. A pasta sheet is placed on the wires, then pressed with a rolling pin, which results in strings of pasta falling into the box below. These look like square spaghetti, and are served traditionally with a lamb or tomato *ragù* (see page 167). The pasta in Molise, by the way, is wonderful, because of the hard wheat grown there, and the water from the high Appennines. It is used to make *laianelle*, special ricotta ravioli served with a lamb or goat *ragù*. Other pasta dishes have vegetable sauces, based on *cime di rapa* (rape tops), or calabrese or purple-sprouting broccoli – all flavoured with garlic and plenty of chilli. A variety of vegetables are cultivated in the region, among them carrots, leeks, artichokes and tomatoes; indeed salads are very popular. And the lentils from Capracolta are almost as good as those of Castelluccio in Umbria.

Other Abruzzan and Molisan specialities include *pizza rustica* and *polenta alla spianatora*. The first is a curious recipe, dating from Renaissance times, which bears no resemblance to today's pizza. It is a savoury pie made with sweetened pastry, *pasta frolla*, usually filled with some local preserved meats, plus some cheese and spices. The polenta dish is another Abruzzan 'feast' (also found in Marche and Basilicata). Soft polenta is poured on to a wooden table around which the diners sit; a meat stew is poured on top, and the diners eat in from the edges towards the middle (see overleaf).

In Molise, the discovery of black truffles in the area of Isernia, has led to their inclusion in regional dishes, helped along by the very scented white truffle oil. There are plenty of wild fungi in the mountains as well. But what characterises this region more than anything else is the variety of cheeses. Pecorino and its by-product ricotta are made in Abruzzi, but in Molise you can also find mozzarella, burrini, scamorza and caciocavallo.

There are festivals and *sagre* all year round in Abruzzi and Molise, but mostly in the province of Campobasso in Molise. In March, in Montorio nei Frenta, there is a 'meal with 13 courses'. In Pietracatella, in May, there is the festival of the Madonna of the Ricotta, the patron of shepherds. In June, in Isernia, there is an onion fair, and in July in Iesi there is the *sagra del grano* (wheat). August is the month with the majority of festivals: wine in Campomarino; peppers and *baccalà* in Frosolone; lamb in Morrone del Sannio; and fish in Termoli. In September in Montelongo there is a *sagra del prosciutto* and in Macchia d'Isernia there is a wine festival. Not one, but numerous 'thanksgivings' in the region ... as you find all over Italy.

Polenta alla Spianatora Polenta on the table

Steaming polenta is poured on to the middle of the *spianatora* (special round wooden table), a *ragù* goes into the middle and everyone tucks in. You will find the same custom in Marche, Basilicata, and in the north of Italy, where the polenta is typically eaten with a stew rather than a *ragù*. Invite some friends round in autumn and winter to share a *spianatora*. You can use other types of meat if you like.

SERVES 6–8

Polenta
600 g polenta flour (or instant polenta)
20 g salt
Ragù
1.2 kg pork (not too lean)
10 tbsp olive oil
4 garlic cloves, finely chopped
salt
100 ml white wine
2 tbsp tomato purée
1 kg mixed red and yellow peppers
2 red chillies, or more
6 tbsp white wine vinegar
To serve
freshly grated Parmesan or pecorino

First, prepare the *ragù*. Cut the pork into walnut-sized pieces. Heat half the olive oil in a pan and fry the meat until browned on all sides. Add the garlic and cook gently for 10–15 minutes, stirring from time to time. Season with salt to taste. Mix the white wine with the tomato purée, add to the pan and cook for a further 20 minutes.

Meanwhile, halve, core and deseed the peppers, then cut into strips. Heat the remaining olive oil in a frying pan and fry the peppers quite briskly until soft, letting only the edges caramelise. Add the chilli (as much as you can take), a little salt and the wine vinegar, and sauté for a minute or two.

Add the peppers to the meat, and taste for salt and chilli. Cook for a further 30 minutes, or until the meat is tender.

Meanwhile, make the polenta. Bring 3.5 litres water to the boil in a large pan, with the salt added. Pour in the polenta and cook, stirring, until thickened and smooth, about 30–40 minutes (or just 5–6 minutes if you've cheated and used instant polenta).

Pour the polenta on to the *spianatora* or a large wooden board, leaving a space in the middle. Pour the pork *ragù* into the middle of the polenta. Sit everyone around, armed with a fork and a big appetite! Hand the grated Parmesan or pecorino separately.

Insalata all'Abruzzese Vegetable and tuna salad

The combination of cooked and raw vegetables in this salad makes it a triumph of flavours. Good ingredients are paramount, so make it in the summer when sweet tomatoes, young courgettes and tender beans are available.

SERVES 4

300 g young courgettes
200 g green beans, trimmed
salt and pepper
200 g tomatoes
1 red pepper
1 sweet red onion
150 g good canned tuna in oil, drained
8 anchovy fillets in oil, drained
8 basil leaves, torn
1 tsp dried oregano
1–3 red chillies, chopped
6 tbsp extra virgin olive oil
2 tbsp white wine vinegar

Quarter the courgettes lengthways, then cut into chunks. Cook the beans in boiling salted water until *al dente*, then drain and cool. Repeat with the courgettes.

Cut the tomatoes into wedges and remove the seeds. Halve, core and deseed the pepper, then cut into long thin strips. Finely slice the red onion.

Put the courgettes, beans, tomatoes, red pepper and onion into a bowl. Break the tuna into little chunks and add to the salad with the anchovies, herbs, and as much fresh chilli as you can take! Toss everything together, adding the olive oil, followed by the wine vinegar. Season with salt and pepper to taste.

Eat the salad at room temperature, with toasted bread.

Calamari Ripieni di Gamberi

Stuffed squid with prawns

This recipe comes from Giulianova in Abbruzi, where it is served in many of the restaurants. I've heard that the idea came from some fisherman who had seen a voracious squid with a whole prawn in its stomach! The rest is easy to imagine.

SERVES 4–6

8 medium squid (about 800 g cleaned weight)
16 small raw prawns, or 8 larger ones, peeled
4 tbsp olive oil
4 tbsp fresh breadcrumbs
2 tbsp finely chopped parsley
1 garlic clove, finely chopped
2 eggs, beaten
salt and pepper
juice of 1 lemon
100 ml dry white wine

Unless they are already prepared, clean the squid, cutting off the heads and beak. Leave the pouches whole, and keep the little bunches of tentacles together; discard the heads. Remove the transparent quill from each body pouch, then rinse.

Chop the tentacles finely, and chop the prawns roughly if they are large. Sauté them together in 1 tbsp of the olive oil for $1\frac{1}{2}$ minutes.

For the stuffing, mix the breadcrumbs with the parsley, garlic and eggs, then add the sautéed prawn mixture. Season with salt and pepper and add the lemon juice. Stuff each squid pouch with a little of the mixture and secure the opening with a wooden cocktail stick.

Put the stuffed squid in a pan with the remaining olive oil. Cook over a low heat for 10 minutes, then turn them. Increase the heat a little and pour in the wine. Cook until this has reduced down, then the squid will be ready. Serve with spinach and some bread.

Triglie Fritte Fried red mullet

I love eating small red mullet, simply fried in olive oil until crisp. As these delicate fish are easily perishable, they are best eaten on the day they are caught, or at least within 24 hours. Very small red mullet don't need to be gutted, but if your mullet are a little larger then I suggest you do so. Allow 3 or 4 fish per person if they are larger.

SERVES 4

20 red mullet, about 50 g each, cleaned and trimmed
olive oil for frying
plain flour mixed with semolina to dust
salt and pepper
lemon wedges to serve

Rinse the red mullet and dry well. Heat a 2–3 cm depth of olive oil in a large heavy-based pan.

Cook the red mullet a few at a time. First dip the fish into the flour mixture to coat, shaking off the excess, then add to the hot olive oil. Shallow-fry on one side first for 2–3 minutes until crisp and golden, then turn and cook on the other side for a few minutes. Drain on kitchen paper and keep warm while you cook the rest.

Season with salt and pepper at the end, just before eating, otherwise you'll lose the crispness. Serve warm, with lemon wedges. Eat them in your hands, as I do!

Pizza Rustica Rustic pie

Any similarity here to a British pie is superficial. The pie is encased in pastry but the inside is characteristically Italian, with a few surprises, such as the sugar and cinnamon. It is a speciality of Teramo in Abbruzi.

SERVES 6

Pastry

400 g plain flour
1 tbsp fresh yeast
2 eggs, beaten
5 tbsp olive oil
1 tsp caster sugar
salt and pepper

Filling

100 g scamorza cheese, in cubes
60 g ham, cubed
12 hard-boiled egg yolks
70 g pieces dry sausage (with chilli)
100g pecorino cheese, grated
4 eggs, beaten
½ tsp ground cinnamon

To make the pastry, put the flour into a bowl or pile into a mound on a surface and make a well in the middle. Mix the yeast with a little water and add to the well with the eggs, olive oil, sugar and seasoning. Gradually incorporate the flour and mix with your hands to make a smooth dough. Cover and leave to rest for 30 minutes.

Heat the oven to 200°C/Gas 6. Meanwhile, mix together all the ingredients for the filling and season with salt and pepper to taste.

Roll out two-thirds of the pastry on a lightly floured surface and use to line a 25 cm flan tin, which is about 3 cm deep. Spoon the filling into the pastry case, spreading it evenly. Roll out the rest of the pastry to make a lid, brush the edge with water and position on top of the pie. Press the edges together to seal and make a hole in the middle to let the steam escape.

Bake for 30 minutes, then lower the setting to 180°C/Gas 4 and bake for a further 15 minutes. Eat warm or leave to cool before serving.

Maccheroni alla Chitarra alla Molisana

Square spaghetti with Molisan sauce

Ready-made *maccheroni alla chitarra* or square spaghetti is available, but you can make your own (see note). The Molisan sauce doesn't take much longer than the pasta to cook.

SERVES 4

400 g *maccheroni* or *spaghetti alla chitarra*
salt and pepper
60 g butter
2 tbsp olive oil
1 onion, very finely sliced
1 garlic clove, finely chopped
150 g Parma ham or other raw cured ham, finely diced
8 basil leaves, torn
3 tbsp coarsely chopped flat-leaf parsley
½–1 red chilli (to taste), chopped
50 ml red wine
150 g *polpa di pomodoro* or chunky passata

For the pasta, put a large pan of salted water on to boil.

For the sauce, heat the butter and olive oil in a pan and gently fry the onion with the garlic until soft. Add the ham and sauté briefly, then add the basil, parsley, chilli and wine. Cook for 3 minutes, then add the tomato pulp and season with salt and pepper to taste. Cook for a further 3 minutes, then the sauce is ready.

In the meantime, cook the pasta in the boiling salted water until *al dente*. Drain the pasta, reserving 2–3 tbsp water.

Thin the sauce with the reserved water if you think it needs it, then toss with the pasta. Serve immediately, with or without grated Parmesan or pecorino.

Note To make your own *maccheroni alla chitarra*, roll out a quantity of egg pasta dough (page 251) to 2 mm thick sheets, cut into 2 mm wide strips and you'll have square spaghetti.

REGIONAL PRODUCTS

SAFFRON Abruzzi is the principal saffron-producing area of Italy, with Sardinia a close second. The saffron crocus, *Crocus sativus*, is grown in the Navelli Valley and, as elsewhere, the stigmas of the flower are picked by hand. Half a million stigmas are needed to make 1 kg of saffron, which explains the high price of this spice. The plant flowers for a mere 2 weeks, and in Abruzzi, the stigmas are only collected in the morning and late afternoon when their scent is at its peak. (When you buy saffron, opt for the strands rather than powdered saffron, which can be adulterated.)

MEAT PRODUCTS Smoked hams are produced at Rionero Sannitico, prosciutto at L'Aquila, and a *mortadella* with one piece of fat running through the middle is made at Campotosto. *Guanciale amatriciano* (cured pork cheek) and *soppressata molisana* (in a rectangular shape) can also be found. *Ventricina del Teramano* is a salami made of coarsely minced fat and lean pork, with the addition of salt, paprika, lots of chilli and lots of fennel seeds. It is eaten crumbled on toast or bread like the *'nduja* of Calabria, preferably with a lot of wine! *Ventricina del vastese* is spicier and coarser, and is sliced.

WINE The Appennines are higher here than anywhere else, and many of the foothills are terraced with vines. In Abruzzi, the Montepulciano grape rules and goes to make a delicious red, Montepulciano d'Abruzzo DOC, and a rosé, Cerasuolo (or Rubino). Molise has two good wines, Biferno DOC, which comes as red, rosé and white, and Pentro d'Isernia, a white. Trebbiano d'Abruzzo DOC is the best-known white and, confusingly, it is not made from the grape of the same name, but from the Trebbiano Toscano (with a little Bombino Bianco).

Other typical regional dishes

Agnello all'arrabbiata A lamb stew, also called *alla diavola*, made with sautéed young lamb pieces, with garlic, rosemary, chilli and white wine

Agnello uovo e limone Lamb stewed with wine and garlic, then served with an egg and lemon sauce, enriched with the cooking juices and flavoured with parsley

Calamaretti crudi Baby squid, cut into small pieces, flavoured with vinegar, oil, onion and lots of chilli, and eaten raw; a speciality of Pescara

Ceci e castagne Cooked chickpeas mixed with roasted chestnuts, with a *soffritto* of garlic and oil

Fritto di bianchi d'uovo Stiffly beaten egg white cooked in boiling water, then cut into pieces, dipped in flour and beaten egg, and deep-fried; a speciality of L'Aquila

Guazzetto alla marinara A fish soup from Pescara, which is flavoured with parsley, garlic, vinegar and lots of chilli

'Ndocca 'ndocca A pork stew (the local dialect name meaning 'cut into large chunks'), which uses all the parts of the pig that can't be used in other ways – the snout, ears, tails, pork skin, etc.

Sanguinaccio alla chietina A pudding based on coagulated pig's blood, cooked in a grape must, with walnuts, chocolate, candied peel and sugar

Spaghetti aglio e olio Abruzzi's famous simple spaghetti dish, flavoured with garlic, olive oil and plenty of chilli

Salame di Noci

Chocolate and walnut salami with candied fruits

Dolci **or sweets are generally reserved for festivities and other special occasions in Italy, rather than served to round off a meal. This *salami di noci* from Molise has some similarities to the *panforte di Siena*. The fact that it's shaped like a salami shows you the love this region has for pork products! You will need two sheets of rice paper to wrap the 'salami'.**

MAKES 2; EACH ABOUT 750 g

- **300 g shelled walnuts**
- **200 g caster sugar**
- **100 g dark, bitter chocolate, broken into small pieces**
- **150 g candied orange peel, finely diced**
- **150 g citron peel, finely diced**
- **1 tsp ground cinnamon**
- **1/2 tsp ground cloves**
- **1 tbsp ground black pepper**
- **200 g dried figs, roughly chopped**
- **200 g dates, pitted and minced**

Crush two-thirds of the walnuts, leaving the others whole.

Put the sugar in a pan with 2 tbsp water and heat gently until the sugar has dissolved. Continue to heat until the sugar syrup just turns golden.

Meanwhile, combine all the other ingredients, including the crushed and whole walnuts, in a bowl. Add the sugar syrup and mix well.

Divide the mixture in two and spoon each portion along the middle of a sheet of rice paper. Roll up in the paper, shaping each into a 'salami'. Leave in a cool place until set.

Serve cut into thin slices, with coffee or Moscato, or wrap decoratively in cellophane for an edible Christmas gift.

CAMPANIA

With its fertile volcanic soil, Campania produces some of the best fruit and vegetables in Italy. The region lies below Lazio, on the Mediterranean coast, and borders Molise, Puglia and Basilicata. Naples is the capital and from here, historically and famously, came pasta, pizza and tomato sauce. Tomatoes were first appreciated in Campania, and the prized San Marzano plum tomatoes are still cultivated. They form the basis of sauces for pasta and pizza, and anything deemed *alla napoletana*. Buffalo mozzarella is another Campanian speciality.

The Romans used to call this region *Campania felix* – or 'happy Campania' and it is indeed a happy place – bright, sunny and home to people who laugh freely. The inhabitants of the region's capital are, however, like another race entirely. The Neapolitans are an admixture of many qualities and characteristics. On the positive side they are generous, spontaneous, passionate, festive, romantic and quick thinking, but they can also be melancholic and rather negative. Perhaps this has something to do with the history of the region, which was dominated by invaders at various times – Greeks, Arabs, French and Spanish – or it may be more to do with the proximity of Vesuvius, and the ever-present threat of another eruption to rival that which destroyed Pompeii. Whatever the reason, the Neapolitans have created a defensive philosophy of their own, based on the concept of *arrangiarsi* (to do it for yourself). This guarantees that they can usually get out of any situation, however tricky.

I understand the character of the Campanians because I was born here, at Vietri sul Mare on the Amalfi coast, and my father came from Benevento, in the centre of the region. Although we moved north when I was very young, we often returned for holidays and much of my formative childhood was spent in the sun – learning, watching, cooking and eating with my grandmother, my aunt and her maid Lina (short for Carolina), who used to be our nanny and who cooked for us. I love Campania and, even after all these years, I find I am still learning about the region and its cuisine.

Inevitably, some of the scenic countryside once cultivated with tomatoes and vegetables has been built on, as I discovered on a recent visit. But as we approached the Amalfi coast, I came across the familiar sight of local farmers selling their wares at the side of the road, including wonderful chillies, lemons and garlic. All is not lost...

CULINARY TRADITIONS & SPECIALITIES

The *mezzogiorno*, or the south of Italy, is dry and mountainous, and the people have always been less affluent and less urban than those of the north. The regions of the south share a chequered history and more than once were united as a kingdom by ruling invaders, including the French and Spaniards. As a consequence, the cooking of the whole of the south has a similar feel to it, primarily what we now think of as 'Mediterranean', focusing on vegetables (with little meat), and featuring tomatoes, olive oil, grain products (primarily pasta), and a preponderance of strong flavours such as garlic, chilli and basil.

Campania reflects that chequered history, and there are reminders of it everywhere: Greek temples with magnificent mosaics at Paestum, still recognisable Roman villas, and the poignant buildings that remain forever petrified at Pompeii and Herculaneum. Amalfi was once one of the four great maritime republics, along with Pisa, Genoa and Venice, and many foodstuffs were imported directly into the region. Although durum wheat was – and still is – grown in the region, it was also imported from Turkey in Renaissance times, and used to make pasta. Spaghetti was invented in Naples (or so it is claimed), where hard wheat, good water from the Appennines, and a warm climate for drying the pasta – came together magnificently. The vertical presses, which force dough through the dies to obtain spaghetti, were once powered by men, then by donkey, and today by modern machinery. Pasta towns, such as Castellamare di Stabbia, Torre del Greco and Gragnano, however, manage to preserve that artisan touch that makes Neapolitan pasta so special.

The spaghetti – or *vermicelli* as it is known here – is often bent in the middle because it is hung over canes to dry. Neapolitans are also very fond of larger pasta shapes like *ziti* (long tubes),

maccheroni (short tubes), *rigati* (macaroni with ridges), *bucatini* (hollow noodles), *penne* (quills), *rigatoni* (large ridged tubes) and *candele* (10–15 cm long tubes). In Campania, pasta is eaten not *al dente*, but *fujenni* – almost undercooked. Smaller pasta shapes are popular as well. You can find *chiocciole* and *lumache* (snails), *conchiglie* (shells), *ditali* and *tubetti* (little thimbles), and the famous handmade *fusilli* (twists). While visiting Campania to research this book, I met Lina, my old nanny, again, and watched her prepare *fusilli* by hand, using a knitting needle – just as she had over 50 years ago when she cooked for me and my siblings.

Lina served her *fusilli* with a long-cooked *ragù* made with tomatoes, and beef, pork or lamb cooked on the bone. In Naples, the *ragù alla napoletana* is as famous as the *ragù bolognese* is much further north. To make it, *braciole* or pieces of beef or veal, large or small, are stuffed with a mixture of garlic, pine nuts, parsley, raisins and a little Parmesan, and gently stewed for hours in a tomato sauce. Pasta is served with the tomato sauce for the first course, then the meat is served separately as a main course. Another famous Campanian speciality is *spaghetti in cartoccio*: cooked spaghetti and seafood are briefly baked in a paper container which, when opened at the table, makes for an explosion of flavours – of the sea and tomatoes! Other pasta dishes include a *frittata di maccheroni*, a pasta omelette, and a *timballo di ziti*, a 'cake' of pasta (both echoes of past French influence).

The other dish associated indelibly with Naples is pizza. Focaccia-type breads had long been made all over Italy (bases topped with olive oil, herbs, etc.) but it was when the tomato was introduced to Italy – and particularly to Naples – that the pizza was created. The bread base became thinner, and the toppings more elaborate, but the simplest are to my mind still the best: the *alla napoletana* (with tomatoes, garlic and oregano), the *Margherita* (tomato, mozzarella and basil), and the *marinara* (garlic, tomatoes, oregano, basil and anchovies). I still love pizza, eating

it in my hands as they do in Naples – it is the quintessential Italian street food. One of my earliest memories of staying in Prata with my grandmother is of a huge ship at Molo Beverello, packed with emigrants departing for America. All had little bundles of possessions, and all were looking for a better life. It was people like these who, between the 1880s and the 1920s, introduced pasta, pizza and ice-cream to the United States.

Tomatoes are the great link between pasta and pizza, and the region's most important crop. It's hard to imagine the Italian kitchen (or indeed any kitchen in the western world) without tomatoes, and the Campanians are wonderfully resourceful with their prized ingredient. My granny in Prata showed me how to make *estratto di pomodoro*, or 'extract of tomato', the most ancient way of preserving concentrated tomato paste for sauces. Ripe tomatoes were minced through a special gadget and deseeded. The pulp was then salted, placed on a long wooden flat container, covered with muslin and left in the sun to dry. Twice a day she would stir the mixture with a wooden spoon. After a few days, when it was dehydrated, the pulp turned dark red. She would then shape it into cubes, stick fresh basil leaves all over, and use them for the rest of the year. I remember eating the extract raw on *bruschetta*, trickled with a little olive oil ... delicious. Like almost every other Campanian family, she would also bottle tomatoes. Special wide-necked bottles were stuffed with quartered ripe San Marzano tomatoes with the addition of salt, fresh basil leaves and water. The bottles were sealed and then sterilised to keep throughout the year. A spaghetti sauce made with *filetti di pomodoro* is particularly good and reminds me of summer.

The fertile volcanic soil of Campania may be perfect for tomato cultivation, but it is also perfect for a multitude of other vegetables, including asparagus (mainly purple in this region), artichokes, cauliflower, *friarelli* (rape tops, or *cime di rapa* as it is known elsewhere), onions, garlic, aubergines, cannellini beans, potatoes, celery, pumpkins, courgettes, and sweet and chilli peppers. Wild mushrooms are also gathered in Campania; even black truffles are found, especially in Bagnoli Irpino, near Avellino. Several ways of preparing vegetables originated in Campania, including: *alla scapece* (marinated); *sott'olio* (preserved in oil); *sott'aceto* (preserved in vinegar); and in *agrodolce* (sour-sweet, cooked in vinegar and sugar). Many vegetables are stuffed too, which is another Arab influence. Vegetable *fritto misto* is found all over Italy, but it is especially delicious here, and is made on special occasions.

The fruits grown in Campania are legion, among them apricots, oranges, lemons, apples, plums and loquats. Chestnuts, hazelnuts, walnuts and pine nuts are also excellent in this region. One of the attractions of places like Monte Vergine (of the Black Madonna) are the vendors who sell the local specialities: *torrone* (see page 179), roasted hazelnuts on a string, and above all *le castagne del prete* (the priest's chestnuts), which are firstly boiled and then dried slightly in the oven, still remaining soft but with an extraordinary taste. Hazelnuts are a speciality, notably in *croccante di nocciole*, made towards Christmas time. The town of Avellino even takes its name from the nut, which is known as *nocciola* or *avellana*.

Another link between pasta and pizza is mozzarella, the famous Campanian cheese, made here only from buffalo milk (see page 179). Pecorino is made too, from the milk of sheep reared in the mountains. Lamb, pork, beef and rabbit are eaten, but meat is not particularly important, the emphasis being on pasta and vegetables. Pork is preserved, though, and there is a good *salame napoli* and a good *salsiccia di napoli*, an excellent *capocollo*, and a few notable hams. A couple of curious Neapolitan dishes are *nervetti* (veal and pork cartilage from the foot, boiled until tender then sliced), and *musso*. From my most recent visit to Campania, I have a lasting image of a man selling *musso* on the street: boiled pig offal (lung, tripe, udder, snout) and veal heads, all lying on ice, sprinkled with salt and lemon juice. We tasted it, with mixed feelings ...

As elsewhere, fish is important on the coast, and anchovies from the Gulf of Naples are particularly well known. They feature in *tortiera di acciughe*: anchovy fillets are lined up on a tray, sprinkled with oregano, garlic, breadcrumbs and oil and baked. Octopus is served freshly poached, *affogato*, in Naples, and another street food I once experienced was *marruzzelle*, or snails – cooked in a tomato sauce – of course. *Spaghetti alla vongole* is common here. And capitone, or a mature eel, is a Christmas treat in Naples, as it is in Rome.

The final thing that defines Campania for me is the coffee. If you visit anyone's house, the first thing you will be offered is a *tazzulella di caffè*, an espresso drunk at any time of day. At home, this would be made in the old-fashioned percolator, a Napoletana, still very much in use today – and indeed, many families used to roast their own green coffee beans in a special pan. That was the perfume of Naples for me! And if you do find yourself in Naples, go and have a coffee and a *babà* or a delectable cake at Gambrino, an old café in the middle of the city.

Campanians, in keeping with their sense of fun and spontaneity, celebrate almost everything they can. In August, they have *sagre* for *pesce azzurro* or 'blue fish' in Agropoli, pecorino cheese in Ceppaloni, prosciutto in Paupisi, and lamb in Santa Croce del Sannio. In September, it is the turn of veal in Apollosa, chestnuts in Contrada and Montella, wine in Trecase and Torrecuso, and chestnuts and truffles in Bagnoli Irpino. In December, in San Bartolemeo in Galdo, sausages and polenta are celebrated in tandem.

Scarola Imbuttunata Stuffed curly endive

This unusual dish, probably of Jewish origin, is likely to appeal to vegetarians. It is typically served as a first course.

SERVES 4

4 heads of curly endive
salt and pepper
6 tbsp olive oil
30 g dried breadcrumbs
Stuffing
1 garlic clove, finely chopped
20 g salted capers, rinsed
8 anchovy fillets, chopped
20 g raisins
20 g pine nuts
50 g pitted black olives, chopped

Heat the oven to 200ºC/Gas 6. Blanch the endive heads in boiling salted water for 7–8 minutes, then drain. Pick off the tough, very green outer leaves so that only the hearts remain. Drain thoroughly, then open out each endive heart to make a cavity in the middle.

To make the stuffing, mix all the ingredients together, seasoning with salt and pepper to taste. Stuff the endive hearts with the mixture and sprinkle with a little olive oil. Fold the leaves together to enclose the stuffing in the shape of a ball, pressing with your hands.

Place the stuffed endive on a baking tray, bases uppermost. Drizzle with the remaining olive oil and sprinkle with the breadcrumbs, then bake for 20–30 minutes. Serve hot or cold.

Polpi Affogati Stewed octopus

For this excellent dish, octopus is cooked in its own juices with tomatoes. You need young octopus, weighing no more than 150 g, and they must also be *verace* – the right kind – identified by the double row of suckers on the tentacles. For me, these are one of the best fish to eat!

SERVES 4

8 tbsp olive oil
8 fresh baby octopus, about 120–150 g each, cleaned
2 garlic cloves, finely chopped
1 red chilli, finely chopped
500 g *polpa di pomodoro* or chunky passata
bunch of flat-leaf parsley, coarsely chopped
salt and pepper

Heat the olive oil in an earthenware pot or casserole (one with a tight-fitting lid). Add the octopus and fry, stirring, for a minute or so. Add the garlic and chilli and fry for a few seconds, then add the tomato pulp.

Cover with a tight-fitting lid and simmer very gently for 20–30 minutes. The octopus will be cooked by now. Open the lid, scatter in the chopped parsley and season with salt and pepper to taste. Serve with toasted bread.

Pizza Margherita

Peppino Brandi, a *pizzaiolo* (pizza-maker), created this recipe for Queen Margherita of Italy in June 1889. He wanted a patriotic pizza – all the colours of the Italian flag – and the Queen loved it! Featuring the best of Campania's products, this simple pizza is one of my favourites.

MAKES 4 PIZZAS

Pizza dough
35 g fresh yeast (or 3 1/2 tsp fast-action dried yeast)
pinch of salt
2 tbsp olive oil, plus extra to oil
600 g Italian 'oo' flour, plus extra to dust
Topping
400 g San Marzano plum tomatoes, or *polpa di pomodoro* (chunky passata)
300 g buffalo mozzarella, diced
12 tbsp olive oil
12 basil leaves, or more if small

To make the pizza dough, blend the yeast with 300 ml warm water and add the salt and olive oil. Leave to stand for 10 minutes. Pile the flour into a mound on a surface and make a well in the middle. Slowly pour the yeast liquid into the well, mixing it into the flour with your hands. Continue until all the liquid is incorporated. Turn on to a lightly floured surface and knead to a smooth dough. Cover and leave in a warm place to rise for 1 hour.

In the meantime, if you are lucky enough to have San Marzano plum tomatoes, halve, deseed and finely chop them; set aside.

Heat the oven to 220°C/Gas 7. Knock the pizza dough back and divide into four. Roll one piece into a ball, then stretch and smooth out to a thin 28cm round on an oiled baking tray. Spread a quarter of the tomatoes or tomato pulp on top and scatter over a quarter of the mozzarella, then drizzle with 3 tbsp olive oil. Repeat to make the other pizzas.

Bake for 8–10 minutes, until the base is crisp and the topping is golden and bubbling. Sprinkle with the basil and serve. Eat warm with your hands, as they would do in Naples.

Other typical regional dishes

Agnello cacio e ova Lamb stew with cheese and egg sauce

Antipasto di Pasqua A structured gastronomic speciality, eaten at Easter, based on green salad, hard-boiled eggs, slices of salted ricotta and salami or *capocollo*

Baccalà alla napoletana Fillets of *baccalà*, dusted with flour, then braised with tomatoes, garlic, capers, black olives, pepper, raisins and pine nuts, often sold on street corners

Costata alla pizzaiola A steak sautéed in oil and then served with a sauce of garlic, tomatoes, pepper, oregano and white wine. It is served in pizzerias, hence the name

Gattò di patate Chopped leftovers of cheese, salami, etc., baked in a potato purée and egg casing, as a 'cake' from the French 'gâteau'

Insalata di rinforzo A salad based on cooked cauliflower, olives, peppers, anchovies, capers, oil and vinegar, to be to be picked at – and to be 'reinforced' or varied as you like. Ideal for counteracting all that sweetness at Christmas

Minestra maritata A thick soup 'marrying' various vegetables like broccoli, chicory and escarole, flavoured with salami, prosciutto or sausage, pork skin, small pieces of caciocavallo cheese and chilli

Mozzarella in carrozza Slices of mozzarella encased in bread, soaked in milk, dipped in flour and egg, then deep-fried

Pastiera alla napoletana A *pasta frolla* or sweet pastry case, with a filling of soaked and cooked wheat grains, ricotta, candied fruit, eggs and spices. Also called *pastiera di grano*

Pasta fritta Deep-fried pieces of yeast dough, with a hidden piece of anchovy inside. There is also a sweet version, known as *zeppole di San Giuseppe*

Sartù A rich timbale of rice, filled with meatballs, sausage, chicken giblets, mozzarella, fungi, peas, etc., and baked. Similar to the *bomba di riso* of Emilia-Romagna

Zucchini alla scapece Fried courgette slices marinated in oil, vinegar and mint

REGIONAL PRODUCTS

MOZZARELLA Buffalo mozzarella is produced in the areas around Battipaglia and Caserta and it has a very special taste. The mozzarella made from cow's milk in many other regions is very much milder. Buffalo milk has a higher percentage of fat (around 6 per cent) than cow's milk (4 per cent fat), which accounts for the creamier taste. Numerous companies in Campania, most artisanal, produce buffalo mozzarella for use mainly on pizzas, in pasta dishes, or eating raw.

SAN MARZANO TOMATOES The San Marzano, a special long-shaped tomato, is the pride and joy of the provinces of Naples and Salerno. Preserving tomatoes in jars, bottles and cans, in various shapes and forms, is a huge industry in this region. Sun-dried tomatoes, tomato pulp and concentrated tomato paste for sauces are important products.

BAKED GOODS *Calzone* is a crescent-shaped folded pizza, often filled with prosciutto or salami, mozzarella, ricotta and Parmesan. *Casatiello*, or *casatello*, is a savoury Neapolitan Easter bread stuffed with cheeses and salami and baked with eggs (still in their shells) pushed into the dough. *Frisella* is a dried bread common to the south, which is used rehydrated in salads, etc. On the sweet side, there are a number of Campanian specialities. *Struffoli* are deep-fried sweet dough balls, coated in syrup and spices, then piled into a pyramid or arranged in a ring. *Sfogliatella* is a puff pastry cake, sold in bars as a snack. It contains cooked semolina, ricotta, candied fruit and spices, or sometimes *crema pasticcera*. *Babba al rum* or *babà* is a sweet yeast dough studded with sultanas, baked then soaked in rum and syrup – much like its French ancestor. *Torrone* is nougat, made with egg white and almonds, originally from Cremona in Lombardy. In Naples, it is enclosed in a Madeira cake casing; in Benevento, the *torrone* is made from hazelnuts and honey.

WINE AND OTHER DRINKS Campania's Taurasi DOCG is a red, made mainly from Aglianico. The Falerno del Massico DOC red is a patient re-creation of the Roman Falernum by the Avallone family, made from Aglianico, Primitivo and Piedirosso. There is a white Falerno too, made from Falanghina. Greco di Tufo DOC is a golden yellow 'white', made mainly near Avellino from the Greco grape by Mastroberardilo. Fiano di Avellino is a fine white wine made from a variety of grapes, including of course Fiano, some Greco and some Trebbiano Toscano. Other drinks made in Campania include anisetta, Strega, the famous herb liqueur from Benevento, and Limoncello – made in Naples from the local Amalfi coast lemons and mandarins.

Ragù alla Napoletana con Fusilli di Lina

Lina's fusilli with Neapolitan meat sauce

In the entire south of Italy, it is customary to extract the maximum possible flavour from a piece of meat – whether goat, lamb, pork, beef or a mixture – with the help of a tomato sauce, enhanced by spices, wine and chilli. This sort of *ragù* helps to flavour pasta of any kind, but especially pasta that is handmade. The fusilli made for me by my old nanny in Avellino epitomises the region's culinary culture, and tastes just wonderful! Neapolitans also eat this sauce with *ziti* – long and large tubular pasta.

SERVES 4

400 g durum wheat flour, plus extra to dust
1 egg, beaten
Ragù
8 slices lean topside of beef
2 garlic cloves, very finely chopped
40 g raisins
3 tbsp coarsely chopped flat-leaf parsley
40 g pine nuts
120 g Parmesan, freshly grated
salt and pepper
50 g lard
4 tbsp olive oil
60 ml dry red wine
150 g tomato purée

First prepare the *ragù*. Lay the slices of beef on a board and top with the garlic, raisins, parsley, pine nuts, half the Parmesan, and some salt and pepper. Roll the beef slices around the filling to enclose and tie with string to secure the *involtini*.

Heat the lard and olive oil in a large pan and fry the *involtini*, turning, until browned on all sides. Add the wine and let this evaporate a little, then add the tomato purée diluted with a little water. Cook on a very low heat for 2–3 hours, adding a little water every now and then to keep the mixture from sticking. (You can prepare this *ragù* a day ahead and reheat it to serve.)

To make the pasta, pile the flour into a mound on a surface and make a well in the middle. Add the egg and a splash of water. Gradually mix into the flour, adding enough water to bind the dough. Knead until smooth, then cover with a cloth and leave to rest for about 30 minutes.

Dust your surface with a little flour and shape the dough a little at a time. Take a little piece of dough and roll it under the palm of your hand to make a baton, about 10 cm long and 3 mm in diameter. With a thin skewer (or a knitting needle, like Lina), press the little baton around the skewer to make a spiral shape. Let the pasta spiral run down and off the skewer, then put on a cloth. Repeat to shape the rest of the dough.

Cook the pasta in a large pan of boiling salted water. When it is ready, drain and mix with a little of the tomato sauce. Serve with the rest of the sauce including the meat, or if you prefer, serve the meat separately as a second course with some vegetables. Scatter the remaining Parmesan over the pasta to serve.

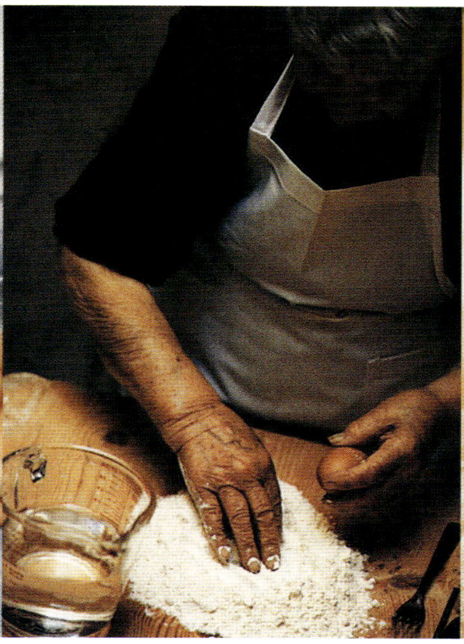

Capretto con Piselli all'Uovo Kid with peas and egg

This wonderful springtime dish is traditionally eaten at Easter, when young lamb and kid are very much in demand. Making egg function as a sauce for meat is quite widespread in the Mediterranean. If fresh peas are unavailable, you can use frozen ones.

SERVES 4–6

1 kg meaty kid or lamb, cut into 5 cm pieces
50 ml olive oil
1 large onion, very finely chopped
50 ml dry white wine
400 g tender garden peas
4 eggs, beaten
3 tbsp finely chopped flat-leaf parsley, plus sprigs to garnish
60 g Parmesan, freshly grated
salt and pepper

Put the pieces of kid or lamb in a pan with the olive oil and onion, and cook slowly to brown the meat on all sides, about 10 minutes. Add the white wine and cook for a further 10–15 minutes. Add the peas and cook for another 10 minutes.

Just before serving, beat the eggs in a bowl with the parsley and cheese. Season the meat with salt and pepper to taste, then remove the pan from the heat. Slowly add the beaten egg mixture, stirring well – the heat of the meat should be enough to turn the egg into a lovely thick sauce. Serve at once, scattered with a few parsley sprigs.

Zuppa di Soffritto Neapolitan soffritto soup

This *cucina povera* dish appeared regularly in Campanian homes during the winter, but is also now seen on posh restaurant menus. It is simply a concentrated *ragù* of pork offal, prepared in advance, then revived with hot stock and served poured over a slice of toasted bread. My mother used to make a lot of this *soffritto* and I remember her taking a few spoonfuls to make lunch from a reddish frozen block kept outside on the balcony. A similar dish exists in Lazio, called *coratella di abbacchio*, which is a delicious lamb offal *ragù*.

MAKES 1 BATCH (20 PORTIONS)

Soffritto
300 g pig's liver
300 g pig's heart
300 g pig's lung
300 g pig's kidneys
100 g pork lard
2 tbsp olive oil
400 g *polpa di pomodoro* or chunky passata
100 g concentrated tomato purée
2–3 hot *diavulilli* chillies, cut into pieces
salt and pepper
To serve
stock
bay leaves
slices of toasted bread

To make the *soffritto*, cut all the pig's offal into very small pieces. Melt the lard with the olive oil in a large pan, and fry the meat ingredients to brown a little. Add the tomato pulp, the concentrated tomato purée, chillies and seasoning, plus some water if necessary – you want it to remain slightly moist, but not too liquid. Cook for 20–30 minutes, stirring occasionally, then set aside to cool. Refrigerate for up to 3 days or freeze in little blocks and defrost as needed.

When the soup is required, take a large spoonful of the cold *soffritto* per person, dilute with hot water or stock to taste, and add one fresh bay leaf per person. Bring to the boil, then simmer for a few minutes. Adjust the seasoning.

Place a hot slice of toast in the bottom of each warm soup plate, pour on the soup and enjoy.

Basilicata

Lying on the instep of the Italian 'boot', with hot, windswept, dry summers, Basilicata is one of the most unsophisticated areas of Italy, and its food reflects this. Peasants still keep pigs and nothing is wasted of the animal, not even its squeak they say! Pork products are prized, especially *lucanica* sausage, and hot dried chilli flavours most dishes. Wheat and olive trees are cultivated to make bread and pasta, and the oil that is so important in local cooking.

Basilicata is bordered by two seas: a narrow strip of the Tyrrhenian Sea to the west, at the Golfo di Policastro; to the south-east there is a larger stretch of coastline around the Golfo di Taranto, on the Ionian Sea. In between lie the southern peaks of the great Italian mountain range, here the Appennino Lucano, and some flatter stretches of land punctuated by a number of rivers flowing down towards the Ionian Sea. Basilicata is bordered to the north by Campania, and to the north-east by Puglia, to which region it actually belonged at one time. The old name of the region, Lucania from *lupus* (wolf), reminds us that this was once Roman territory; the more modern name comes from the Greek for 'royal'. There are two provinces only, Potenza and Matera.

The inhabitants of Basilicata, known as the Lucani, are a mixed population of eastern origin. They have been quite reticent about mixing with the rest of Italy, not least because for so many years the region was cut off and secluded, far from any centres of power. Roads and communications have now been established, amazingly only since the 1980s, and the area has much to offer in culinary terms. Although the produce is much the same as elsewhere in southern Italy, the cuisine is based entirely on local ingredients and it is interestingly inventive.

I have many fond memories of Basilicata. I spent a holiday in Maratea, a pleasant little town with good beaches on the Tyrrhenian Sea, while writing my first book over 20 years ago. I recall a plaque on a wall in Maratea, which claimed that if you said a prayer on that spot, you would have 300 days of *'indulgenzia plenaria'*, in other words, 300 trouble-free days ... long enough to write a book! Ricotta is a speciality of the region and I remember watching the local farmer preparing his for sale. He scooped the fresh curds into a little cone-shaped woven basket of reeds – a handmade cheese drainer – then covered his cheese with a small fresh vine leaf.

And while filming for my TV series further east in Basilicata, we came across Accettura, a small village in the centre of a sea of green hills and valleys, part of the Pollino Mountains. By chance, the annual celebration of the *matrimonio degli alberi* (the marriage of trees) was taking place. From two opposite sides of the village, two teams of young and very strong men, with the aid of bulls, each hauled in a huge full-grown tree, one an oak deprived of all its branches, the other, a holly tree in full leaf. They bound them upright in the piazza, one above the other, almost grafting them together, then tied notes of paper to the branches. Quite what this symbolised, I didn't know, but then some 12 marksmen fired at the trees to detach the paper. Thereafter everyone celebrated, and I can still remember the festive meal I ate in the local *trattoria*. This included *maccheroni al ferretto*, a hand-rolled pasta with a rich, slow-cooked *ragù* of tomatoes, lamb, pork and *pezzenta*, a unique Basilicatan salami (see page 192). The dish was sprinkled with salted ricotta, a hard cheese that is the local substitute for Parmesan. I can still taste it today.

As you drive towards the Golfo di Taranto in the summer, there are golden wheat fields on either side of the road, contrasting wonderfully with the green of the olives. Here and there are reminders of *Magna Grecia* ('Great Greece', the Greek Empire), in the forms of temple and theatre ruins, as well as Norman castles and villages. You might stop at the roadside to buy a '*gnumaridd* (see page 191) or something else grilled and always spiked with chilli.

CULINARY TRADITIONS & SPECIALITIES

What I find particularly special about Basilicata is that almost everything is still produced in the old, established way. The Lucani appreciate the value of a traditional culture, and realise it isn't possible to improve on customs that have developed organically over the centuries.

Pork is the meat that rules and almost every family has at least one pig. The personalised, good feeding guarantees excellent fresh meat and equally good meat products, most of them still made at home. Meat-processing companies do exist in Basilicata, but only on a small scale. Apart from the sausages and salami (see page 192), Basilicata has two pork specialities that epitomise *cucina povera* (peasant cuisine). *Sugna* is lard obtained by rendering pork fat, used for cooking and to preserve fresh sausages, but also eaten as a 'spread'. Before embarking on long trips, shepherds would mix the lard with flavourings – fennel, salt, spices and the ubiquitous *peperoncini* (chilli) – and spread this on toasted bread, when it becomes *sugna forte*. The other by-product of rendering pork fat is *ciccioli*, which are pork scraps or scratchings. These crisp but juicy tiny bits of meat and fat are wonderful eaten hot with bread (something my mother used to give us in Piedmont, but then she came originally from the south).

Wheat is one of the main agricultural products of Basilicata and it is used to make the famous bread of Matera, which is not dissimilar to Puglia's equally well-known bread (see page 206). Before homes had ovens, the large rounds of dough (*panella*) were shaped at home, then baked in the local baker's oven. These huge loaves would last a family for a whole week. Nowadays the breads are smaller, but no less tasty. Local wheat products, such as bread sticks, *taralli* (savoury round biscuits) and *lingue* (sweet biscuits), are dispatched to Turin, Milan and other parts of Italy, where they are much appreciated. Wheat is also used to make pasta, and there are a few types that are particular to Basilicata. One is *strascinati* (or *strascinari*): this is wheat flour dough enriched

Grano al Sugo Wheat grains with a tomato and meat sauce

This simple recipe probably originates from Greece, where I have sampled many dishes using whole grains such as wheat. It is an interesting dish, which includes a very simple *ragù* made of lamb and pork.

SERVES 4

300 g wholewheat grains, soaked in cold water for 24 hours
150 g lean pork
150 g lean lamb
6 tbsp olive oil
1 small onion, finely chopped
500 g *polpa di pomodoro*, or chunky passata
1 hot chilli, chopped
salt and pepper
100 g mature pecorino cheese, freshly grated

Drain the wheat, place in a pan and cover with fresh water. Bring to the boil, then cover and simmer for 40–50 minutes, or until tender.

Cut the pork and lamb into very small pieces. Heat the olive oil in a pan, add the chopped meats with the onion, and fry, stirring, until browned on all sides. Add the tomato pulp and chilli and bring to a simmer. Cover and cook slowly for 30–40 minutes. Season with salt and pepper to taste.

Drain the cooked wheat and toss with the *ragù*. Serve in warm bowls, sprinkled generously with grated pecorino.

Baccalà con Peperoni alla Griglia

Baccalà with grilled peppers

I came across this *baccalà* speciality in Matera. I have replaced the *peperoni cruschi* with grilled strips of pepper, which may not be quite authentic, but they are easier to prepare and equally tasty. To desalt *baccalà*, soak the chunks of meaty fish, skin-side up, in cold water for 24 hours, changing the water a couple of times.

SERVES 4

- **800 g soaked and desalted *baccalà***
- **1 large, fleshy red pepper, about 200 g**
- **8 tbsp olive oil**
- **1 red chilli, finely chopped, or more if you like**
- **80 g black olives, pitted**
- **2 tbsp coarsely chopped flat-leaf parsley**

Cook the *baccalà* in boiling water for 20 minutes or more, depending on thickness, until soft.

Meanwhile, char-grill the red pepper until the skin blackens. Peel away the skin, deseed and cut the flesh into strips.

Drain the *baccalà* and reduce the flesh to flakes, getting rid of any bones. I keep the skin as I like it, but you can get rid of that too, if you prefer. Add the olive oil and chilli, the olives and parsley, and mix well. Serve topped with the grilled red peppers.

with *sugna* (lard), rolled to a thin sausage over an implement called a *cavarola*, and cut into lengths to a rough macaroni shape. Lasagne, *fusilli* and other shapes are common, and the *ragù* or sauce is usually based on tomatoes, with bits of meat, and lots of chilli. The wheat grain itself is eaten with a *ragù* (see page 187).

Peppers, both hot and sweet, are probably the defining characteristic of the region's cooking. Sweet peppers, ripened in the hot summer sun, appear in many dishes – in *peperonata*, in pickles, with pork and with *baccalà*. In part of the Matera province, dried red sweet peppers are deep-fried until crisp. These *cruschi* are then crumbled on to food, mainly pasta, as a flavouring. Strings of chillies drying in the sun decorate virtually every house, and dried chillies are used to flavour olive oil. The peppers come in many strengths, ranging from mild to very hot, and there are several names for them in the local dialect, among them *frangisello*, *diavulicchio* (of the devil), *cerasella* (little cherry) and *pupon*.

The Pollino Mountains are rich in both game and wild fungi, and Basilicata's wild oyster mushrooms are especially good. Almost every little food shop offers a speciality of some sort, from preserved fungi to cheeses and salami, or indeed grappa made with local soft wild fruit such as strawberries, blueberries and raspberries. The volcanic soil around Monte Vulture ensures not only healthy vines for the wine (see page 192), but also many vegetables, including chickpeas, borlotti and cannellini beans from Sarconi, destined for the region's thick soups.

Fish doesn't feature strongly in Basilicata cooking, except around the Golfo di Taranto, where it is often combined with beans and pasta – a wonderful marriage between land and sea. The coastal plain here is very fertile, and apart from wheat and vegetables, it produces some of the best fruits of the region, among them apricots, peaches, grapes, oranges, tangerines, strawberries, clementines, and the more unusual prickly pear.

There is a marvellous saying in this region, 'he who eats bread lives, he who drinks wine never dies!' and the Lucani take every opportunity to celebrate their love of food and wine. There is a famous fish festival during the first ten days of August in Maratea. In Miglianico, on the second Sunday in September, there is a festival dedicated to the cactus fruit – the prickly pear. In October the *vendemmia* is celebrated in Venosa, while in Barile, a festival is dedicated to Aglianico wine and chestnuts.

Other typical regional dishes

Baccalà e peperoni cruschi *Baccalà* cooked in water then sprinkled with chilli and crispy deep-fried sweet peppers

Cicoria in brodo di carne Blanched wild chicory, enriched with pieces of prosciutto and pecorino, and served in beef broth

Cotechinata Rolls of pork skin stuffed with garlic, parsley and chilli, which are fried, then baked with a tomato sauce

Gnocchetti alle erbe di monte Little potato dumplings with a wild herb sauce

'Gnumaridd A little bundle of offal tied up with *budello* (gut) and roasted, also found in Puglia, Calabria and Sicily

La pigneti Lamb very slowly cooked with potato, salami and cheese in a special earthenware pot, its lid sealed with clay (not dissimilar to a Moroccan tagine)

Lagane e ceci A mixture of pasta and chickpeas, also known as *ciceri e tria*, common in Puglia too

Panzarotti A chickpea purée mixed with chocolate and spices, then deep-fried or baked and eaten cold

Peperonata alla carne di maiale Peppers in vinegar cooked with pork

Piccione al sugo Pigeon stuffed with its offal, breadcrumbs, parsley, egg and tomato, then baked

REGIONAL PRODUCTS

PORK PRODUCTS *Pezzenta* is a salami made with the less valued parts of the pig – lung, liver and other offal – flavoured with garlic, fennel, spices and a preponderance of chilli. The name comes from *pezzente*, the Italian for 'tramp' or 'miser', so it's definitely a poor man's salami. The best *lucanica* (mildly spiced sausage) comes from Latronico and dates back to Roman times. When fresh it is either roasted or grilled, or crumbled to use in *ragùs*. *Lucanica* is available smoked and dried, too. Good prosciutto and *capocollo* (the cured neck or shoulder of pork) are also made in Basilicata. And Lagonegro e Lauria produces an excellent *soppressata*, a salami made from a mix of pork meat and fat, and spices like fennel and chilli.

CHEESES Caciocavallo, a semi-hard cow's milk cheese, is made here, as it is over much of the south of Italy. Ricotta is also produced, as is cacioricotta, an 'aged' version, which although still soft, is stronger in flavour. Salted ricotta is pressed and dried to become hard enough to grate. Canestrato di Moliterno is a soft sheep's milk cheese, while manteca o butirro is a caciocavallo-like cheese ball with butter in the middle; similar cheeses are found in Campania and Calabria.

WINE AND OTHER DRINKS The small amount of wine produced in Basilicata mostly comes from the Aglianico grape (probably introduced by the Greeks). The best wine is Aglianico del Vulture DOC, a rich red made from grapes grown on the east-facing slopes of the extinct volcano, Monte Vulture. The best makers of this wine have also produced an oak-aged Aglianico, called Canneto. *Vino cotto* is reduced grape juice, but in Basilicata they also make a similar intensely flavoured fig syrup, called *vino cotto di fichi*. And Basilicata's famous digestif is Amaro Lucano.

Vellutata di Funghi Cardoncelli

Mushrooms with cannellini bean purée and rice

A curious recipe from Basilicata, where all the ingredients are produced locally, except the rice. *Cardoncelli* belong to the same family as oyster mushrooms. They grow wild in the south of Italy, but they are also cultivated.

SERVES 4

200 g dried cannellini beans, soaked in cold water overnight
8 tbsp olive oil
2 garlic cloves, chopped
1 thick slice of Parma ham (with fat) or pancetta, about 100 g
1 onion, finely sliced
200 g *cardoncelli* (or oyster mushrooms), cleaned and sliced if large
200 g risotto rice
salt and pepper
80 g mature pecorino cheese, freshly grated

Drain the soaked beans. Heat half the olive oil in a pan and fry the garlic with the ham or pancetta for a few minutes. Add the cannellini beans and enough water to cover generously, then cook for a couple of hours until soft.

Remove the ham or pancetta from the beans. Purée the cannellini beans with some of the cooking liquor in a blender or food processor to a pulp. Transfer to a bowl. Chop the ham and stir into the bean purée; keep warm.

Heat the remaining olive oil in another pan and gently fry the onion until soft. Add the mushrooms and fry gently for 5–10 minutes until softened.

At the same time, cook the rice in salted water until *al dente*. Now combine the three mixtures – the bean purée, the mushrooms and the rice. You should have a very tasty soupy rice, almost like a wet risotto. Check the seasoning and scatter plenty of pecorino over. Humble and delicious.

Peperoni Mandorlati

Pan-roasted peppers with almonds

I once ate peppers cooked like this in Lecce, in neighbouring Puglia, and I remember how good they tasted. I like to eat them as part of an antipasto or as a side dish to grilled lamb. My mother cooked peppers in a similar way, but without the raisins and almonds. Sweet, meaty peppers are essential.

SERVES 4

4–6 yellow peppers
6 tbsp olive oil
2 garlic cloves, finely chopped
20 g caster sugar
40 g raisins
30 g slivered almonds
3 tbsp white wine vinegar
salt and pepper

Halve, core and deseed the peppers, then cut into strips. Heat the olive oil in a pan and fry the pepper strips, stirring from time to time, until they are soft and beginning to caramelise at the edges, about 20–25 minutes.

Add the garlic, sugar, raisins and almonds. Stir-fry for a few minutes longer, then add the wine vinegar and let it evaporate. Season with salt and pepper to taste. Serve hot or cold.

Maiale e Peperoni Pork and pickled peppers

We used to cook this dish regularly in winter. It relies on very meaty peppers called *pepacelle*, which have been preserved in vinegar during the summer. For this we use a *damigiana* (demijohn), or a big flask with an opening at the top large enough to take the peppers. Alternatively, you can fry fresh peppers until soft, then add vinegar at the end, as I have done here. The combination of pickled peppers and pork is a truly peasant dish, but it is also one for gourmets.

SERVES 4

40 g lard
9 tbsp olive oil
600 g diced pork (lean and fat), or fillet, cut into medallions
3 garlic cloves, finely sliced
1 red chilli (optional), finely chopped
salt and pepper
600 g meaty red peppers
4 tbsp white wine vinegar

Melt the lard with 3 tbsp of the olive oil in a pan, and fry the pork on all sides until brown. Add the garlic, chilli if using, and some salt and pepper. Sauté until the pork is cooked, about 20–25 minutes.

Halve, core and deseed the peppers, then cut into slices. Heat the remaining olive oil in another pan and fry the peppers until soft and caramelised at the edges. Add the wine vinegar and season with salt.

Add the peppers to the meat (or add sliced pickled peppers at this stage) and toss to mix. Cook, stirring, for a further 5 minutes to let the flavours combine.

Serve as a main course. We eat it with bread.

Puglia

This hot southern region, which runs from the 'spur' down to the bottom of the heel of the Italian 'boot', is also known as *il granaio d'Italia* (the Italian granary) and *l'orto d'Italia* (the vegetable garden of Italy). This is because most of Puglia is a flat plain, with vast acreages given over to grains, vegetables and fruit. Most of the grain is hard durum wheat, used to make some of Italy's best pasta and bread. Once considered 'poor' from a food perspective, Puglia is now wealthy because of the wheat, olive oil, and fruit and vegetable cultivation.

I have known Puglia all my life. When I was a child, I often visited relatives living in Lecce, in my summer holidays. As the son of a stationmaster, I always travelled by train, usually with my head stuck out of the window for most of the journey, gathering black smoke from the steam locomotive! The landscape was much the same then as it is now: endless plantations of green olive trees and huge golden wheat fields, standing out in stark contrast between red-earthed tobacco fields and serried ranks of vines. The region is characterised by its deep colours, those of the sea and sky, those of the earth – from ochre to red to black – and the green of the massive olive trees. Some of these are a thousand years old, and still producing prized olives, which in turn produce even more precious oil.

Among those trees, specially around Alberobello and Martina Franca in the Valle d'Itria, there are strange circular buildings with conical roofs – painted white and immaculately kept. Constructed from loose stones, these ancient buildings are the *trulli*, in which farmers house their cattle. Their origin goes back far into Puglian history, when the region was dominated successively by Swabians, Normans, Spaniards, French and, before that, Greeks, Lebanese, Turks and Saracens. Puglia's historical charm depends partly on relics such as these, and in the fortifications along the coast, the castles, churches and other religious buildings. Also of interest are the *masseria*, farms once owned by a *signore* or local dignitary who employed people to cultivate crops and to share in the proceeds. Most of the *masseria*, which were abandoned in the past century, have now been refurbished and become tourist attractions, offering accommodation and selling olive oil, preserves, vegetables, fruit and wines – all produced on the premises. Puglia has hidden itself from tourists for a long time, but it is inviting for those in search of something new and special. It still offers unspoilt bays and beaches, but I wouldn't like to say for how long ...

CULINARY TRADITIONS & SPECIALITIES

Most of the region faces east across the Adriatic, and the style of cooking is eclectic, reflecting the centuries of alien influences. The eastern Puglian ports of Bari and Brindisi were – and are still – the gateways to eastern Europe and beyond, to Croatia, Greece, Albania and Turkey. The curve of the Gulf of Taranto, from the tip of the heel up into the instep of the Italian boot, is on the Ionian Sea. The city of Taranto itself, an important military port, is known for its extensive cultivation of good quality mussels and oysters.

Vegetables, fish and pasta are the primary characteristics of the cuisine – all accompanied by the famous Puglian bread. Wheat is the main crop and it is ground locally into flour, which is used to make the bread and pasta. Bread is particularly popular in Puglia, especially around Altamura. The huge Pugliese loaves were once made on a weekly basis, and the dough taken to the local baker to be cooked. The dough is a mixture of durum and a softer wheat flour, which lends a unique flavour and texture. It is mostly eaten fresh of course, but is also baked hard as *fresella* (see page 206). Puglian pasta is paler than other Italian pastas partly because of the local wheat grain, and also because the pasta is pressed through bronze dyes. These leave a certain roughness on the surface of the pasta, which enables the sauce to adhere better. This pasta, because of the 'harder' gluten, usually takes much longer to cook and it is a bit chewy, but delicious.

The most popular pasta shape is *orecchiette* (little ears), known as *recchie* or *recchietelle* in the local dialect, and a speciality of Bari. Other pastas are *cecatelli* or *cavatieddi* (double ear), *strascinate* or *stagghiotti* (ridged rectangles), *festoni* (lasagne/pappardelle with one wavy edge), *fusilli* (spirals), and *laganelle* (pasta strips). There are said to be more pasta shapes in Puglia than anywhere else in Italy, and my own pasta producer in San Severo, Signor Pazienza, offers literally hundreds of shapes. Most pasta in Puglia is eaten with a simple tomato sauce, or vegetables such as *cime di rapa*, broccoli or rocket, or chickpeas, or salted ricotta or, occasionally, with a heavier and long-cooked meat *ragù*.

Chiancarelle con Cime di Rape

Small orecchiette with rape tops

Of the many traditional Puglian *orecchiette* dishes, this one from Foggia is very good and couldn't be easier. *Chiancarelle* is Puglia's small version of *orecchiette*. Purple-sprouting broccoli works well in place of *cime di rape*.

SERVES 4

350 g *chiancarelle* or *orecchiette* pasta
salt and pepper
500 g trimmed *cime di rape* rape tops), or purple-sprouting broccoli
3 garlic cloves, sliced
1 red chilli, chopped
6 tbsp olive oil
6 anchovy fillets

Add the pasta to a large pan of boiling salted water and cook for 6–7 minutes. Add the *cime di rape* and continue to cook until the pasta is tender, another 5 minutes or so.

Meanwhile, fry the garlic and chilli in the olive oil for a few minutes. Just before the garlic starts to brown, take the pan off the heat, and add the anchovies, stirring to dissolve them.

Drain the pasta and vegetables and toss with the garlic, chilli and anchovy mixture. Taste for seasoning and serve.

Vegetables are grown all over *il tavoliere di Puglia* (the table) from the north at the Gargano (the spur) right down to my childhood stamping ground of Lecce, and further, right down to the Capo Santa Maria di Leuca on the Ionian. Tomatoes are grown everywhere. In season they are tied in bunches and hung on the walls of country houses, or balconies in the towns and cities, where they keep fresh through winter. These *pomodorini*, with their tough skins and sweet flavour, are used in the best and simplest pasta sauces. Acres of tomatoes drying in the sun are a typical sight in Cerignola, just south of the Gargano, and of course, they find their way to all parts of the world. Here too grows a very special olive, the Bella di Cerignola which is eaten in the wonderful antipasti offered here. Many of the vegetable dishes reflect the influences of countries to the east, and the bean and pulse purées have been likened to those of Greece and the Middle East.

The Gargano is also the home of cultivated mushrooms, like oyster, button and *cardoncelli* (king oyster). An unusual vegetable that grows wild all over Puglia (and is cultivated) is the bulb of the grape hyacinth – *lampascioni* or *lampasciuoli*. It looks like a small squat onion, has a bitter taste, and must be blanched well before cooking further. It is usually preserved in vinegar and salt, or made into a jam with *saba*. Puglia grows a truly amazing array of vegetables – curly and flat endive, salad leaves of all types, spinach, cauliflower, broccoli, *cime di rapa*, fennel, artichokes, onions from Aquaviva, peppers, carrots, potatoes, cardoons, celery, lentils, chickpeas, broad beans, cannellini beans (eaten fresh and dried) – you name it and they have it. Around Brindisi, *cicoria*, a prized green, is cultivated and also gathered wild for use in many dishes.

Fruit are cultivated too, among them peaches, nectarines, tangerines, oranges, lemons, melons, cherries, apricots, grapes, quinces, apples, figs, prickly pears, loquats, *carrube* or carob (the pods of which children chew like sugar cane) and a host of nuts, including almonds, walnuts, peanuts and chestnuts. These products appear in many guises. As a child in Lecce, I remember the little stalls on the side of the road selling mulberries or figs on fresh fig leaves, freshly picked and cleaned prickly pears, and wonderful almond milk made by squeezing fresh almonds and sugar.

Indeed it seems to be a tradition in Puglia that fresh foods are turned into 'new foods', or preserves. Many vegetables are pickled in vinegar or cured in the local olive oil. Fruits are made into jams and preserved in other ways. While holidaying in the Murgia, I invented my own non-cooked jam – only feasible in a place where the sun shines all the time! I shredded ripe peaches, mixed them with an equal amount of sugar and put them in the sun under muslin to deter wasps and flies. I stirred the mixture a couple of times a day, and after 5–6 days it had dehydrated to form a delectable jam. It kept well in jars – I found it was still good a year later!

Meat is popular, notably horsemeat rather than beef, which isn't suited to the hot climate. Donkey meat was also once eaten. Pigs in the Murgia, the hilly part of Puglia that divides the region from Basilicata, are allowed to roam freely and eat acorns, chestnuts or whatever is available in the *macchia* or undergrowth. Their meat, which tastes wonderful, is used to make offal dishes and preserved meats, chief among them *capicollo* (see page 206). The Pugliesi eat *involtini* of offal which is 'off limits' for most foreigners because they contain lungs, heart, testicles, liver, etc; these are usually tied up with intestines and grilled. Goat, poultry, game birds, and lamb are eaten too, but the main products of the region are its sheep's cheeses (see page 206).

Fish is abundant all over Puglia and especially on the coast, where there are many *brodetti*, offering mixtures of fish from either the Adriatic or the Ionian Sea. Squid are eaten, as are octopus (sometimes raw) and squill fish, a langoustine-like shellfish, known as *caratieddi* in Puglia (*canoci* in Venice, *spanocchio* in Naples and *cicala* in Tuscany). Sea urchins are found mainly on the Adriatic side, while mussels (and oysters) are more common on the Ionian, particularly around Taranto. The combination of fish and vegetables is interesting here, and they are sometimes served with pasta as well as in the *orecchiette, broccoli e cozze* (pasta 'ears' with mussels and broccoli). One thing I like about fish restaurants in Puglia is that, by law, menus must state whether the fish is fresh or frozen.

Most of the annual celebrations in Puglia are dedicated to wine. At the end of May there are open cellars in most wine-producing towns, and festivities extend to the end of the year. In March *Gnumarieddi* are celebrated in Cisternino, melon in Brindisi in August, grapes in several places in September, and in Fasano, there are many gastronomic exhibitions around Christmas.

Tiella di Patate e Funghi

Timbale of potatoes and mushrooms

The *tiella*, or *tegame*, is comparable to the French tian, but the dish dates right back to the Spanish occupation. This delicious combination of potatoes and mushrooms is eaten as a starter or accompaniment. You can make it richer if you like by pouring on some single cream before baking, though I prefer it pure and simple.

SERVES 6

- **2 large potatoes, about 600 g, peeled**
- **300 g *cardoncelli* (oyster mushrooms) or fresh porcini**
- **1 large onion, about 300 g**
- **120 ml olive oil**
- **3 tbsp coarsely chopped flat-leaf parsley**
- **salt and pepper**
- **50 g dried breadcrumbs**

Heat the oven to 200°C/Gas 6. Slice the potatoes and mushrooms. Thinly slice the onion into rings. Oil a shallow ovenproof dish.

Layer the potatoes, mushrooms and onion in the dish, drizzling each layer with a little olive oil and sprinkling with parsley, salt and pepper. Scatter the breadcrumbs over the top and drizzle generously with olive oil. Bake for 40–50 minutes.

Allow the timbale to stand for a few minutes before serving.

Peperoni Arrotolati Stuffed rolled peppers

Peppers and aubergines are the main players in the Pugliese cuisine. Peppers are fried, dried, regenerated, roasted, cooked with tomatoes, stuffed, grilled, preserved in vinegar … there's no limit to their versatility. I ate this dish for lunch in a *trattoria* in Lecce. It was so exhilaratingly good that I decided to make it for myself.

SERVES 4–8

4 large, fleshy red and/or yellow peppers
20 g dried breadcrumbs
olive oil
Filling
1 tbsp pine nuts
4 tbsp fresh breadcrumbs
1 tbsp finely chopped flat-leaf parsley
1 tsp capers
3 tsp raisins
8 anchovy fillets, finely chopped
2 tbsp olive oil
salt and pepper

Heat the oven to 200ºC/Gas 6. Roast or grill the peppers for about 10 minutes until the skin is charred and can be peeled off easily.

Meanwhile, mix all the ingredients together for the filling, seasoning with salt and pepper to taste. Set aside.

Peel away the skin from the peppers, then halve or quarter lengthways, depending on size. Remove the seeds.

Lay the pepper pieces on a surface and divide the filling between them. Roll up to enclose and secure with a wooden toothpick or cocktail stick. Place on a baking tray, sprinkle with the dried breadcrumbs and drizzle with a little olive oil. Bake for 15–20 minutes.

Serve the stuffed peppers warm or cold, with a bowl of olives on the side if you like.

Infanticelle di San Nicola in Cartoccio

Sea bream in a bag

Dorade **or** ***orate*** **is the real name of the fish used in this recipe; small ones are called** ***infanticelle*** **(from infants). St. Nicolas is the patron saint of Bari and this is where the recipe originated. If you can't find very small bream, buy 4 larger ones, about 300–400 g each, and put two in each parcel.**

SERVES 4

8 small sea bream, 200 g each, gutted and cleaned
2 lemons, sliced
salt and pepper
2 garlic cloves, peeled
2 tbsp chopped flat-leaf parsley
olive oil to drizzle

Heat the oven to 200ºC/Gas 6. Tear off two large sheets of foil and place on baking trays. Rinse the sea bream and pat dry.

Lay a sliced lemon, overlapping, in the middle of each sheet foil, then arrange 4 fish on top. Season with salt and pepper, add a whole garlic clove to each package and scatter over the parsley. Drizzle with a little olive oil.

Bring the edges of the foil up over the fish and fold together to seal. Bake for 20–25 minutes, or a little longer if your fish are bigger. Serve warm.

Other typical regional dishes

Agnellone al ragù Young lamb slow-cooked in a tomato *ragù*, eaten with pasta

Bracioline Slice of beef, lamb, pork or horsemeat rolled and stuffed with prosciutto, parsley, pepper, pecorino, and sometimes pine nuts and sultanas. Slow-cooked in a tomato sauce, to flavour pasta

Brodetto A 'little broth' eaten at Easter, not of fish, but of pieces of braised kid with asparagus, finished with beaten egg and grated pecorino

Caldariello Lamb slowly cooked in milk and oil with garlic and wild fennel, served on bread

Cappello da gendarme Stuffed pizza shaped as a hat, filled with cooked courgettes, aubergines, meat, eggs and mozzarella; a speciality of Lecce

Carteddate Baked boat-shaped Christmas sweet flavoured with *vino cotto* and cinnamon, or fried and then dipped in honey and sprinkled with cinnamon and sugar. Also known as *cartellate*

Cazzmarre Little *involtini* of lamb offal tied up with gut and baked; also called *gnumarieddi*

Ciceri e tria Ancient dish of chickpeas and pasta flavoured with fried onions, typical of Lecce

Cozze arrecanate Mussels in their half-shell, lined up on a tray, covered with breadcrumbs, oregano, a little tomato juice, garlic and olive oil, and baked in the oven

Fenecchiedde Blanched wild fennel, sautéed with oil, garlic and fillets of anchovies; a Christmas speciality of Bari

Melanzane alla campagnola Char-grilled aubergine slices, marinated with extra virgin olive oil, garlic, mint, basil and parsley for 6 hours

Minestra maritata 'Married soup', comprising blanched escarole, wild fennel, celery, pancetta, pecorino and beef stock, usually baked. Versions also found in Campania, Calabria and Basilicata

'Ncapriata di favi e foggi Puréed cooked dried broad beans with cooked chicory, drizzled with extra virgin olive oil; similar to the *maccù* of Sicily

Peperoni verdi Fried whole small green peppers seasoned with salt, and eaten whole, seeds and all

Recchie a ruchetta e patate Rocket, quartered potatoes and *orecchiette*, flavoured with garlic and chilli fried in olive oil

Sgombro all'aceto Mackerel fillets wrapped in muslin, blanched, then steeped in vinegar for an hour. Served drizzled with olive oil, chopped garlic and mint ... delicious

Zuppa di pesce alla gallipolina A mixture of fish such as *rascasse*, prawns, mussels and squid, cooked with tomatoes, oil, a little vinegar, and onion to make a thick soup similar to *bouillabaisse*

REGIONAL PRODUCTS

BREAD AND BAKED GOODS Pugliese bread has an interesting flavour and texture, and is perhaps the best in Italy. It can also be eaten as *fresella* – double-baked slices with a biscuit-like texture, invented by farmers to make their bread last. In the summer, many Pugliesi eat *fresella* softened with tomato juice or water, and topped with sliced tomatoes, a little garlic, olive oil and a sprinkling of oregano or basil. *Taralli* is the other famous Pugliese bread speciality. These little dough rings, flavoured with fennel seeds, are immersed first in boiling water until they surface, and then baked until crisp. They are the equivalent of the *grissini* of Turin.

OLIVE OIL Puglia produces more olive oil than any other region in Italy, both for its own abundant use, and also for export (some goes for blending to other regions). It is made variously from Corantina, Frantoio, Oliarola Barese and Leccino olives, and is mostly of very good quality. Puglian olive oil is not as bitter or peppery as Tuscan oil, because the olives are collected later, when they are more mature. The Pugliesi use their olive oil for everything, including preserves.

CHEESE Great Puglian cheeses include pecorino, caciocavallo, provolone and mozzarella. There is also burrata, a heavenly cheese unique to Puglia, made with cow's milk on the outside (similar to mozzarella), with filaments of mozzarella combined with double cream inside. It must be eaten very fresh and is irresistible. Pecorino cheese is made with sheep's milk and is available in various forms. The youngest pecorino, the *marzuolo*, is made with milk collected during March, and is particularly tasty because of the new grass. Then there is *caciotta* (soft and fresh), then *pecorino fresco* (slightly aged, but still soft), and finally *stagionato*, which is aged until hard, intense in aroma and flavour, and used instead of Parmesan for grating. Puglia's fresh sheep's milk ricotta tastes exquisite, and there is also a *ricotta salata*, an aged and salted ricotta for grating.

PORK PRODUCTS These include pancetta, *sopressata*, *coppa*, salami and ham. Puglia's *sopressata* is prepared *a punta di coltello*, the meat cut with the tip of a knife, rather than minced. There is also a *salsiccia di Lecce*. In Martina Franca on the hills above Grottaglie, I ate the best *capicollo* (neck of pork, slightly smoked) I've ever tasted. And if you are ever in this locality, visit the two excellent butcher's shops (Fratelli Ricci and Romanelli) to buy local specialities. All of these are usually eaten as antipasti, which is especially good in Puglia. There is a curious Easter custom in Bari: eggs are brought to the church where they are blessed, then boiled at home and eaten with *sopressata* and orange slices, as an antipasto.

WINE AND OTHER DRINKS The wines of Puglia were once strongly alcoholic and produced in large quantities – mostly destined for the north to become part of blends. Nowadays, the production has lessened and the style of the wines is lighter. In general, the wines are now good enough to compete with the best in the world. Names like Salice Salentino, Copertino, Castel del Monte and Primitivo di Manduria are all white wines made with grapes like Negro Amaro, Bombino Bianco, Trebbiano, Primitivo, Bianco d'Alessandro, Verdeca, Locorotondo and Aleatico di Puglia. Cacce'mmitte of Lucera is a curious rosé wine made from the pulp of red grapes. There are also Gioia del Colle, Gravina, Martina Franca Moscato (sweet) of Trani, Nardo', Rosso Barletta, San Severo, Squinzano and many more. When in Puglia, always drink the local wine. *Saba* is a *vino cotto*, the cooked-down must of grapes, used in southern Italy to make biscuits, cakes, etc.

Calzone Pugliese Onion pie

The *calzone* of Puglia is quite different from the more familiar *calzone* of Naples, which is essentially a folded pizza. The Puglian version looks more like a pie or giant pasty. I have made plenty of these pies, using the excellent red onions of Acquaviva delle Fonti, similar to those of Tropea. Also known as *pizza di acqua viva*, they are traditionally eaten to celebrate the feast days of the two saints, Dottori Cosimo and Damiano.

SERVES 4–6

Pastry

400 g plain flour, plus extra to dust
100 ml olive oil, plus extra to oil
1 egg, beaten
100 ml dry white wine
salt

Filling

3 tbsp olive oil
1 kg red onions, sliced
160 g salty ricotta cheese
50 g pecorino cheese, freshly grated
4 eggs, beaten

To make the pastry, put the flour in a bowl and make a well in the centre. Add the olive oil, egg and white wine, and gradually mix into the flour to make a dough, adding water if necessary, and a pinch of salt. Wrap in cling film and chill for 30 minutes before rolling. Meanwhile, heat the oven to 200°C/Gas 6.

For the filling, heat the olive oil in a pan and cook the onions until soft. Allow to cool, then mix with the ricotta, pecorino, and most of the eggs (save a little for glazing).

Roll out the pastry on a lightly floured surface to a 3 mm thick round and place on an oiled baking tray. Pile the filling on to the centre of the pastry, and fold over to enclose the filling in a half-moon shape. Press the edges together to seal and brush with the reserved egg. Bake for about 20 minutes.

This pie can be eaten warm or cold.

Cutturidde Soupy lamb or mutton stew

I always like curious or less well-known recipes, and this one intrigued me. Incidentally, mutton with its full flavour is now fashionable again, and is ideal for this rustic dish.

SERVES 4

1 kg mixed pieces of lamb (medium fat, some on the bone)
300 g *pomodorini* (or vine-ripened cherry tomatoes), halved
1 onion, finely chopped
200 g mature pecorino cheese, diced
2 tbsp finely chopped flat-leaf parsley
salt and pepper

Put the lamb, tomatoes and onion in a pot, cover with water and cook with the lid on, very slowly and gently, for an hour.

Add the pecorino, parsley and some seasoning, and cook for a further hour, or until the meat is tender. Check the seasoning.

Serve the stew with bread, for mopping up the juices.

Calabria

This beautiful region, which forms the 'toe' of Italy, comprises mainly mountains that drop abruptly to white sandy beaches and the sea, together with some fertile plains – both low and high. There are plenty of cultivated citrus groves and vegetables, plus excellent wild fungi and chestnuts in the autumn. Chilli flavours meat and fish dishes, and an array of Mediterranean seafood is caught along the extensive coastline, to be enjoyed locally and abroad.

Calabria is the fore part of the Italian 'boot' with its capital, Reggio di Calabria, situated right at to the 'toecap'. The island of Sicily is a half-hour journey from here by *traghetto* or boat. Calabria's only land border is with Basilicata, to the north; to the west and east are the Tyrrhenian and Ionian Seas respectively. Calabria is rich in history, having experienced invasions with cultural influences through the ages by the Arabs, Greeks, French and Spaniards among others – much like Sicily and Puglia. We know the Greeks were here because Homer mentions Scylla and Charybdis, the opposing maritime hazards on the Strait of Messina, which separates Calabria and Sicily.

The Appennino Calabrese, the end of the great Italian mountain range, covers most of the region. The only flattish land is near the sea in the area of Trebisacce in the north-east, and on the great plateaux of Sila in the north and Aspromonte in the south. This geography is one of the reasons why Calabria was regarded as the 'extremity' of Italy for such a long time. It was difficult to get into or out of the region, and agriculture was subsistence. For many years Calabria and other southern regions were given help by the more industrialised northern regions, almost as if they were underdeveloped, and were rather perceived as 'takers'. Today, though, Calabria has become hugely successful in agriculture – as it should, with its fertile earth and wonderful weather.

Thankfully, people from this region no longer feel compelled to seek work and wealth elsewhere, historically in Lombardy, Piedmont and Veneto, or abroad. Indeed I have met Calabrese all over the world, even in Australia and New Zealand. My lasting memory, though, is of a group of Calabrese onion pickers in a field in Tropea happily singing *'Calabresella Mia'*, a popular love song, in the sun. I wasn't far from Capo Vaticano and on the horizon was the silhouette of the volcanic island of Stromboli ... an unforgettable, breathtaking sight.

CULINARY TRADITIONS & SPECIALITIES

Like all of the other southern regions of Italy, Calabria's traditions and culinary specialities have been formulated by location and weather, by geography, and by the incursion of different cultures. Because of its Mediterranean climate and mild winters, it is a major area of fruit and vegetable cultivation. Because of its long coastlines, seafood is an important ingredient in the cuisine. And because of the proximity of Sicily, there are many similarities in dishes and in ingredients.

As in Basilicata, many households still keep a pig for their own use, and the annual slaughter calls for a big celebration. A *norcino* (pork butcher) is called in to do his business, then neighbours and friends are invited round for a pork feast. The rest of the animal is preserved as salami, etc (see page 217). *Involtini*, 'little parcels', are made from offal of pork (and sometimes kid and lamb), and tied together with a piece of gut before being grilled. Here in Calabria these are known as *gnunerieddi* or *gnunerielli*. Pork offal even forms the basis of a breakfast dish in this region. *Murseddu* (or *morseddhu*) consists of pork tripe and other offal slowly cooked in red wine, and then served in a pocket of bread, a pitta (the Greek influence). This was once served in *trattorie* along with a glass of wine – a fine way to start the day – but nowadays you'd be more likely to have a brioche and a cappuccino ...

Wild boar are hunted in the mountains, and sheep and goats are kept throughout the region. All are eaten, but the production of milk for cheese is the main purpose of the latter two (see page 217). After pork, seafood is the next most important source of protein. The seas around Calabria and Sicily teem with fish, particularly tuna and swordfish. From springtime to the end of summer, the entire south-west coastline is involved in swordfish fishing, using long boats called *lontre*, especially constructed for harpooning. A lookout sits on top of the main mast (about 7 metres high) and shouts out to the harpoonist, who stands on an extended bridge at the prow of the boat, ready to shoot his deadly weapon. Apparently the fish swim in pairs and swordfish hunters choose to kill the female first. This means that they can grab the male as well, as he, rather than escaping,

continues to swim around the same area, searching for his missing mate. If the male is caught first, the female takes the sensible route rather than the romantic one and flees! There are endless swordfish recipes in Calabria, many of them shared with Sicily, and many showing Arabic influences in ingredients and combinations (with the addition of raisins, pine nuts and orange juice, for instance).

Tuna are caught between May and June in the Golfo di Sant'Eufemia, between Pizzo Calabro and Tropea. In Pizzo Calabro and Vibo Valentia preserving tuna in oil is a thriving industry. The roes are also salted and pressed to make *bottarga*. Other fish caught are bonito, mackerel, sardines and anchovies. A speciality of the opposite side of the region, from Ciro, near Crotone, is known as *mustica* or *rosamarina*. This is the young of anchovies and sardines – *neonato* or *bianchetti* – which is salted, dried and then preserved in olive oil with plenty of chilli. This extremely hot paste is spread on bread as an appetiser, and a generous drink is invariably needed!

Although Calabria is far south, it isn't a dry place lacking vegetation, far from it. When you travel though the region, with the exception of fields of golden wheat, everything appears green. One of the main crops is citrus fruit, and citrus orchards are everywhere, among them oranges, lemons, citrons and bergamot oranges. The latter is bitter, and its oil is extracted for use in the food and drink industry – the flavouring of Earl Grey tea, for example. Both the rinds of the bergamot orange and the *cedro* or citron, a quince-shaped lemon, are preserved – mostly candied – for use in desserts, which are similar to those of Sicily.

On every piece of ground that is accessible in Calabria vegetables are cultivated. Broccoli grows well here (hence its other name, calabrese), as do potatoes, cherry tomatoes (there is a dried tomato industry), and celery. The principal vegetable of the region is aubergine (another influence from Sicily), and there is a wealth of recipes involving the vegetable – the Calabrese version of *parmigiana di melanzane* is very special indeed. Perhaps the best-known vegetable, though, is the red onion from Tropea, so sweet it can almost be eaten raw like an apple. It is either kept until mature, or eaten younger, as *cipollotti*, when it resembles a rather large spring onion.

In the mountains, and particularly on the high plains of Sila in the north, there are chestnuts and many wild fungi. Sila, an area of trees and lakes rather similar to Switzerland, boasts two varieties of porcini, black and white truffles, and saffron milkcaps, known here as *sanguinello* or *fungo sanguigno* because of the reddish tinge of the milk. And around Saracena in Aspromonte to the south, mushrooms are cultivated in a type of tuff stone, which is porous and, if kept moist, acts as a good basis for fungal spores. There is even some rice grown in the centre of the region, watered, I presume, by the rivers coming down from the mountains. And one of the most unusual crops is liquorice, a legume like a purple-flowered bean. It is the roots that are used, and in Italy they sell little batons of these for children to chew. Although grown mainly for use in confectionery, the Calabrese also make a delicious liqueur from the plant, called Liquirizia. Another prolific crop in Calabria is the fig, which is eaten fresh or dried – sometimes baked with orange blossom honey, or stuffed with walnuts, or enveloped in citron, orange or chestnut leaves. There are not many sweet things, but the Calabrese love biscuits cooked with *vino cotto* and with cinnamon (an Arabic influence). They eat these on special occasions.

Festivals take place throughout the year in Calabria. In February, sausages – *salsiccie* and *polpette* – are celebrated in Castrovillari and Acri. *Prosciutto* and '*nduja* are revered later, in August, in Aireta and Spilinga respectively. March sees a festival of oils and essences in Reggio di Calabria, and of oranges in Trebisacce in May. *Pesce azzurro* (blue-skinned fish) and the famous red onion are both honoured in July in Tropea, and the entire Calabrian cuisine is celebrated in Crotone in September. October welcomes wild chestnuts in Acri, Cellara and Bianchi, and wild mushrooms in Camigliatello and Silo.

Brodo Pieno 'Full broth'

A valuable soup for a chilly evening, which is hardly the norm in Calabria, (except in Sila), but then people living in warmer climes have a different interpretation of cold! Wherever you are, it's the perfect dish when you want to warm up in a gentle way.

SERVES 4

800 ml very good chicken or vegetable stock (pages 250–1)
3 eggs, beaten
4 tbsp fresh fine breadcrumbs
2 tbsp finely chopped flat-leaf parsley
pinch of freshly grated nutmeg
6 tbsp Parmesan or mature pecorino cheese, finely grated
salt and pepper

Bring the stock to the boil in a pan.

Mix the eggs with the breadcrumbs, parsley, nutmeg, cheese and salt and pepper to taste.

Drop teaspoonfuls of this mixture into the boiling broth. Simmer until they rise to the surface, then serve. The soup is quite delicious.

Cipolle di Tropea e Pecorino

Baked red onions stuffed with pecorino

The onions of Tropea can be eaten raw in salads, or cooked. I decided to cook them with pecorino here, combining two wonderful Calabrian ingredients.

SERVES 4

4 large Tropea onions (or equivalent)
salt and pepper
4 tbsp olive oil, plus extra to drizzle
50 g smoked pancetta, very finely chopped
100 g fresh, young pecorino cheese, diced

Heat the oven to 200°C/Gas 6. Peel off the papery onion skins. Cut a slice off the top of each onion to reveal all the inner circles, then, using a melon baller, excavate everything apart from the 3 or 4 outer layers, leaving an onion casing; reserve the flesh. Boil the onion casings in salted water for 10–12 minutes. Drain and cool.

Meanwhile, chop the excavated onion flesh finely. Fry in the olive oil with the pancetta and lots of black pepper until soft.

Mix the fried onions with the diced cheese and use to fill the onion cavities. Stand the onions in a baking dish, drizzle with olive oil and bake for 20 minutes. Serve as a starter.

REGIONAL PRODUCTS

PORK PRODUCTS Salami, *capocolli* (preserved pig shoulder), ham, *soppressate* (short, coarse salami, thought by some to be best here), and various other preserved meats are found in Calabria. Most are still artisan products, rather than made on an industrial scale, and all are flavoured to some extent with spices, primarily chilli and fennel seeds. The fresh *salsiccie calabresi* are excellent. One unusual speciality is *'nduja* or *'ndugghia*, which is a soft, fierce and fiery salami mix of pork offal and fat, red peppers and chilli peppers, aged a little in a skin. It is spread on bread and eaten as a snack, or as part of the southern Calabrian version of antipasto, *il piattino* (little plate). It can also be used as part of a sauce for pasta or in a *battuto*, the basic flavouring for stews.

CHEESES Sheep's milk pecorino is Calabria's main cheese, and that from Crotone is reputed to be the best. Caciocavallo is a cow's milk cheese – named after the horse because the cheeses are hung in pairs astride a pole, as if riding. It is eaten young or grated when mature. A salted ricotta called abbespata comes from Sila and Crotone, and is usually grated. Ricotta calabrese condita is a variation on ricotta, with salt and chilli added before drying to give it a *piccante* flavour. Also from Sila is giuncata, the name coming from *giunco*, a bendable reed, which is used to make little cheese-draining baskets. Butirro is a strange cheese shaped like scamorza with a caciocavallo-like layered exterior enclosing a centre of butter. In fact it was 'invented' as a way of preserving butter in the hot south, and is also made in Basilicata. Some buffalo mozzarella is also produced in Calabria.

WINES The most famous wine of Calabria is Cirò DOC, and it has been around since the time of Ancient Greece. It was once known as Cremissa, and was served, so they say, to Olympic winners. The best is the red, made from the Gaglioppo grape, with Trebbiano Toscano and Greco Bianco; there is also a rosé and a white, the latter made from Greco Bianco and Trebbiano Toscano grapes. A white wine, Greco di Bianco DOC, is made from the Greco grape and comes from Bianco, in the south, where it is grown on low terraces overlooking the sea. It is a *passito* wine – made from dried or semi-dried grapes – so it is quite strong and sweet. Chardonnay and Cabernet grapes have recently been introduced to the region.

Insalata di Bosco Silano Salad from the Sila woods

The best porcini and truffles come from Sila, the high plain of Calabria, which resembles Switzerland. As I am passionate about the world of wild fungi, I dedicate this recipe to all the mycophiles of the world.

SERVES 4

10 of the finest fresh porcini or ceps, young and solid
5 black summer truffles, about 100 g in total, peeled thinly
6 tbsp extra virgin olive oil
juice of 1 lemon
salt and pepper
3 tbsp finely chopped flat-leaf parsley
lemon wedges to serve

Make sure the porcini are impeccable, with no larvae inside. Clean them and slice them very thinly. Arrange the porcini slices on individual serving plates in a flat circle, leaving a space in the middle.

Cut the truffles very thinly, and use these slices to cover the centre of each plate. Mix the olive oil with the lemon juice and brush gently on to each slice. Sprinkle with salt and pepper and finally scatter over the chopped parsley.

Serve the mushroom salad with lemon wedges. Toasted bread and good wine are ideal accompaniments.

Linguine alla Mollica

Linguine with anchovies, capers, olives and breadcrumbs

The Italian composer, Ruggero Leoncavallo, who wrote *I Pagliacci* among other operas, was very partial to this dish. It is traditionally eaten on Christmas Eve in Calabria.

SERVES 4

300 g *linguine* (also called *lingue di passero*)
salt and pepper
12 tbsp olive oil
60 g pitted black olives, chopped
2 small red chillies, finely chopped
1 tbsp salted capers, rinsed
6 anchovy fillets
60 g fresh breadcrumbs

Add the *linguine* to a large pan of boiling salted water and boil until *al dente*.

Meanwhile, heat half of the olive oil in a pan, add the olives, chillies, capers and anchovies, and heat, stirring to dissolve the anchovies. Drain the pasta as soon as it is ready and toss into this sauce.

At the same time, heat the rest of the olive oil in a large non-stick pan and fry the breadcrumbs until slightly brown.

Now mix the dressed pasta into the breadcrumbs. Fry for a few minutes, until a crust forms underneath. Invert on to a warm plate, so the crusted side is on top. Cut into portions with a knife and serve.

Pesce Spada a Ghiotta Braised swordfish

Calabria is the place in Italy to eat swordfish, and in Bagnara this recipe is common in both family homes and restaurants. In Calabria and Sicily, a *ghiotta* means 'extremely desirable to eat'. The fish is cooked in a rich tomato sauce, which you will find not only here, but also in Messina, on the other side of the 'pond'. The best part to use for this dish is the *ventresca*, the belly of this big fish.

SERVES 4

8 thin slices fresh swordfish, about 60 g each
4 tbsp olive oil
1 onion, finely chopped
500 g *polpa di pomodoro* or chunky passata
salt and pepper

Stuffing

5 tbsp fresh breadcrumbs
30 g salted capers, rinsed and chopped
50 g pitted black olives, chopped
2 tbsp olive oil
4 tbsp orange juice

To make the stuffing, mix all the ingredients together and season with pepper to taste.

Lay the slices of swordfish on a surface and divide the stuffing mixture between them. Roll up tightly to enclose the filling and secure with wooden cocktail sticks.

Heat 3 tbsp olive oil in a large frying pan, add the swordfish rolls and fry gently, turning carefully, until brown on all sides. Remove from the pan, and set aside.

Add a little more olive oil to the pan, and fry the onion until soft. Add the *polpa di pomodoro* and cook gently for 20 minutes. Season with salt and pepper to taste. Place the fish rolls in the sauce, and heat gently for 5 minutes to let the flavours mingle.

Serve the braised swordfish rolls at once. Green beans are a suitable accompaniment.

Other typical regional dishes

Capretto farcito Milk-fed goat, boned out, stuffed with pasta and sauce, and baked

Ciambrotta A stew based on peppers and aubergines, like ratatouille; a similar dish called *cianfotta* is found in Campania

Ghiotta della vigilia Fish, usually swordfish or *baccalà*, in a sauce of onions, raisins, capers, etc., its name coming from the Arabic *ghatta*; traditionally eaten on Christmas eve

Maccaruni di casa Homemade macaroni flavoured with a rich meat *ragù*, also known as *scivateddi infirrittati*

Mariola Thin omelette enriched with cheese, herbs, chilli and bread, cut into very small strips and served with a soup

Melanzane sott'olio Aubergine slices 'cooked' in a marinade of vinegar, then preserved in oil for use in antipasti

Parmigiana di melanzane Baked layered aubergine and mozzarella slices with tomato sauce. Hard-boiled eggs and small meatballs are sometimes added before baking

Pasta con l'uovo fritto Pasta abundantly flavoured with grated pecorino and *peperoncino*, served topped with fried eggs

Polpettoni in agrodolce Huge meatballs of minced veal and pork with egg, garlic and parsley, fried then baked with tomato purée diluted with *vino cotto*

Sardi arriganati Sardines (without heads) baked with oil, garlic, vinegar and oregano. Red mullet are cooked in the same way

Crucette di Fichi al Forno

Baked honey figs

Calabria holds many memories for me, not least the wonderful baked dried figs. They were called *crucette* (little crosses), because the figs were cut open and twisted together in pairs to make a little cross. I didn't have the patience for that, so here is the single version.

MAKES 30

juice of 2 oranges
3 tbsp honey
30 good quality large, soft dried figs
30 half walnuts or whole blanched almonds
30 small pieces tangerine, orange or citron peel

Put the orange juice in a pan and dilute with about 75 ml water. Add the honey and bring to the boil. Add the figs to the pan and cook gently for about 15 minutes until they begin to swell. Drain, reserving any liquor, and spread the figs out on a tray. Leave to dry for a day.

Heat the oven to 200°C/Gas 6. Make an incision in each fig, and insert a nut and a piece of tangerine, orange or citron peel in each slit. Close tightly and bake for about 25 minutes, until caramelised and brown.

At the end, I drizzle the reserved orange and honey syrup over... delicious.

Sicilia

Sicilian cooking is really quite unique, compared to the other Italian regions. Centuries of invasion have exposed the island to a variety of culinary influences, which have enriched the cuisine. Arab and Greek influences are significant and responsible for the introduction of olives, almonds and citrus fruits, for example. Pasta and vegetables form the basis of Sicilian cooking, and fish is more dominant than meat. Sweet things are popular, among them *cassata*, *cannoli*, sorbets and ice-creams.

Sicily is the largest island in the Mediterranean (closely followed by its northern neighbour, Sardinia) and the 'football' at the 'toe' of the Italian 'boot'. Its position, central in the Mediterranean and close to Africa, has made the island irresistible to a succession of invaders over the centuries, among them the Phoenicians, Carthaginians, Greeks, Arabs, Spanish, Normans and French, and of course many mainland Italians, including the Etruscans and Romans. Sicily was once considered so important strategically and geographically that large swathes of Italy and other parts of Europe were governed from here.

Sicilian cooking has benefited from this long multi-ethnicity. That the basis of the cuisine is vegetables and fish is due to the Greeks, who introduced olives and vines, while the Normans (originally from Scandinavia) brought *baccalà* (salted and dried cod) and *stoccafisso* (dried cod), and taught the Sicilians how to bake. The primary influence, though, was that of the Arabs, who came from Muslim Spain and from North Africa, and who stayed for centuries. They introduced lamb and goats (suited to drier terrain), and taught the Sicilians how to make cheese and to preserve and dry foodstuffs (raisins and sultanas from grapes, for instance). They cultivated new vegetables and fruits, and were said to be responsible for introducing the concept of pasta. Inevitably the conquering rulers and rich landowners who lived in cities, such as Palermo and Syracuse, ate a sophisticated diet, while the peasants who worked the land had to make do with what they could get – *cucina povera.*

Sicily may be separated from mainland Italy by the narrowest of straits, that of Messina, but it has a style of cooking of its own. There has been talk for many years of a bridge to conjoin Calabria and Sicily (prevarication is typical of Italian politics), but I'm sure that Sicily's cuisine will remain unique even if the bridge were to become a reality.

Pasta lies at the heart of Sicilian cooking today, and it was from here that pasta was to spread all over southern Italy, then to the north, then to the rest of the world. Macaroni and *vermicelli* were the first shapes, but *anelli* or *anellini* (ring-shaped pastas), also became popular. These are still used to make the Sicilian version of pasta pie, *pasticcio* or *pasticciata*, but they are seldom found elsewhere in Italy. Other Sicilian pasta dishes are sauced mainly with fish and vegetables, brought together in such a way that they can become quite rich. *Pasta con le sarde*, a speciality of the capital, Palermo, is a richly flavoured dish of short tubular pasta, fresh sardines and wild local fennel, generally with pine nuts and sultanas added. Herbs lend flavour to many pasta sauces, mostly fresh ones, except oregano – one of the few herbs that is improved by drying (shown above). Pasta, usually a longer type, is also served with a sauce of tuna, another Sicilian fish (as it is in Calabria), often with an added chilli kick. Another pasta dish common to both regions is *con la mollica* or *muddica* – fish and pasta with a final sprinkling of fresh breadcrumbs mixed with garlic, parsley and olive oil.

The local durum wheat used to make pasta is also used to make bread, which Sicilians are very fond of, and couscous – an introduction from North Africa. The semolina *cuscusu* in Sicily is flavoured with saffron, and accompanies a fish stew. Rice was also once grown here, when Sicily wasn't as dry as it is today, and a couple of notable rice dishes date back to that time. In Catania, the province and town overshadowed by Mount Etna, you'll find *ripiddu nivicatu* (black risotto), which is served shaped like the volcano itself, topped with ricotta (the snow) and with a streak of chilli sauce down the side! *Arancini*, or fried rice balls are eaten all over Italy, but they originated here. These are now eaten hot or cold in the hand – as a 'fast food' whenever hunger strikes. This type of eating, known as *tavola calda*, has become a characteristic of the Sicilian way of eating.

The seas around Sicily – the Ionian, Tyrrhenian and Mediterranean – are rich with fish, primarily tuna, swordfish and sardines. These are eaten both fresh and preserved. Swordfish are harpooned in the waters between Calabria and Sicily, and thin slices are rolled around a stuffing to make *involtini di pesce spada*, which are either grilled or simmered in a tomato sauce. Swordfish steaks are grilled, as are *spiedini* (skewered chunks of fish), and both are often served with *salmoriglio*, a sauce of olive oil, lemon juice, herbs and garlic. Swordfish is also eaten raw in thin slices as *carpaccio*, and smoked. Tuna is caught, mainly around Mazara del Vallo, a fishing port on the north-west coast. It is prepared like swordfish, and the fish is also smoked, *mosciame*, as in Sardinia. But it is the sardine that is truly celebrated here. *Sardine alla beccafico*, or *sarde a beccaficu* (sardines like 'fig-peckers') is a famous dish of baked, rolled sardines with their tails in the air, to resemble little birds. Sardines are also stuffed with raisins and pine nuts, baked and sprinkled with orange juice at the end. Other seafood found here includes *branzino* or *spigola* (sea bass), sea urchins and octopus, which are sold freshly cooked in the Vucceria market in Palermo.

Canning sardines and tuna are huge industries in Sicily, but there is another famous preserved fish – *bottarga*. Also associated with Sardinia, this air-dried and salted tuna or grey mullet roe is prepared and canned in Sicily (and Liguria). It is usually served in thin slices seasoned with lemon juice and olive oil as an appetiser, or crumbled over pasta or scrambled eggs. *Baccalà* and *stoccafisso* (known in Sicily as *pescestocco*) are linked to the production of natural salt from the province of Trapani, in the north-west of the island. Here huge purpose-built ponds or pans are used for the evaporation of seawater, to produce salt that may not be immaculately white, but is pure and full of minerals.

Meat isn't eaten a lot in Sicily, although it is used in meatballs and meat rolls (a good way of using the rather tough beef), and goat and lamb are made into stews. For special occasions *farsumagru* (see page 229) are made. Black pigs are bred in the Messina province and pork is made into fresh sausages and some hams and salami, notably *salame di Sant'Angelo di Brolo*, the chilli-flavoured *fellata* or *salame di San Marco*, and a *supprissatu*. Game is popular in the region, particularly rabbit, and in common with other southern regions, offal is loved. *Involtini*, little parcels of lamb offal known as *stigghiole*, are often made with the intestines of milk-fed lambs and grilled over charcoal. In the Vucceria market, in the centre of Palermo, they sell *milza* (spleen) that is charcoal-grilled, then sliced and fried with chilli, and served in a roll like a hot dog. Try it if you dare!

Although Sicily consists primarily of mountains, the soil is extraordinarily fertile and many fruits and vegetables flourish in the dry, bright heat. Some are intensively cultivated, primarily those introduced by the Arabs, such as aubergines and spinach. Other vegetables that are widely grown include garlic, broccoli (which means 'cauliflower' in Sicily), artichokes (including a special local one, the Spinosa di Palermo), carrots, onions, tomatoes, broad beans, celery and pumpkin. The most famous Sicilian vegetable recipe must be *caponata* (see page 230), which is entirely based on local ingredients, including capers. Those from Sicily and the nearby islands of Lipari and Pantelleria are the best in the world, and these are the capers you find salted in jars. Tomatoes in Sicily are made into a super-concentrate, *estratto* (or *strattu*) *di pomodoro*. Six times more concentrated than the usual tomato paste, this product is used to bolster the flavour of tomato sauces. Sicilian aubergine specialities include the well-known *parmigiana di melanzane* (see page 230). Wild vegetables are a speciality of the island too, and wild fennel, asparagus and fungi are used in many dishes.

A host of fruit and nut trees were introduced by the Arabs, among them apricots, all the citrus, figs, almonds, hazelnuts, walnuts and pistachios, as well as pine nuts and indeed sugar. Sicily is today famous for her orange and lemon trees (and produces some 90 per cent of Italy's lemons), and citrus fruit are used in many dishes, sweet and savoury. The rind is used too, candied in the way the Sicilians were taught by the Arabs, and used in the famous Sicilian *cassata*. There are two types of *cassata*. The original is a cake made with marzipan, ricotta and dried and candied fruit; the other version is an ice-cream based on the same ingredients. Once made only at Christmas time by nuns, *cassata* it is now enjoyed all year round. A smaller version, *cassatina*, is available in Sicilian bars and cafés.

The Arabs were credited with the creation of ice-cream, and there are romantic stories about snow from Etna being mixed with fruit pulp to make *granite* and sorbets. The concept spread all over Italy, particularly to Naples, and beyond. Indeed, it was a Sicilian, Procopio Coltelli, who introduced real ice-cream to France when he opened a shop in Paris in the early 17th century. The Café Procope is still there, and Italian ice-cream, particularly that of Sicily, is still considered to be the best.

Nuts feature in many Sicilian pastries and biscuits, especially almonds which are prolific all over the island. Marzipan, or what the Italians call *pasta di mandorla* or *pasta reale* (almond paste), is formed into coloured fruit and other shapes, one of the specialities of Sicily. These are still made by nuns, particularly in Palermo. The most famous pastry of the island, *cannoli alla siciliana* (see page 229), was originally made as a celebratory treat at *Carnevale*. Fruit and nuts figure in many other Sicilian dishes, including a magnificent honey made from lemon and orange blossom, and a *mostarda* based on prickly pears. Interestingly, Sicily is the only region able to grow pistachio nuts – in the rich soil at the foot of Etna. At Noto, in the Syracuse province, a pistachio paste is made, as well as *cedro* (citron) paste, quince paste and many ice-creams flavoured with flowers.

Sicily is full of wonderful things to see and do, and Sicilians like to eat well and celebrate. One of the most curious traditions is the San Giuseppe's Day celebration (in March), in the hilltop town of Salemi near Trapani. Every year, the locals adorn the church with hundreds of shapes – flowers, fruit, vegetables, saints, ladders, fish, etc. – all baked from bread dough ... it must take them ages! They also have a special meal, *La cena di San Giuseppe*. Otherwise, there are the usual sausage, ricotta, soft fruit, chestnut and wine festivals at appropriate times of the year. Less usually, in Agrigento, they have a *sagra del mandorlo in fiore* (almonds in flower festival) in February; a *sagra delle nespole* (loquat feast), in Trabis, Palermo, in May; an ice-cream feast in Noto, Syracuse, in August; and, in the same month, a *sagra* of couscous in San Vito in Capo, Trapani.

Other typical regional dishes

Arancini Rice balls, filled with a *ragù* of meat, or butter and cheese, then coated in breadcrumbs and deep-fried

Cannoli alla siciliana Tubes of special fried pastry, filled with ricotta cheese, candied fruit and chocolate

Cuscusu Couscous from Trapani, flavoured with seafood

Farsumagru A huge slice of beef stuffed with all sorts of goodies – ham, cheese, sausage, eggs, garlic, onion, etc. – and then rolled and braised or baked in a tomato sauce; the name literally translates as 'false lean'

Maccaruni di casa Handmade pasta similar to fusilli, traditionally served with a rich sauce of meatballs, sausage, chicken, salami and tomatoes, and topped with grated salted ricotta

Maccu Dried broad bean purée, eaten as a side dish, flavoured with olive oil

M'panata A sort of *calzone* stuffed with either cooked vegetables or meat and baked, named after the Spanish *empanada*

Pasta alla Norma Spaghetti dressed with tomato sauce and slices of fried aubergine, to honour Vincenzo Bellini, the composer of *Norma*

Pasta con le sarde Pasta dressed with wild fennel and fried sardines

Pesce spada a ghiotta Swordfish cooked with tomatoes, olives and capers, equally popular in Calabria (see page 220)

Sarde a beccafico Baked sardines stuffed with breadcrumbs, pine nuts, parsley, garlic and raisins

Caponatina di Melanzane Sicilian aubergine relish

This is one of Sicily's most popular and versatile aubergine dishes. You can eat it with bread, as part of an antipasto, or as a side dish with hot or cold meats or fish. This is the original recipe, from Palermo. A *caponatina* is a 'small' caponata. Ideally you want the pale violet type of aubergine, without too many seeds.

SERVES 4–6

600 g meaty aubergines
salt
6–8 tbsp olive oil
1 large onion, sliced
2 celery hearts (inner heads only), cut into little chunks
500 g ripe tomatoes, chopped
100 g pitted green olives
60 g salted capers, rinsed
100 g slivered almonds
2 ripe but firm pears, cored, peeled and sliced
1/2 tsp ground cinnamon
1/2 tsp ground cloves
50 g caster sugar
50 ml white wine vinegar

Cut the aubergines into cubes, the size of a walnut. Immerse in salted water for 1 hour, then drain, squeezing the water out. Pat the aubergine cubes dry.

Heat about 6 tbsp of the olive oil in a sauté pan and fry the aubergine cubes until golden. Scoop them out with a slotted spoon and set aside. Adding more oil to the pan if necessary, fry the onion until soft, then add all the other ingredients, apart from the sugar and vinegar. Simmer for about 20 minutes.

Add the aubergines to the mixture with the sugar and wine vinegar. Taste for salt and cook for another 10–15 minutes. *Caponata* can be eaten warm but it is also delicious cold.

Milinciani alla Parmigiana

Timbale of aubergines with Parmesan and tomato

Many people believe this simple recipe originates from Emilia-Romagna, but it was born in Sicily. It appears in various guises and is often simply called *parmigiana di melanzane*. Serve as a starter.

SERVES 6

3 large meaty aubergines
3 eggs, beaten
salt and pepper
flour to dust
olive oil for frying
15 basil leaves
250 g Parmesan, freshly grated
Sauce
1 garlic clove, finely chopped
5 tbsp olive oil
800 g *polpa di pomodoro* or chunky passata
4–5 basil leaves, torn

Cut the aubergines into 1 cm slices and immerse in cold water for 1 minute, then drain and pat dry. Season the eggs with salt.

Dust the aubergine slices with flour and then dip into the beaten egg. Heat a film of olive oil in a large frying pan and fry the aubergine slices until golden on each side. Drain on kitchen paper and set aside. Heat the oven to 200°C/Gas 6.

To make the sauce, fry the garlic in the olive oil, then add the tomato pulp and basil. Simmer for 15–20 minutes, then season with salt to taste.

To assemble the timbale, spread 2–3 tbsp of the tomato sauce over the bottom of a suitable baking dish. Cover with a layer of aubergine slices, some more sauce, a little basil and plenty of Parmesan. Repeat until the ingredients are used up, finishing with tomato sauce and Parmesan. Bake for 20 minutes until golden and bubbling. Leave to stand for 5 minutes or so, then serve cut into squares.

Panelle con Frittella Chickpea fritters

Panelle **are a speciality of Palermo, where the fritters are often eaten in a *panino* (roll). Here they are served with a fresh vegetable stew, comprising artichokes, peas and broad beans – the perfect Sicilian complement. When fresh peas and broad beans are not in season, you can use frozen ones.**

SERVES 4

Panelle

300 g chickpea flour

1 tsp aniseed

salt and pepper

3 tbsp coarsely chopped parsley

olive oil for frying

Frittella

4 tbsp olive oil

200 g onions, finely sliced

300 g fresh young and tender artichoke hearts, halved

275 g podded tender garden peas

300 g podded broad beans

3 tbsp chopped flat-leaf parsley

1 tbsp salted capers, rinsed

To make the *panelle*, in a saucepan, mix the chickpea flour with the aniseed, some salt and pepper and 500 ml water until smooth. Slowly bring to the boil, stirring, and cook, stirring, for 8–10 minutes until the mixture thickens, then mix in the parsley. Pour on to an oiled baking sheet or marble surface and flatten to a 1 cm thickness. Leave until cool and set.

In the meantime, prepare the *frittella*. Heat the olive oil in a large saucepan and fry the onions until soft. Add the artichoke hearts, peas, broad beans and about 100 ml water. Cover and cook for 15–20 minutes until all the vegetables are soft. Add the parsley and capers, and season with salt and pepper to taste.

Cut the set chickpea mixture into rounds or diamonds and shallow-fry in olive oil until golden on each side. Drain on kitchen paper, then serve the fritters with the vegetable stew.

Pasta n'Casciata Pasta timbale

This impressive pasta timbale contains tomato sauce, *polpette* or little rissoles, Parmesan, mozzarella or caciocavallo cheese, slices of salami, etc. It requires a fair amount of preparation, so I suggest you make it for a special occasion.

SERVES 8–10

Ragù

1 large onion, sliced
6 tbsp olive oil
150 g pancetta, diced
600 g minced beef
100 ml red wine
1 kg *polpa di pomodoro* or chunky passata
100 g podded fresh (or frozen) peas
5 basil leaves, torn
2 tbsp tomato purée
salt and pepper

Dumplings

200 g minced pork
200 g minced beef
1 garlic clove, chopped
2 eggs, beaten
2 tbsp chopped flat-leaf parsley
1 tbsp dry breadcrumbs
2 tbsp freshly grated Parmesan
olive oil for deep-frying

To assemble

1 kg *candele* or *ziti* (long and large *maccheroni*)
24 hard-boiled quail's eggs, shelled
280 g salami, sliced
200 g caciocavallo or provolone dolce cheese, sliced
20 g podded peas, briefly sautéed
6 eggs, beaten
200 g Parmesan, freshly grated

First make the *ragù*. Fry the onion in the olive oil for a few minutes, then add the pancetta and cook briefly. Add the minced meat and fry, stirring, to brown evenly. Add the wine and allow to evaporate, then add the tomato pulp, peas and basil. Dilute the tomato purée with 4 tbsp water and stir in. Cook very slowly for 2 hours. Season with salt and pepper to taste.

Heat the oven to 190°C/Gas 5. To make the dumplings, mix together the minced meats, garlic, eggs, parsley, breadcrumbs and Parmesan, and season with salt and pepper. Shape into dumplings, the size of large olives, with your hands. Heat the olive oil for deep-frying in a suitable pan and fry the dumplings until golden. Drain well on kitchen paper.

Add the pasta to a large pan of boiling salted water and cook for about 7–8 minutes; it must still be decidedly *al dente*. Drain thoroughly.

Line the inside of a deep ovenproof bowl, measuring about 25 cm across the rim, with some of the long pasta pieces. Toss the rest of the pasta with some of the *ragù*.

Layer the hard-boiled quail's eggs, salami, sliced cheese, peas, dumplings and pasta in *ragù* in the bowl. Finish with the *ragù* and pour the beaten eggs all over. Scatter the Parmesan on top, cover with foil and bake for 30 minutes. Then remove the foil and cook for another 30 minutes to form a crust.

Allow the timbale to stand for about 40 minutes before turning it out on to a plate. Cut into wedges and serve.

REGIONAL PRODUCTS

Sicily's primary products are fruit and vegetables, but there are also some good cheeses and wines.

CHEESES Pecorino siciliano may not be as famed as the sardo, toscano and romano, but this sheep's milk cheese is delicious nonetheless. It can be eaten the day after it is made, when it is fresh, creamy and called *tuma*. As it ages, it becomes harder and stronger, until it can be grated. In the inland province of Enna, pecorino is made with the addition of whole black peppercorns and saffron, and is called *piacentinu* or *piacintinu*. Ricotta is made throughout the region, as a by-product of pecorino production. It comes fresh, as ricotta salata al sole (dried in the sun) and ricotta salata al forno (dried in the oven). Fresh ricotta is the mainstay of Sicilian desserts. Canestrato is a semi-cooked cow's and sheep's milk cheese, which is pressed by hand into a *canestro* (basket) to drain and assume a basket shape; it is eaten both fresh and matured. Caciocavallo is also made on the island.

BREAD AND BAKED GOODS Sicilian bread is heavier than elsewhere because it is made with durum wheat. *Guastedde* is a special bread roll, which is eaten with a variety of fillings, but famously with *milza* (fried spleen) – sold in the Vucceria market in Palermo. In Enna, there is a very pleasant and unusual focaccia, which is filled with salami. Hard and dry biscuits are made all over Sicily, for dipping into a sweet dessert wine, such as Moscato or Marsala (see below). They include *mustazzoli* (or *mostacciolo* elsewhere) and *tarallo* (also *taralluccio* or *tarallino*).

WINES Cool climates are said to be better for white wines, hotter areas for reds, but Sicily has turned that on its head, being best known for her crisp whites, grown mostly on the west of the island. Names like Alcamo, Corvo, Etna, Regaliali, Terre di Ginestra, Vigna Gabri and others are associated with both whites and reds. The island is most famous for its fortified wine, Marsala, of which there are several types and colours (including Vecchio Samperi and Joséphine Doré). *Passito* wines, made from dried and semi-dried grapes, are perfect with Sicilian pastries. The best known come from the neighbouring small islands – Malvasia from Lipari, and Moscato from Pantelleria.

Coniglio alla Partuisa Stewed rabbit from Ragusa

Rabbit is popular all over Italy, but the origin of this Sicilian dish lies in the cuisine of Iberia. You can use farmed rabbit, although a wild one would give a better flavour.

SERVES 4

1 rabbit (wild is best), about 1.2 kg, cleaned
flour to dust
6 tbsp olive oil
1 onion, finely chopped
2 garlic cloves, finely chopped
2 tbsp tomato purée
4 tbsp white wine vinegar
100 g pitted green olives, chopped if large
100 ml white wine
1 celery heart, finely diced
1 tbsp salted capers, rinsed
salt and pepper
2 tbsp chopped flat-leaf parsley

Cut the rabbit into chunks, discarding some of the bones, and dust with flour. Heat the olive oil in a pan and fry the rabbit until browned on all sides. Add the onion and garlic, and cook for a few more minutes.

Dilute the tomato purée with about 6 tbsp water and add to the pan with the wine vinegar. Stir, then cook for 15 minutes. Add the olives, wine, celery and capers, and season with salt and pepper. Cover and cook slowly for a further 30 minutes until the rabbit is tender, adding more water if needed.

Sprinkle with parsley and serve with polenta, *spätzle* (page 48), or puréed, boiled potatoes and spinach.

Insalata di Limoni e Arance

Orange and lemon salad

The Sicilians have a penchant for including citrus fruit in savoury salads. This salad is made with those lemons that have a very thick skin rather like *cedri* (citrons), and these have less acidity than normal lemons. The use of blood oranges in season makes the dish very special, and it will accompany pork and veal roasts wonderfully.

SERVES 4

- **2 large oranges**
- **4 thick-skinned lemons**
- **salt and pepper**
- **handful of feathery fennel leaves, or celery leaves**
- **2 tbsp olive oil**

Using a very sharp knife, peel the oranges and lemons, removing every bit of white pith, as well as the rind.

Cut the fruit into slices and arrange decoratively on a plate. Add salt and pepper to taste and scatter over the fennel or celery leaves. Drizzle with the olive oil.

Cassata Semifredda Sicilian ice-cream

This is the easier ice-cream and candied fruit version of *cassata*, as opposed to the elaborate, rich sponge, which is more time-consuming. My former head chef, Andrea Cavaliere perfected this *cassata* recipe – it is a *semifreddo*, with a superb soft texture.

SERVES 8–10

- **200 g egg whites (about 4)**
- **70 g caster sugar**
- **100 g ricotta cheese (best quality)**
- **20ml milk (plus a little extra to soften ricotta if needed)**
- **400 ml double cream**
- **100 g thin honey, warmed**
- **100 g mixed candied citron and orange peel, chopped**
- **50 g pine nuts, toasted**
- **50 g dark, bitter chocolate, chopped**
- **80 g skinned pistachio nuts**
- **8–10 red candied cherries**

Whisk the egg whites until stiff, then gradually whisk in 50 g of the sugar. In another bowl, fluff the ricotta with a fork, adding a little milk to soften if it is too firm. Whip the double cream in another bowl until thick.

Fold the honey into the whisked egg whites, followed by the whipped cream and ricotta. Then fold in the chopped candied peel, pine nuts and chocolate. Spoon into a 1.2 litre bowl or bombe mould, cover and chill in the freezer for 12 hours.

Before serving, whiz the pistachio nuts with the remaining 20 g sugar and 20 ml milk in a blender to make a sauce.

To unmould, dip the bowl into hot water for a few seconds to release the *cassata* then turn out on to a plate. Cut into wedges, using a warm knife.

Put a little pistachio sauce on each plate, lay a wedge of *cassata* in the centre, decorate with a cherry and serve.

SARDEGNA

Sardinia, the second largest island in the Mediterranean, has one of the most insular regional cuisines in the whole of Italy. It has developed slowly over the centuries, stemming from waves of invasion and rule by outsiders. Sheep are vital to the economy and pecorino cheese is an important product. Inland, all kinds of game and lamb, pork and kid are eaten, while around the coastline, the emphasis is on fish and seafood.

Sardinia and its people are beautiful, mysterious, unbowed, but full of pride, and somehow shy... reminding me of a wild horse galloping freely. To generalise, you could say that Sardinians are reserved and seem to get on with life without expecting anything from anybody. The origins of this trait lie in the distant past, and remnants can be seen today in the *nuraghe*, ancient tower-like buildings, used to house cattle and artefacts; they are even used as tombs. Found mostly in the north of the island, these impressive constructions (reminiscent of the *trulli* of Puglia) are built of huge chunks of granite and display construction techniques of a culturally advanced society, although little is known about their builders.

Since then Sardinia has been ruled by many nations and civilisations, which have left tangible influences on food as well as language and life. The Phoenicians, Carthaginians and Romans controlled the island at various times. Incursions by the Spaniards and other Italians followed, leaving their traces. The Byzantines, for instance, are thought to have introduced cheese, and the Arabs brought rice and almond pastries. The Arabs who came were mainly from mainland and Muslim Spain, and even today the names of various dishes are typically Catalan, while in the north of the island, some of the coastal dialects have Piedmontese, Genoan, Pisan and Sicilian traces.

If the history of Sardinia has a mixed ancestry, so too do the natives. The original inhabitants fled to the interior, leaving the coastline to the invaders over the centuries, and as a consequence the language and customs of the two are divergent. Many original Sardinians became shepherds – even today a third of Italy's sheep are pastured on the island. There is also a dual identity to the cooking: the most traditional Sardinian food is based on ingredients from the land, while fish is eaten more by the incomers. It has even been said that true Sardinians don't care for the sea or seafood at all!

Sardinia has changed enormously over the last 50 years or so, as it has discovered tourism – or vice versa. The north coast of the island, in the province of Sassari, is where the most beautiful gold to reddish beaches are, lined by pink granite rocks eroded by wind and sea into the most fantastic shapes. The sea between Sardinia and Corsica is crystal clear, its colour ranging from deep blue to emerald green, hence the name 'Costa Smeralda'. The Aga Khan has invested a great deal of money here, and the rich flock to the resorts and luxury villas, while the sea is home to many floating schooners and yachts from elsewhere in Europe.

CULINARY TRADITIONS & SPECIALITIES

No Italian meal would be served without bread, and in Sardinia there are said to be over 500 different types, reputedly one from every village. The most typical and famous perhaps is the paper-thin, crisp *pani carasau*, also known as *carta di musica*, supposedly because it rustles like music manuscript paper! This evolved as a food for the shepherds, because it lasted well in its dried form. They ate it softened with hot water and flavoured with thin slices of fresh pecorino as *suppas*. A richer version of today is the *pane frattau*, with the addition of eggs and tomatoes. Sardinia also boasts one of the largest loaves in Italy, the semolina-based *civraxiu*, which can weigh over 3.5 kg.

Although Sardinians generally prefer bread to pasta, the local wheat is also used in several original pasta-like dishes, learned from mainland Italy. The most ancient, possibly introduced by the Romans, is *fregula* or *fregola* – large semolina granules, rather like a rough couscous. Other well-known regional pasta dishes include Sardinian ravioli, called *culingiones* or *culurzones* (see page 243), and *malloreddus* (little bulls) or *gnocchetti sardi*, which are served with a rich meat *ragù* or simply with tomato sauce (see page 244). *Casca* is a local couscous-type dish, similar to

the Sicilian *cuscusu*, but with a more pronounced spice taste. Rice was introduced by the Arabs and is still grown on the island; there are a few typical rice dishes flavoured with the local saffron.

It is the main course of a Sardinian meal, though, that reveals the differences between customs and ingredients of the coastline and the interior. Hearty meat-eating is characteristic inland, and lamb, pork, kid, wild boar and many other game animals and birds are eaten. They are typically roasted or grilled, or boiled and marinated, or made into a *ragù* for pasta. Meats were once roasted by shepherds in covered pits – *caraxiu* – a technique said to have been devised by poachers to avoid detection during cooking! This is a unique Sardinian way of cooking larger animals. A big hole is dug in the earth and lined with aromatic wood such as oak. A fire is lit and when it is glowing charcoal and cooled a little, it is covered with branches of myrtle. The prepared animal is then lowered on to this bed and covered with more myrtle, rosemary and other wild herbs. Earth is spread on top, and a huge bonfire lit on top of that. After a few hours the animal is ready to be eaten and relished by the local community. Nowadays, spits are used, and the most famous dish is *porceddu* (roast suckling pig), a speciality of the Barbagia. Once, while visiting shepherds in the mountains of the Barbagia, I saw how to baste a roasting pig with a piece of lard that had been set alight, dropping hot fat on to the meat as it melted.

Around the coastline, though, it is quite different. The present-day Sardinian fishermen are descended from Genoese, Neapolitan, Sicilian, Arab and Spanish settlers, and coastal dishes reflect this. The famous fish stew of Sardinia, *burrida*, for example, is related to the Genoese *buridda*; a similar fish soup, *cassola*, is linked to the original Spanish *cazuela*. And there is a wealth of recipes using all the Mediterranean fish available, including swordfish, tuna, sardines, octopus, squid, cuttlefish, clams, mussels and, perhaps less familiarly, sea anemones, sea urchins and sea dates. Lobster has become a speciality and Sardinia is one of the few places in Italy where it is common. Eel is eaten here too, as is the deep-sea *cernia* or grouper. Tuna are caught and eaten fresh, or preserved in oil in jars and cans, or air-dried to make a local speciality, *mosciame*.

Buttarica e Uova Salted mullet roe and scrambled eggs

Both mullet and tuna roe are cured in salt and air-dried to make *bottarga*, an expensive speciality in Sicilia and Calabria, as well as Sardinia. The eggs of mullet are more delicate than those of tuna and usually the *bottarga* is sliced on to food, as it is here.

SERVES 4

12 eggs, beaten
2 tbsp finely chopped parsley
1 tbsp mascarpone or thick double cream
salt and pepper
2 tbsp olive oil
100 g mullet *bottarga*, cut in thin slices

Beat the eggs in a bowl and fold in the parsley and mascarpone or cream. Season with pepper and just a little salt (as the *bottarga* will be salty).

Heat the olive oil in a pan over a low heat and pour in the egg mixture. Stir constantly until the mixture start to thicken, then remove from the heat and stir a little bit more until the eggs are softly scrambled and creamy.

Divide the scrambled eggs between warm plates and sprinkle with the slices of *bottarga*. Eat with bread.

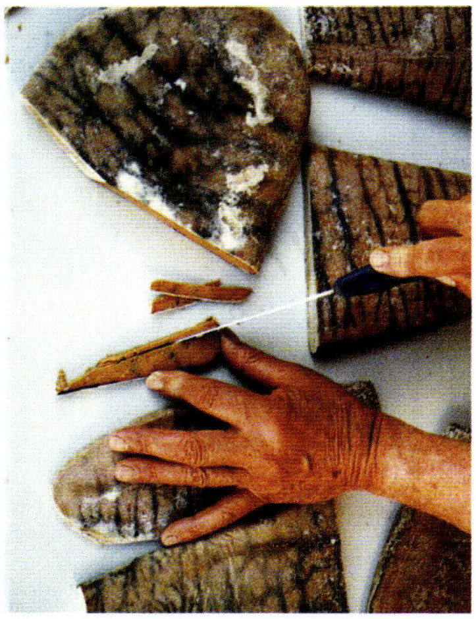

The most characteristic flavour of Sardinian antipasti, though, is probably that of *bottarga* or *buttariga*, the salted and pressed roes of grey mullet or tuna (shown left). The technique may have been learned from the Sicilians, but, the Sardinian version is now considered the best. *Bottarga* is sliced very thinly and served with olive oil and lemon juice as a starter; it is also grated over pasta, rice and scrambled egg (see above). Mullet fillets are also salted and preserved with samphire.

Sardinia is rich in vegetables and fruit. The prime garden produce are the *carciofo di Sardegna*, an artichoke that grows around the towns of Samassi, Serramanna, Oristano, Ittiri and Valledoria, and the *pomodoro di Sardegna* in the Campidano. The olive oil from Cagliari is excellent, and honey is available in the mountains to the centre and north. Vines are planted all over the island, and fruit and nut orchards abound, among them peaches, almonds and oranges. Wild foods feature in the cooking as well, particularly chestnuts, figs, prickly pears, fungi and fennel. The most significant flavouring – myrtle – is also wild, and its use in cooking is virtually unique to Sardinia. The bush grows wild all over the island, and the highly aromatic leaves are wrapped around meats, or cooked together with them; they also form part of the covering of a traditional *caraxiu* (see page 241). Saffron is another characteristic Sardinian flavouring (see page 248). And to season all, natural sea salt is produced near Cagliari, in special pans used for the evaporation of seawater.

Pastries are a tradition in Sardinia, again introduced by the Arabs, and they make good use of almonds and local flavourings such as vanilla, saffron and honey. An island speciality is *sebadas, seadas* or *ravioli fritti sardi con miele*, which are little fried pecorino pastries, served with honey (see page 249). *Anicini* (sweet anise biscuits) may have originated in Umbria, but they are famous here, typically eaten dipped into the local strong red dessert wine, Monica di Sardegna.

The Sardinians are proud of their wine, and there are celebrations everywhere in the month of September – in Calasetta, Magomadas, Monti, Tempio and Villasalto. Monserrato also celebrates sweets at the same time, as does Quartu Sant'Elena in October, with an exhibition of grapes, breads and sweets. Earlier in the year, at Uri in March, they honour the triple combination of artichokes, olive oil and wine – very Sardinian, indeed very Italian!

Culurzones Sardinian ravioli

***Culurzones* or *culingiones* are best described as a sort of plaited ravioli, and they are stuffed with various different fillings in Sardinia. I like this version with potatoes, mint and plenty of cheese. Spinach, eggs and pecorino is another popular filling, and sometimes the *culurzones* are served with a meat or tomato *ragù*.**

SERVES 4

Pasta dough

300 g Italian '00' flour
1 egg yolk

Filling

800 g boiled potatoes, drained
200 g fresh pecorino cheese
50 g mature pecorino cheese
120 g Parmesan, freshly grated
3 tbsp olive oil
3 tbsp chopped mint leaves
pepper

To serve

salt
50 g butter
8–10 sage leaves, shredded
10 saffron strands, steeped in 1 tbsp warm water
freshly grated pecorino or Parmesan

For the filling, mash the potatoes smoothly in a bowl. Crumble in the fresh pecorino and grate in the mature pecorino. Add the Parmesan, olive oil, chopped mint and pepper to taste. (No salt because of the cheese.) Mix thoroughly and set aside.

To make the pasta dough, mix the flour, egg yolk and 120 ml water together to obtain a smooth dough. Cover and set aside to rest for 20–30 minutes.

Roll out the pasta on a floured surface to a 2 mm thickness and cut out 10 cm rounds. Re-roll the pasta trimmings and cut more rounds.

Fill and shape the ravioli one by one. Place a small ball of the filling (the size of a small cherry) in the middle of a pasta round. Starting at the front edge, lift this on to the filling, covering half of it. With the other hand, now lift the lower left side of the pasta over the filling, then the lower right. Repeat folding in left and right again. You should obtain a sort of plaited ravioli, and then you just squeeze the top together to seal. Repeat with the rest of the dough and filling.

When you are ready to cook, bring a large pan of salted water to the boil. Add the *culurzones* and cook for 6–8 minutes.

In the meantime, heat the butter, sage and saffron in a pan until the butter is melted. Drain the pasta and toss with the flavoured butter. Serve sprinkled with pecorino or Parmesan.

Malloreddus Little bulls

Don't worry, this is the name of a specific pasta shape, and has nothing to do with the real animal. *Malloreddus* come in many different sizes, and I have chosen to use a minimal one here. It is also called *gnocchetti sardi* and is often flavoured with saffron, which is cultivated on Sardinia.

SERVES 4

2 garlic cloves, finely chopped
6 tbsp olive oil
1–2 red chillies (optional, but recommended), chopped
500 g cherry tomatoes, halved
100 g *polpa di pomodoro* or chunky passata
5 basil leaves, torn, plus extra to garnish
salt and pepper
300 g small *malloreddus* pasta (or other saffron pasta)
100 g pecorino cheese, grated

Put the garlic in a pan with the olive oil, and chilli if using, and fry for a few minutes. Add the fresh tomatoes and tomato pulp. Stir briefly to amalgamate, bring to a simmer and cook gently for 15–20 minutes. Add the basil and season with salt and pepper to taste.

Meanwhile, cook the pasta in a large pan of boiling salted water until *al dente*. Drain and toss with the sauce. Serve generously covered with grated pecorino and scattered with a few basil leaves ... delicious.

Quaglie Arrosto Roasted quail

Sardinians are fine hunters and birds of all kinds and sizes are traditionally cooked either at home in the oven or outdoors on a spit. Quail is now a protected bird, so you will need to use farmed quail for this very easy recipe.

SERVES 4

8 quail, cleaned and oven-ready
flour to dust
50 g butter
50 ml olive oil
1 large onion, finely chopped
100 ml dry Vernaccia or other dry white wine
100 ml chicken stock (page 250)
1 rosemary sprig
6 sage leaves
salt and pepper
freshly grated nutmeg

Heat the oven to 190°C/Gas 5. Dust the quail with flour. Heat the butter and olive oil in a heavy-based pan and brown the quail for about 30 seconds on each side. Transfer to a roasting pan. Add the onion to the frying pan and fry, stirring, over a medium heat until softened, then add to the quail.

Pour the wine and stock over the quail and add the rosemary, sage, and some salt and pepper. Cook in the oven for 20 minutes, then transfer the quail to a warm dish and set aside.

Discard the herbs and pass the cooking liquor through a sieve into a pan. Reheat, add a little nutmeg and check the seasoning. Pour over the quail and serve.

Sardinian's would eat just bread with this, but you may prefer to serve it with a green salad or some peas and broad beans tossed in butter with a little grated pecorino cheese.

Pernice alla Sarda Partridge Sardinian style

When I was in Sardinia I couldn't believe the luxury of eating partridges this way, cold. They prepare thrushes in a similar way, marinating the cooked birds with myrtle leaves and salt for a few days before eating them. This is hunters' food in Sardinia, but you should be able to buy partridges from your butcher during the game season, or you could, at a pinch, use quail instead. Serve as a little antipasto or snack.

SERVES 4–6

- **1 litre chicken or vegetable stock (pages 250–1)**
- **4 partridges, cleaned**
- **8 tbsp extra virgin olive oil**
- **4 tbsp white wine vinegar**
- **3 tbsp coarsely chopped flat-leaf parsley**
- **3 tbsp salted capers, rinsed and chopped**
- **few rosemary sprigs**
- **salt and pepper**

Bring the stock to the boil in a large cooking pot, add the partridges and simmer for 25 minutes until tender. Drain and allow to cool, then quarter the birds.

Mix the olive oil, wine vinegar, parsley and capers together in a shallow dish and add the rosemary sprigs. Add the cold partridge pieces and turn to coat with the mixture. Cover and leave to marinate in the fridge for at least 6 hours before eating, turning the birds occasionally.

Season the partridge pieces as you eat them, with your hands naturally. The traditional accompaniment is *carta da musica*, the thin Sardinian bread made more crispy in the oven and sprinkled with the oil of the marinade.

Risotto alla Sarda Sardinian risotto

This tasty pork, veal and tomato risotto is flavoured with Sardinia's prized saffron. This was a surprise risotto for me, but it's excellent.

SERVES 4

- **about 800 ml beef stock (page 250)**
- **6 tbsp olive oil**
- **1 small onion, finely chopped**
- **150 g lean minced pork**
- **150 g lean minced veal**
- **300 g risotto rice**
- **3 tbsp red dry wine**
- **200 g *polpa di pomodoro* or chunky passata**
- **pinch of saffron strands**
- **salt and pepper**
- **40 g butter**
- **60 g mature Pecorino cheese, freshly grated**

Put the stock in a pan on the hob and bring to a simmer; keep it at simmering point.

Heat the olive oil in a flameproof casserole or heavy-based pan, add the onion and fry until soft. Add the minced pork and veal, and fry, stirring from time to time, until it is browned and cooked.

Add the rice and stir for a minute or two, then add the wine and let the alcohol evaporate. Add the tomato pulp, saffron and a ladleful of the stock. Stir continuously over the heat, adding stock a ladleful at a time as each addition is absorbed. After 15 minutes, check for the required texture: the rice should be tender, but with a firm bite in the centre, and the risotto should be moist. Taste for seasoning.

When ready take off the heat, mix in the butter and serve, sprinkled with grated pecorino.

REGIONAL PRODUCTS

CHEESE Sardinia's most famous cheese is its ewe's milk pecorino, which comes in several forms – fresh, salted, drained as canestrato etc. Fiore sardo or cacio fiore is a semi-hard cheese from the central part of Sardinia. Pecorino sardo is made all over the island and is smaller than the pecorino romano, supposedly of Lazio but also produced in the Sardinian provinces of Cagliari, Sassari and Nuoro. Goat's cheeses are also made, and the caprino is aged as well as eaten fresh.

SAFFRON This is a major crop on the south of the island, and 19 of the 25 acres cultivated nationally are here in San Gavino Monreale. In my opinion, Sardinian saffron, with its long, dark and very scented pistils, is the best in the world.

WINE AND OTHER DRINKS Sardinians have been making wine for thousands of years, and the majority of vines in Sardinia are distinctive from those found in other regions of Italy. In fact, some of the varieties, such as Cannonau (Spain's Garnacha) and Torbato, are virtually extinct in the Iberian peninsula, their place of origin. The wines are excellent, starting with the white (really straw yellow) Vermentino di Gallura from the north, the only wine to have the accolade of DOCG and ideal with fish. Other whites are Vernaccia di Oristano (sherry like, made rather like Marsala), Nuragus di Cagliari, Malvasia di Bosa and di Cagliari, and several Moscato wines. The reds are dominated by the Cannonau grape, and the Cannonau di Sardegna is eminently drinkable, available dry, medium and sweet. There is also a Cannonau *passito* wine, Anghelu Ruju. Carignano del Sulcis is another red made from a Spanish grape, Carignan. A *sapa*, the Sardinian equivalent of *saba*, is made from grapes, and there is also a fine myrtle liqueur, Mirto. Filu di Ferru is a good grappa.

Other typical regional dishes

Angiulottus Ravioli, filled with meat or ricotta, or other cheese, served with tomato sauce

Aranzada Candied orange peel mixed with toasted almonds in the shape of a *torrone*, a speciality of Nuoro

Arrosto a caraxiu Meat roasted in a hole in the ground, flavoured with myrtle and other wild herbs

Burrida A fish soup originally from Liguria, but very common in Sardinia

Casca Steamed couscous, flavoured with minced meat, peas, cauliflower and strong spices

Cassola A fish soup of Spanish origin

Cordula Entrails of baby lamb or goat, bound together with gut and then roasted, similar to those of Sicily, Puglia and Calabria

Filatrotta cum sa zibba Eel cooked simply with samphire

Gallina al mirto Chicken boiled in broth, then put into a container with lots of myrtle to flavour for 48 hours; eaten cold

Impanadas Baked stuffed pastry, similar to a *calzone*, which takes its name from the Spanish *empanada*. The filling is usually salami, artichokes, peas and olives, but may also contain pork or eel

Lasagna de isposus A 'wedding lasagne' of pasta layered with pork or veal *ragù*, topped with pecorino

Lepudrida A soupy mixture of legumes and meat such as pork or beef, with pieces of ham added, from the Spanish *olla podrida*. A speciality of Cagliari

Pastu mistu A large animal stuffed with a smaller one – often a turkey stuffed with a hare or chicken and herbs and spices – roasted under the earth like *arrosto a caraxiu*; also called *piocu a caraxiu*

Pisci scabecciau Mullet fried and marinated with vinegar, oil and garlic, from the Spanish *escabeche*

Sebadas Giant ravioli with pecorino and honey

Of the many Sardinian sweet specialities, these sweet ravioli (also known as *seadas*) are something out of the ordinary. They bring together two typical and excellent regional products, fresh pecorino cheese and orange blossom honey. A good glass of Monica di Sardegna is the perfect complement.

SERVES 4

4 rounds fresh pecorino cheese, 10 cm in diameter, 5 mm thick
olive oil for deep-frying
120 g orange blossom honey, warmed

Sweet pasta dough
150 g Italian '00' plain flour
1 egg
1 egg yolk
pinch of salt
1 tbsp caster sugar

To make the pasta dough, pile the flour into a mound on a surface and make a large well in the centre. Put the egg, egg yolk, salt and sugar in the well and beat lightly with a fork. With your hands, gradually mix in the flour. When the mixture has formed a dough, knead it well with the palms of your hands for about 10 minutes, until it is very smooth and elastic. Cover and leave to rest for 20 minutes.

Roll out the pasta dough on a lightly floured surface to a 2 mm thickness and cut out 8 rounds, each 15 cm in diameter. Put a cheese round on each of 4 pasta rounds, brush the pasta edges with a little water, then top with the other pasta rounds. Press the edges together to seal.

Heat the olive oil in a suitable pan and deep-fry the ravioli until golden, about 7–8 minutes. Remove and drain well on kitchen paper. Serve hot, drizzled with honey.

Basic recipes

A good stock can make all the difference to the flavour of a dish and it's well worth getting into the habit of making your own stocks. However, there are good stock products available now, so don't be deterred from preparing my recipes if you haven't any homemade stock in the freezer, or the time to make some. Tubs of fresh stock are available from good fishmongers, butchers and supermarkets.

My basic pasta dough is also included here, although you will come across several other pasta recipes – made with or without egg – throughout the book.

Brodo di Pesce Fish stock

Fish stock forms the basis of most fish soups and seafood risottos. Use the heads and bones of white, rather than oily, fish to make the stock – your local fishmonger will probably be happy to supply you with the heads of larger fish, which are normally not sold.

Makes about 2.2 litres

1.2 kg white fish heads and bones
salt and pepper
2–3 celery stalks, coarsely chopped
2 carrots, cut into chunks
bunch of flat-leaf parsley
1 onion, halved
2 garlic cloves, peeled
1 tsp fennel seeds

Wash the pieces of fish under cold running water, then place in a saucepan with 3 litres lightly salted water. Bring to the boil and skim away the froth from the surface. Add all the remaining ingredients and leave to simmer gently for 40 minutes. Strain the liquid through a sieve into a bowl, check the seasoning and allow to cool.

On cooling, this stock tends to set into a jelly. Chill and use as required within 1–2 days, or freeze.

Brodo di Gallina Chicken stock

Chicken stock forms the basis of many soups, risottos and other dishes. Indeed some Italian soups consist of little else apart from a good broth with some small pasta cooked in it, or eggs, as in the famous *stracciatella* of Lazio. Ideally, use a 2- to 3-year old bird.

Makes about 3 litres

1 chicken, about 2 kg
salt
2 carrots, cut into chunks
1 onion, halved
2–3 celery stalks, coarsely chopped
4 bay leaves
1 tbsp black peppercorns

Put the chicken in a large pan and cover with 4 litres lightly salted water. Bring to the boil and skim off the froth from the surface. Add the remaining ingredients and allow to simmer gently for 1½–2 hours, skimming occasionally. Strain the stock into a bowl, check the seasoning and allow to cool.

Remove the solidified fat from the surface. Keep the stock in the fridge and use within 4 days, or freeze.

Brodo di Carne Beef stock

A beef stock should be made from the meat of a mature animal, and a bone with marrow can be added if you want to thicken the broth. If the full flavour of the beef is to be savoured in the stock, it is advisable to mince the meat first.

Makes about 3 litres

1 kg stewing beef and some bones
salt
2 carrots, cut in pieces
1 onion, halved
2–3 celery stalks, coarsely chopped
4 bay leaves
1 tbsp black peppercorns

Put the meat in a large pan and cover with 4 litres lightly salted water. Bring to the boil and skim off the froth from the surface. Add the remaining ingredients and allow to simmer for 2–3 hours, skimming occasionally. Strain the stock into a bowl, check the seasoning and leave to cool.

Remove the solidified fat from the surface of the stock. Keep in the fridge and use within 4–5 days, or freeze.

Brodo di Vegetali Vegetable stock

A nutritious vegetable broth is a good alternative to a meat-based stock. Choose vegetables with a distinctive flavour, such as celery, fennel, etc. Avoid potato as this will make the stock cloudy.

Makes about 1.2 litres

1.3 kg mixed vegetables (carrots, celeriac, celery, fennel, onion, parsnip, etc.)
1 garlic clove, chopped
bunch of flat-leaf parsley
2 bay leaves
few thyme sprigs (or other herbs)
salt and pepper

Prepare and roughly chop the vegetables and put them into a pan with the garlic, herbs, seasoning and 1.7 litres water. (Keep the vitamin-rich water from cooking green vegetables to use here.) Bring to the boil and simmer for 20 minutes or so until the vegetables are tender.

Strain the stock into a bowl and allow to cool. Keep in the fridge and use within 3 days, or freeze.

Note This broth can be turned into a soup, simply by puréeing the cooked vegetables and mixing the purée back into the broth with a little cream.

Pasta all'Uovo Egg pasta dough

The ideal proportions for homemade pasta dough are 1 large egg to every 100 g flour, but variations in temperature, humidity and flour absorbency affect the consistency and you may need to vary the quantity of flour slightly. Aim for a dough that is perfectly smooth and elastic, yet firm after kneading.

Makes about 600 g

400 g Italian '00' flour, plus extra to dust
4 large, very fresh eggs
large pinch of salt

Pile the flour in a mound on a surface and make a well in the middle. Break the eggs into the well and add the salt. Stir the eggs into the flour, with a fork at first, and then with your hands, until it forms a coarse paste. Add a little more flour if too moist.

Now knead the pasta dough, either using a pasta machine or by hand until it is smooth and workable, not too soft but not too hard. To knead by hand, lightly flour the surface and your hands, and knead the dough with the heel of one hand, pushing it away from you and folding it back towards you; do this for 10–15 minutes. Cover the dough with a cloth and rest for 15–30 minutes before rolling out.

Divide the dough into 4 or 5 portions. If rolling by machine, pass the dough through the rollers, a portion at a time, decreasing the gap between the rollers each time, so that the dough becomes thinner and longer. Repeat this until you obtain the desired thickness: 3–4 mm for lasagne and cannelloni; 1.5–2 mm for stuffed pasta; even thinner for finer pasta. Then either pass through the cutting rollers to make various sizes of ribbon, or cut into sheets. If rolling by hand, gently roll out a portion at a time on a lightly floured surface to the required thickness, rolling away from you and giving the dough a quarter-turn after each rolling. To cut ribbons, fold the sheet of pasta into a loose roll and cut it into ribbons of the desired width.

For stuffed pasta, such as ravioli, use the pasta straightaway. If you are making lasagne or ribbon pasta, place on a floured cloth to dry for 10 minutes or so before cooking.

Cook fresh pasta in a large saucepan, allowing 1 litre water per 100 g pasta, plus 2 tsp salt. When you put the pasta into the pan, give it a quick stir to prevent it from sticking together. (It is only with lasagne, which must be immersed one sheet at a time, that you need to add a few drops of oil to the water.) Cooking time varies according to the kind of pasta, its thickness and whether it is stuffed, but homemade pasta ribbons will take about 3 minutes. Stir a few times cooking, preferably with a long-handled wooden fork.

Test the pasta when you think it should be almost done: it is ready when it is *al dente*, and slightly resistant. A few moments before it reaches that stage, take the saucepan off the heat, add a glass of cold water, and leave for a couple of seconds. Then drain the pasta (perhaps saving a little of the water in case a sauce needs it), and return immediately to the saucepan or a preheated dish. Mix it with a little sauce and perhaps some grated cheese. Serve immediately.

Index *Recipes are in upper and lower case type*

Acknowledgements

My unreserved thanks go to:
Priscilla, my wife, for her inspirational visual and style input; Alastair Hendy, who travelled with me in Italy, for outstanding photography; Tanya Marzola, my P.A., for endless typing; Susan Fleming for making sense of my 'English'. And to my publisher Quadrille, and those who have made the book possible: Alison Cathie, Jane O'Shea, Mary Evans, Janet Illsley and Clare Lattin.

For inspiration and motivation:
I owe a special thanks to Pellegrino Artusi, to whom this book is dedicated. I came across his book, *La Scienza in Cucina e L'Arte di Mangiar Bene*, published in 1891, only 10 years ago and discovered that we shared the same philosophy. This inspired me and gave me enormous encouragement to write this book and further my appreciation and enjoyment of Italian food and customs.

I am also very grateful to:
bmi for providing my excellent flights to Milan and Naples direct from London Heathrow
Albino Barberis of Alba Gold for the comfortable travelling through Italy
Enzo Zaccarini for all the vegetables and fruit from Italy
Guiseppe from Enotria Wines Ltd for the wines used for cooking
Carluccio's for groceries
Marco Vineis, Gastronomica Ltd for cheeses and salami
Wild Harvest for mushrooms
Southbank for fish
Yorkshire Game for meat and game
Andrea Cavaliere, who was my head chef at The Neal Street Restaurant for many years, for various tastings
The Touring Club of Italy's guides for their excellent travelling tips
The Slow Food publications for information

Thanks to the following friends in the regions for hospitality, help in searching for products and tips:
Carlo, Rosalba and Anna Carluccio, Ivrea
Famiglia Bava, Cocconato
Fabrizio, owner of Trattoria del Ponte, Cocconato
Sandrino and Birba of Sandrino Tartufi, Asti
Giulio Gallo, Torino
Giulia Riberi and Luisa, Torino
Associazione Pescatori del Garda, Garda
Gabriele Ferron (rice), Verona
Giorgio Gioco, my friend, from 12 Apostoli, Verona
Giovanni Gregoletto (wines), Conegliano
Antonio and Servilia Alzetta, Pordenone
Pinuccia of Ristorante S. Giovanni, Casarza Ligure
Gian Paolo Belloni of Zeffirino, Genova
Miriam of La Buca Restaurant, Zibello
Hotel Locanda del Lupo, Soragna
Massimo for Culatello, Diolo
Ferrari Prosciutti, Felino
Claudio Basler from Altesino Montalcino (wines)
Marchese Leonardo Frescobaldi, Firenze (wines)
Benedetto Franchi of Gastronomia, Roma
Ristorante Sabatini, Roma
Donatella Limentani, Pavoncello Roma
Mario Fortunato, Roma
Maria Maresca from Espresso, Roma
Sonia and Carla Gentile, Avellino
Lina Fasulo (my old nanny), Prata P.U.
Mastro Berardino wine, Avellino
Baldo, owner of La Cambusa Restaurant in Positano
Caffe' Gambrinus, Naples
Antonio and Silvia Accito, Matera
Donna Maria Pignatelli, Grottaglie
Franco Fasano, Grottaglie
Famiglia Cantore, Gioia del Colle
Francesco Carluccio, Lecce
Famiglia Rallo (Donnafugata), Marsala
Luigi of Albergo su Gologone Oliena
Laura and Nardo Cacciatore Sicari from Santa Rita
Pino Medaglia, Vibo Valenzia.

Photographic credits:
All photography by Alastair Hendy except: p10 André Martin; p112 and p116 kindly supplied by ©Altesino; p234 © Donnafugata/ Pasquale Modica; 240 (left) PUBLIPHOTO/ Roberto Moro.

Illustration credits:
Map of Italy, p6, by Owen Dwelly design; drawing of Antonio, p5, by Milton Patrick.

Piemonte e Valle d'Aosta
LOMBARDIA
Trentino-Alto Adige
Friuli-Venezia Giulia
Veneto Liguria
Emilia-Romagna
TOSCANA Umbria
Marche LAZIO
ABRUZZi e MOLiSE
CAMPANIA Basilicata
Calabria Puglia
Sicilia SARDEGNA